DECODING
DESPAIR

Mariam Khayretdinova

DECODING DESPAIR

How AI is Reshaping **Psychiatry**

WILEY

Copyright © 2026 by John Wiley & Sons, Inc. All rights reserved, including rights for text and data mining and training of artificial intelligence technologies or similar technologies.

Published by John Wiley & Sons, Inc., Hoboken, New Jersey.

No part of this publication may be reproduced, stored in a retrieval system, or transmitted in any form or by any means, electronic, mechanical, photocopying, recording, scanning, or otherwise, except as permitted under Section 107 or 108 of the 1976 United States Copyright Act, without either the prior written permission of the Publisher, or authorization through payment of the appropriate per-copy fee to the Copyright Clearance Center, Inc., 222 Rosewood Drive, Danvers, MA 01923, (978) 750-8400, fax (978) 750-4470, or on the web at www.copyright.com. Requests to the Publisher for permission should be addressed to the Permissions Department, John Wiley & Sons, Inc., 111 River Street, Hoboken, NJ 07030, (201) 748-6011, fax (201) 748-6008, or online at http://www.wiley.com/go/permission.

The manufacturer's authorized representative according to the EU General Product Safety Regulation is Wiley-VCH GmbH, Boschstr. 12, 69469 Weinheim, Germany, e-mail: Product_Safety@wiley.com.

Trademarks: Wiley and the Wiley logo are trademarks or registered trademarks of John Wiley & Sons, Inc. and/or its affiliates in the United States and other countries and may not be used without written permission. All other trademarks are the property of their respective owners. John Wiley & Sons, Inc. is not associated with any product or vendor mentioned in this book.

Limit of Liability/Disclaimer of Warranty: While the publisher and the author have used their best efforts in preparing this work, including a review of the content of the work, neither the publisher nor the author make any representations or warranties with respect to the accuracy or completeness of the contents of this work and specifically disclaim all warranties, including without limitation any implied warranties of merchantability or fitness for a particular purpose. No warranty may be created or extended by sales representatives, written sales materials or promotional statements for this work. The fact that an organization, website, or product is referred to in this work as a citation and/or potential source of further information does not mean that the publisher and authors endorse the information or services the organization, website, or product may provide or recommendations it may make. This work is sold with the understanding that the publisher is not engaged in rendering professional services. The advice and strategies contained herein may not be suitable for your situation. You should consult with a specialist where appropriate. Further, readers should be aware that websites listed in this work may have changed or disappeared between when this work was written and when it is read. Neither the publisher nor author shall be liable for any loss of profit or any other commercial damages, including but not limited to special, incidental, consequential, or other damages.

For general information on our other products and services or for technical support, please contact our Customer Care Department within the United States at (800) 762-2974, outside the United States at (317) 572-3993 or fax (317) 572-4002.

Wiley also publishes its books in a variety of electronic formats. Some content that appears in print may not be available in electronic formats. For more information about Wiley products, visit our website at www.wiley.com.

Library of Congress Cataloging-in-Publication Data:

Names: Khayretdinova, Mariam author
Title: Decoding despair : AI's potential to reshape psychiatry / Mariam Khayretdinova.
Description: Hoboken, New Jersey : Wiley, [2026] | Includes bibliographical references and index.
Identifiers: LCCN 2025038034 | ISBN 9781394305933 hardback | ISBN 9781394305957 adobe pdf | ISBN 9781394305940 epub
Subjects: LCSH: Artificial intelligence—Medical applications | Psychiatry
Classification: LCC R859.7.A78 K6645 2026
LC record available at https://lccn.loc.gov/2025038034

Cover Design: Wiley
Cover Image: © koyu/Getty Images
Author Photo: Courtesy of the Author
Printed and bound by CPI Group (UK) Ltd, Croydon, CR0 4YY

C9781394305933_051225

To my husband, Ivan, who always supports me in every wild endeavor, and to all innovators brave enough to try changing the world.

Contents

Introduction ... ix

PART I — Psychiatry ... 1

Chapter 1   The Patient's Journey ... 3
Chapter 2   Diagnostic Roulette ... 23
Chapter 3   Treatment, Pharma, and the Brain ... 41
Chapter 4   Psychiatry as a System ... 69

PART II — Artificial Intelligence ... 91

Chapter 5   The Fundamentals of AI ... 93
Chapter 6   It Is All About the Data ... 115

PART III — Innovating Psychiatry with AI ... 133

Chapter 7   Innovation Starts with Data ... 135
Chapter 8   Revealing the Nature of Mental Disorders ... 159
Chapter 9   Innovations Within Reach ... 185
Chapter 10   Afterword or Afterworld ... 205

Glossary	*215*
Notes	*231*
Acknowledgments	*251*
About the Author	*253*
Index	*255*

Introduction

Trigger Warning: This book discusses topics including suicide, mental illness, and emotional distress, which some readers may find disturbing or triggering. Please exercise discretion.

During one of my rare trips home in 2017 I was having dinner with my best friend when he first told me about Jay, a woman he had been searching for his whole life. She was independent, smart, ambitious, and always joyful—a bundle of energy that brought out the best in him. I had never seen him shine like that before, nor had I ever heard him speak about anyone with such admiration. I knew then that he had made one of the most important decisions of his life, and soon enough, I would meet his wife-to-be. A few months later, I finally met Jay. When I think of her now, the first thing that comes to mind is her smile—that radiant, contagious smile that lit up the room the moment she descended the stairs to greet my husband and me. I remember thinking, "Wow, what a presence."

As I got to know her better, I realized how truly sophisticated and multilayered she was. Jay had a way of revealing her warmth and friendliness to others, while carefully guarding the deeper parts of herself. She was a dreamer, with vivid imagination and a crystal-clear sense of what she wanted from life. An ambitious achiever, she held herself to incredibly high standards—whether in her career or in her personal relationships. Every detail mattered to her. Together with my friend, she built what looked like an enviable life—young, successful, and striking.

As I continued to follow her life from that distant view, I noticed how her presence drew others in. Jay wasn't just focused on her own goals; she was also a magnet for others. She had a close-knit circle of friends—her "Hyenas," as they liked to call themselves. Jay had created a special club for them, where they met regularly, trying out new activities, from art workshops to wellness retreats. Her energy and ideas were the glue that kept it going. Yet even as the center of this group, she sometimes seemed to bear the weight of keeping everyone inspired. Her friends admired her deeply, but there were moments when I wondered if she ever felt overwhelmed by the role she played in their lives.

Throughout her career, she had founded several startups and held C-level positions, constantly striving for excellence. Her lifestyle seemed, by all measures, exemplary: she worked out regularly, ate healthily, and practiced meditation. Even her social media reflected this—her posts often featured her parents, showing a close bond and sense of being loved. Her smile, laughter, and infectious joy always shone through in everything she shared with the world.

At times, however, I couldn't help but notice certain aspects of her life that left me with mixed feelings. There were moments when the relentless drive for perfection—the carefully curated social media posts, the endless stream of activities, and her constant glow of positivity—felt almost too much. I found myself wondering if, beneath the surface, there was more going on than she let on. It seemed as though she was striving too hard, investing so much energy into maintaining that flawless image. Her presence, while magnetic, could occasionally feel overwhelming. Yet, even in my private moments of doubt—when I questioned whether her need for attention or her busy lifestyle might be masking something deeper—one thing always felt genuine: her energy. Her joy, her smile, and the light she brought into a room never seemed forced. That was real.

Then, four years later, I received a message from my friend: "Jay killed herself."

I stared at the screen, emotionless, as if the words couldn't register.

By the time it happened, I was already deeply embedded in the world of psychiatry, so I no longer asked the question most people instinctively ask: "why?" We instinctively seek reasons—something or someone to blame. We want a clear, understandable explanation because, for many, the simple answer—a mental disorder—doesn't feel like enough. And that's understandable. We see seemingly perfect individuals, leading what appear to be enviable lives, and it's hard to believe they could feel suicidal. Even when they share their struggles, it's often difficult for us to fully grasp their depth. Let's be honest—many of us project our own perceptions onto others, unintentionally downplaying what they reveal. So, when we learn that someone has taken their own life, we search desperately for a reason strong enough to explain the "why."

This relentless search for "why" is just one facet of a much larger, multifaceted problem—a widespread lack of knowledge and deep understanding of mental health. In a world filled with technological and medical advances, it's hard to accept that psychiatry remains decades behind. Science continues to struggle in linking the symptoms of mental disorders to research, often failing to produce consistent, replicable results. Meanwhile, most people's understanding of mental illness is shaped by literature, movies, and social media—sources that often present distorted or oversimplified views, reinforcing stereotypes rather than offering real understanding.

As psychiatry stagnates, suicide rates continue to rise at an alarming pace. Jay's story is just one of millions, yet it reflects the reality we face. Mental disorders don't have simple explanations and can't be reduced to one-dimensional answers. Jay wasn't dealing with socio economic struggles, nor did she lack access to care. She wasn't battling substance abuse, nor was she facing extreme life circumstances like poverty, incarceration, or terminal illness. With her confident demeanor and positive outlook, she didn't fit the stereotypical image of someone struggling with mental health. Yet, despite having none of the "usual" factors, she still died by suicide.

Jay's decline didn't happen all at once. At first, the changes in her seemed subtle, even understandable given the pressures everyone felt. In February 2022, the world was shaken by the outbreak of war. Like many, Jay felt her anxiety spike; she sensed a deep, inexplicable fear that overshadowed her usual confidence. Her husband convinced her that they should temporarily leave the city to escape the uncertainty. They relocated to a remote area in another country, hoping a change of scenery might bring peace. Jay tried to keep up with her work and routines remotely. She took on multiple roles, working from dawn until late into the night, pushing herself relentlessly as if her worth depended on being constantly busy. Her friends believed she was simply coping, finding ways to manage her fears by keeping herself absorbed in work.

But when she returned home that spring, Jay was different. She became erratic, impulsive, and oddly ambitious in ways that her friends could barely recognize. She began sharing plans that sounded surreal, even delusional. She told them she had a "special destiny"—to become the country's first female president, no less. She spoke of rooting out corruption at her workplace, believing she was the only one who could hold executives accountable. She grew deeply invested in an almost mystical view of herself, consulting a shaman who fed into her fantasies by assuring her that she had a purpose larger than anyone understood. The shaman even gave her a talisman to "protect" her on her journey, a symbolic gesture that Jay took to heart, embracing this belief in her own exceptionalism.

Her close friends started noticing more erratic, grandiose behavior by late spring. Jay's mood swung wildly, from ecstatic highs to quiet lows, and she began to fixate on her own significance, talking about a "spiritual awakening" and claiming she'd unlocked her "third eye." She saw signs everywhere that she was "chosen" or "enlightened," and she spoke as if she'd been granted insight into things others couldn't see. It was as if a switch had flipped, and she was no longer grounded in the reality that once defined her.

Soon, her actions matched her words. Jay suddenly left her husband, announcing it was time for her to make drastic changes in her life. She abruptly quit her job to start a new role in a salon chain that turned out to be nothing more than a shell operation. This dramatic career shift, fueled by impulsive decisions and unrealistic ambitions, threw her friends and family into confusion. To them, it was as if Jay was now living in a world of her own, consumed by visions of her own greatness.

In May, Jay took a spontaneous trip to Israel, an experience that added yet another layer to her increasingly unpredictable behavior. She met strangers, donated money freely, and engaged in conversations with a conviction that seemed almost surreal. She even told a friend she had encountered a man in a wheelchair who "radiated divine light" after she gave him money. She insisted he rose and walked alongside her, declaring she would be his "queen."

Alarmed, her friends and family suggested she see a professional. At first, Jay consulted a psychologist—an unlicensed counselor, someone who failed to recognize the gravity of her symptoms. Instead, the psychologist interpreted Jay's behavior as "spiritual growth" and encouraged her, further reinforcing Jay's delusions rather than challenging them. This continued for weeks, with her delusions growing unchecked.

Finally, after a chaotic few months, Jay's friends staged an intervention, pushing her to seek medical help from a psychiatrist. The psychiatrist diagnosed her with a manic episode featuring psychotic symptoms, and she was admitted to a psychiatric facility. She was prescribed mood stabilizers and antipsychotics, but the medication seemed to drain her of the intense energy that had been driving her mania without addressing the underlying issues. Her initial mania subsided, but she began spiraling into a depressive state.

Released in late June, Jay's once-grand visions were replaced by self-doubt and fear. She confided to friends that she felt like a shell of herself, convinced the medications had robbed her of her intelligence, her cognitive abilities, and her very identity. During a trip to Italy that summer, her friends noticed the drastic change. Jay, still only in her thirties, had previously navigated the world with ease, but now was suddenly plagued by small, seemingly irrational fears. She worried about finding her gate in the airport and even expressed anxiety about being alone in public spaces. It was as if she'd become someone else—a woman deeply insecure, haunted by the belief that she had lost everything that once made her who she was.

By September, her depressive symptoms had deepened into a bleak hopelessness. Jay's friends and family tried to support her, but she seemed unreachable, convinced that her life had no future. She attempted to return to work, only to find herself incapable of handling even the simplest tasks. Each failure reinforced her sense of worthlessness. Despite her family's efforts, despite friends checking in on her, she continued to slip away from them emotionally.

Around this time, Jay confided to a friend that she no longer wanted to live. The friend immediately reached out to Jay's father, pleading with him to take her words seriously. But her father, believing it to be a passing phase or "seasonal depression," dismissed her friend's concerns. Jay's words were seen as nothing more than a symptom of temporary sadness. In reality, Jay had started meticulously researching suicide methods. She wanted a way that was certain and painless. Her search history showed she had considered jumping from high places, speeding into traffic, and, ultimately, methods that required specific equipment. She was thorough and precise, determined to find a way that would end her life without risk of survival.

By October, she made her first suicide attempt. She traveled to her father's country home, drank heavily, and tried to hang herself. Her father discovered her unconscious before the attempt could succeed, and she was rushed to the hospital. Following this, she was briefly hospitalized and placed under observation. She was released again with a minimal support plan, having been deemed a "low suicide risk." Doctors, trusting the results of a standard risk assessment, believed she had stabilized.

Friends tried to stay hopeful, but some sensed that Jay's reassurances were a front. A close friend who visited her in the hospital reported to others that she seemed "better," talking about plans to sell her car and get back on her feet. But one friend, who had known Jay for years, wasn't convinced. Jay's silence toward those closest to her, her refusal to answer certain messages—these were warning signs her friends recognized too late.

On the day she was discharged from the hospital for the final time, Jay completed a series of suicide risk questionnaires, a standard procedure. Her answers, combined with the doctors' evaluation, led to the conclusion that she was at "low risk" for suicide. With this assessment, she was released into her family's care, her file marked with that confident but tragically mistaken classification.

Just a couple of hours after she was discharged, Jay told her family she needed to fuel up her car. But instead, she drove to an isolated spot, equipped with all the supplies she had meticulously prepared over the previous weeks before her hospital stay. Jay fatally intoxicated herself with helium. She left a note, carefully explaining her reasons with an unsettling clarity. This was not an impulsive act; it was the last step in a plan she had orchestrated in detail, a plan that her loved ones—and even the mental health professionals she had just seen—were powerless to prevent.

Following her death, however, even the record of her passing became blurred with denial and cultural stigma. Her death certificate made no mention of suicide. This omission reflected, in part, her family's inability to accept the unbearable loss and the stigma associated with acknowledging her suicide. But it also had a cultural weight: if her death was classified as suicide, she would be denied a church funeral, as the church traditionally withholds rites from those who die by their own hand. Her death, therefore, was viewed through a religious lens—not as a tragic end to a battle with mental illness but as an irreversible sin.

Systemic Failure in Psychiatry

Jay's tragic story might initially appear as merely a rare, unfortunate convergence of events—her personal struggles, specific societal pressures, cultural attitudes within her immediate family, insufficient medical oversight, ineffective medications, and sheer bad luck. Yet, when we look carefully at each of the factors contributing to her death, it becomes clear that they are not simply random coincidences. Rather, her case painfully highlights systemic flaws deeply embedded within psychiatry itself: the persistent difficulty in recognizing early mental health deterioration; the entrenched stigma preventing open discussions; repeated encounters with unqualified professionals and pervasive misinformation; delayed access to proper mental healthcare; poorly chosen treatments leading to severe side effects and medication nonadherence; ineffective hospitalization guided by inadequate assessment tools, resulting in premature discharge; and the absence of proactive interventions capable of interrupting her meticulous preparation for suicide. Each step in her tragic journey exposes fundamental weaknesses in how the psychiatric system currently operates.

We might prefer to think Jay's case is just a rare and tragic exception, but unfortunately, global statistics suggest otherwise. Her story is not an isolated incident; it fits into a much larger, deeply troubling pattern. In fact, suicide has become one of the leading causes of death worldwide for young people aged 15–29, taking over 700,000 lives every year.[1] Each of these deaths is not only an immeasurable personal loss but also a stark indicator of critical weaknesses within our current psychiatric care systems.

These alarming statistics point unmistakably toward one conclusion: psychiatry today remains fundamentally ineffective and urgently requires innovation. Mental health disorders affect nearly one billion people worldwide—approximately one in every eight individuals globally—making mental illness one of the greatest public health challenges of our time.[2] Anxiety disorders and depression are particularly widespread, affecting hundreds of millions of lives. Yet, the impact of these conditions extends far beyond the individual sufferers—it touches their families, friends, colleagues, and entire communities. Each untreated or inadequately managed mental health issue creates ripple effects, disrupting relationships, impairing workplace productivity, and weakening social cohesion. Ultimately, what begins as an individual struggle evolves into a truly global crisis.

Beyond the immeasurable human suffering, the global economic burden of mental illness is immense. According to a comprehensive report published by the Lancet Commission on Global Mental Health and Sustainable Development, mental disorders are projected to cost the global economy as much as $16 trillion between 2010 and 2030.[3] This enormous figure is driven largely by lost productivity, healthcare expenditures, and substantial economic disruptions resulting from untreated or inadequately managed mental health conditions. Each year, mental health issues lead to the loss of approximately 12 billion productive working days worldwide, further exacerbating poverty, straining healthcare resources, and hindering economic growth.[3]

Such staggering economic impacts reflect not only the individual challenges posed by mental illness but also its profound societal implications. When mental health is neglected, entire communities and economies suffer, perpetuating cycles of poverty, disability, and social fragmentation. The true cost of failing to address mental health comprehensively reaches far beyond financial terms—it encompasses the social fabric and resilience of societies globally.

These statistics collectively underscore two critical points. First, psychiatry as a field is clearly in urgent need of innovation and significant transformation. The sheer scale of human suffering and economic burden makes it evident that the existing approaches are simply ineffective. Yet, despite the urgency and magnitude of these issues, we've seen very little meaningful progress over the past several decades. This lack of advancement highlights an even deeper problem: psychiatry is caught in an exceptionally complex web of interconnected challenges, making it extremely difficult to pinpoint clear starting points or simple solutions. If the path toward meaningful innovation and improvement were straightforward, these issues would have already been resolved.

The Hope That AI Presents

There is hope, however, and it lies in the rapid technological advancements we've witnessed over recent decades—particularly in the field of artificial intelligence. Unlike psychiatry, which has seen limited meaningful progress in recent years, AI has evolved dramatically, experiencing transformative breakthroughs in algorithms, data processing, and computational capabilities. Today's AI systems are vastly more powerful, sophisticated, and effective than those developed even just a few years ago.

Machine learning algorithms have proven revolutionary in various industries, profoundly reshaping fields such as healthcare, finance, transportation, and communications. These transformations were enabled by the enormous growth in available data, improvements in computational resources, and the continuous innovation in AI methodologies. Where traditional methods struggled to manage complexity, AI now routinely identifies patterns and solutions with impressive speed and accuracy. This rapid development in artificial intelligence brings new optimism and momentum—especially to disciplines like psychiatry, which have remained largely stagnant.

Psychiatry's deeply rooted and complex challenges may seem overwhelming, but the rise of AI provides genuine hope precisely because it introduces fundamentally different tools and approaches. It represents an entirely new perspective, driven by data and algorithms rather than subjective assessment alone. Such technological advancements are already beginning to disrupt established practices in other medical fields, and there's no reason psychiatry should remain an exception.

This optimism is not simply theoretical. We've already seen how quickly AI has reshaped multiple industries, delivering results that seemed almost impossible not long ago. Tasks like reliably transcribing speech, instantly translating languages, or precisely recognizing patterns in complex images, once distant goals, are now routine tools we barely notice in our daily lives. The speed and effectiveness with which AI has transformed these areas strongly suggest psychiatry could soon experience similarly meaningful progress.

This book is written for those who believe that change in psychiatry is not only necessary but also possible. It's for innovators, researchers, clinicians, entrepreneurs, and anyone passionate about improving mental healthcare who sees the urgent need for fresh thinking and meaningful innovation. Psychiatry today stands at a crossroads, marked by daunting challenges, yet brimming with untapped opportunities. My goal with this book is to spark inspiration, provoke thoughtful reflection, and ignite new ideas about how we can collectively transform mental healthcare.

Through exploring the intersections between modern psychiatry and rapidly evolving technologies, particularly artificial intelligence, I illustrate how we can approach existing challenges differently. Rather than simply highlighting the numerous problems within psychiatry, this book seeks to deepen your understanding of their complexity and encourage you to recognize the immense potential technology offers for addressing them. By thoughtfully combining our insights into the current psychiatric system with emerging technological possibilities, I hope to inspire innovative thinking and spark meaningful new solutions.

How This Book Is Organized

This book is structured into three distinct parts, each serving a unique purpose and building progressively toward meaningful innovation in psychiatry. The primary goal of the first part is to closely examine how the world of psychiatry operates today—not just superficially identifying its well-known flaws and shortcomings but also probing deeper to understand the underlying causes that perpetuate them. I genuinely believe that clear insight into the nature and origin of a problem is always the first and most essential step toward developing truly effective solutions.

In the initial chapters, we will explore psychiatry thoroughly from the patient's perspective. By carefully following the patient's journey—from the initial moment they sense that something is wrong to their eventual encounter with professional care and treatment—we will uncover the complex, multifaceted obstacles patients face along the path to recovery. This exploration will span various critical dimensions, from deeply embedded cultural and social attitudes to the technical and methodological issues within existing diagnostic practices. My aim here is not only to highlight difficulties but also to expose how these issues manifest in real-life scenarios, shaping patient experiences in profound and often hidden ways.

We will analyze where these challenges originate, pinpointing the deeper systemic issues responsible for common problems such as inaccurate diagnoses, ineffective medications, and inadequate treatment strategies. By taking this step-by-step journey through the patient's eyes, we gain a direct understanding of psychiatry's internal struggles and shortcomings. In doing so, we move beyond mere symptoms of dysfunction, instead uncovering root causes—critical insights that can meaningfully guide future innovation.

However, to fully grasp the complexity and interconnectedness of these issues, we will shift our perspective in the fourth chapter. Here, we step back from individual patient experiences and adopt a broader, system-level view. Psychiatry does not function in isolation; it is an intricate network of relationships between numerous players, including hospitals, clinicians, pharmaceutical companies, regulators, professional associations, insurance companies, and many others. Understanding these interconnected relationships—and the motivations and limitations of each participant—is essential. It enables us to identify where systemic friction occurs, providing valuable insights into the often overlooked obstacles innovators may encounter when trying to implement meaningful changes.

My hope is that this first part will prove valuable even to seasoned professionals in mental health, individuals who might already be familiar with many of these challenges. By carefully gathering and presenting these interconnected elements as a unified picture, readers may achieve a new depth of understanding. Seeing psychiatry comprehensively as a cohesive system—rather than a fragmented series of problems—might inspire unexpected ideas and illuminate areas previously overlooked or underestimated. Ultimately, a clear and holistic view of psychiatry—one that fully appreciates its intricacies, shortcomings, and potential—will serve as a powerful foundation, enabling us to rethink and reshape the future of mental healthcare in meaningful, lasting ways.

The second part of this book is dedicated entirely to artificial intelligence: its true potential, realistic capabilities, and inherent limitations. Today, the term "AI" has become almost ubiquitous, appearing everywhere from daily news headlines to casual conversations, which can lead to misconceptions about its genuine possibilities. To successfully implement any technological innovation, we must clearly understand both what it can realistically achieve, and the specific conditions required for it to function effectively in real-world scenarios.

In this section, I will present a broad overview of artificial intelligence, helping you navigate its promises, capabilities, and constraints. We'll address important questions such as: What exactly can AI achieve today, and what remains out of its reach? What challenges might arise when trying to apply AI-based solutions in complex fields such as psychiatry? Furthermore, since data is the lifeblood of artificial intelligence, we will also examine why quality data matters so greatly, what constitutes robust and reliable data, and what infrastructure we need to successfully integrate AI-driven approaches.

If you are already an expert in artificial intelligence, this part might seem familiar or perhaps less relevant. However, if your experience with AI is primarily through everyday apps, interactions like ChatGPT, or news snippets, this section is designed specifically for you. My goal here is not to provide a deep technical education on artificial intelligence, but rather to offer a realistic, clear-eyed perspective on what AI can—and cannot—do. I aim to equip you with essential knowledge, empowering you to recognize both opportunities and pitfalls when considering AI for tackling psychiatry's complex challenges. Ultimately, this section seeks to give you a grounded understanding, preparing you to thoughtfully harness AI's potential as we explore innovative solutions in mental health.

Finally, in the third and concluding part of this book, we will attempt to bring all the pieces together, combining the deep understanding of psychiatry's complex challenges established earlier with the clear-eyed perspective on artificial intelligence discussed in the second section. Here, we'll explore precisely how AI could transform this troubled industry and discuss the specific ways that emerging technologies might address some of psychiatry's most pressing issues. This is where theory meets practice—where we'll envision concrete scenarios in which AI-driven innovations could realistically take hold and fundamentally shift how mental healthcare is delivered.

Importantly, I will also speculate on the potential sequence and timelines for these innovations, taking into account the unique systemic constraints that shape the pace and scope of change within mental healthcare. Recognizing the intricate network of stakeholders, incentives, and regulatory frameworks, we'll consider which advancements are likely to occur first, and which may face greater hurdles or delays. By examining these pathways critically, we'll form a realistic sense of how transformative change could unfold within the complex environment of modern psychiatry.

In addition to addressing these major shifts and fundamental innovations, we'll also explore several interesting, practical applications of AI that—while perhaps not revolutionary—can significantly enhance current clinical and administrative processes. These incremental improvements have the potential to bring immediate and tangible benefits, paving the way for broader acceptance and smoother integration of more ambitious solutions in the future.

At the conclusion of this book, I warmly invite you to imagine with me the ideal future of psychiatry—a world in which technology and human insight work seamlessly together. How would this transformed field look, and what positive impacts might we see in the lives of patients, their families, and communities at large? By envisioning this future clearly, we not only gain inspiration but also clarify the goals we should strive toward today.

Ultimately, my greatest hope is that upon completing this book, you will come away not only with a deeper understanding of psychiatry's current problems but also with confidence in our collective potential to overcome them. More importantly, I want you to leave equipped with your own fresh ideas, strategic insights, and practical visions for implementing innovations that will truly thrive within the complexities of the psychiatric ecosystem.

Jay's story—and the millions like it—leaves us with a clear truth: our understanding and treatment of mental health can't remain in this state. We need solutions that don't just react but anticipate, that don't merely treat but transform lives. In this book, we'll explore how AI could open doors that psychiatry has struggled to crack for decades, offering new ways to diagnose, treat, and, maybe someday, even prevent the mental health crises that devastate so many. Each of us has a part to play in this journey. Whether you're here to learn, innovate, or simply understand, we're building a movement that pushes mental healthcare forward—one that can't afford to leave anyone behind. Together, we'll question what's possible and imagine a future where stories like Jay's are no longer inevitable.

PART I
Psychiatry

1 | The Patient's Journey

It was one of the roughest days in my battle with depression. I had a brutal mental breakdown. My emotions were overwhelming—anxiety, sadness, frustration—rising in me all at once. I couldn't contain the pain. I burst into tears, completely lost, unsure what to do with myself. After several hours of emotional catharsis, I felt drained—frustrated, foggy, and unable to make sense of what was happening or what to do next. Then, right in the middle of it, my phone buzzed. A text.

I had been waiting for that message for four months. A renowned professor, clinical psychologist, and businesswoman I'd been hoping to meet—someone who might be interested in investing in my company—finally had a time slot that evening. The timing felt almost cruel: just slightly off, arriving when I was barely able to function. But I couldn't miss the opportunity. Or at least, that's what I told myself.

The problem with depression—unlike other illnesses—is that it doesn't feel "legitimate." There's no cast, no fever, no visible marker that confirms you're unwell. You can still walk, talk, and show up. So when your mind is clouded, your emotions are flat, and life itself feels remote and hollow, it's easy to dismiss the experience as self-indulgent. Not a valid reason to pause. Especially when a business opportunity is at stake—one you might regret missing.

So I did what many of us do. I washed my face, put on makeup, dressed properly, and headed down to Tribeca for the meeting.

The restaurant was loud and crowded, overstimulating for someone who could barely hold her thoughts together. Navigating through the noise, weaving past people, feeling the weight of it all—it only amplified my state. And then I saw her. The rock star of the mental health industry.

As I began presenting my team's work on improving mental health, I shared my personal story. This wasn't just a business project—it had grown directly out of my own experience with mental illness. I had poured years of my life, my savings, my energy, and yes, even my mental health into it. I told her I had struggled with depression for quite some time, had been on various medications for over four years, and had finally managed to get off them.

The moment those words left my mouth, something shifted. It was as if an invisible wall suddenly rose between us. I sensed the change and tried to steer the conversation back to business. But it didn't go well—at all. I made a few more attempts to salvage the meeting, asking about her work, hoping to learn from her experience. But it didn't land.

As I was beginning to wrap things up, she abruptly turned the focus back to me.

"You know, you shouldn't be stupid," she said. "You need to get back on your medication. SSRIs are like an inhaler—you take them to live normally. You're a smart girl, you know how they work. They just increase your serotonin. Don't think they mess with your brain—they simply help you not miss out on opportunities because of a fuzzy mind. You don't need all these emotions. I mean, sure, if you were a novelist or an artist—maybe they need that drama to create. But you? You don't need it. So just get back on the pills."

I was speechless.

I mumbled something back, thankful the meeting was finally ending.

* * *

Where it all begins

It always starts with the patient. Every medical discovery, every shift in care—starts there. They're the first to notice when something feels off—subtle shifts that may go unnoticed by everyone else. They're the ones making that initial, often difficult call to a doctor, struggling to put into words concerns they may not fully understand themselves. Their journey is deeply personal, unique to each individual, yet familiar in how it forces every patient to step into the same complex, often overwhelming system in search of answers.

And it's never easy, especially in psychiatry, because what they find can be inconsistent, ambiguous, and, at times, frustratingly incomplete.

Patients are the drivers of healthcare. They are not cases to be analyzed or conditions to be solved—they are people, living with the effects, successes, and inevitable shortcomings of their care. They describe their symptoms, follow treatment plans, manage side effects, and carry the emotional weight of hope, uncertainty, recovery, and too often, frustration. Their well-being, relief, and outcomes are what ultimately define success in healthcare.

To understand psychiatry—or any area of medicine—we have to start at the center: the patient and their journey. Each journey is a story of its own, marked by highs and lows. This idea of the "patient journey" represents a shift toward **patient-centered care**—a philosophy that places the individual, not just the diagnosis, at the heart of treatment. It encompasses everything: the first unsettling symptoms, the diagnosis, treatment attempts, setbacks, and long-term management. It serves as a lens through which we can examine the entire landscape of psychiatric care, connecting all aspects of the system and revealing where it falls short.

Because in the end, what matters most is simple: does the patient feel better?

To make sure we capture the full range of complexities and pinpoint as many shortcomings as possible in the psychiatric field, the first three chapters of this book will closely follow the patient's journey, step by step. We'll carefully examine each stage, identifying the specific difficulties patients encounter along the way. This detailed exploration will provide a solid foundation, enabling us to delve deeper into where these challenges originate—and how, potentially, they could be addressed.

The Power of Stigma

Maria is 27, a business consultant at a tech startup. A year ago, her life took a sharp turn. After an unexpected divorce, she returned to her hometown and had to rebuild everything from scratch—finding a new apartment, starting fresh in a new job, and working to regain her stability.

Now, she's proud of the life she's creating, especially her work. She thrives on complex challenges, enjoys her grounded, funny team, and loves the travel that keeps her meeting clients around the world. Despite the sudden loss that left her with almost nothing, she took control and managed to rebuild. After a year, things are finally falling into place: a beautiful apartment, a job she loves, supportive friends and family, even a promising new relationship. By all accounts, she should feel happy.

But lately, something feels off. At first, she brushed it aside as a passing phase—just a few bumps in the road. She found herself lying awake at night, unable to sleep. She began binge eating when stressed, growing frustrated with her usual workout routine, and gradually pulling back from plans with friends. Probably, I'm just tired, she thought. Ignoring the nagging thoughts was easier than facing what they might mean. Here comes the first step of the patient journey—awareness. Maria has noticed her symptoms, but she's choosing not to seek help. This stage is heavily shaped by cultural beliefs and social conditioning. In Maria's environment, talking about feeling drained or even hinting at depression is often dismissed as laziness. Mental health stereotypes loom large; mental illness is associated with extreme, unsettling characters—like those in *One Flew Over the Cuckoo's Nest*. Patients like Maria often prefer to keep quiet, ignore the symptoms, and push forward, hoping this phase will simply pass on its own.

But mental health, like any other area of medicine, relies on timely intervention. The earlier we seek treatment, even in the form of prevention, the better our chances of avoiding serious consequences. The problem is that mental health concerns are perceived differently. If Maria had noticed a skin rash or unexplained weight gain, she'd likely be more concerned and less willing to ignore it.

Here, we face the first and perhaps the most powerful obstacle in a patient's journey to treatment—**stigma**. But what is stigma?

Erving Goffman, in his book *Stigma: Notes on the Management of Spoiled Identity* (1963), defines it as "an attribute that is deeply discrediting," something that reduces a person "from a whole and usual person to a tainted, discounted one."[1] It's not just about the condition itself; it's about the gap between who someone is and how they are perceived.

Sociologist Graham Scambler, who studied the stigma of epilepsy, expands on this by distinguishing between **enacted stigma** and **felt stigma**.[2] Enacted stigma is external—it's the discrimination, exclusion, and unfair treatment that people with mental illness face from others. Felt stigma, on the other hand, is internal. It's the shame, the expectation of rejection, the fear that speaking up will lead to judgment. And sometimes, this internalized stigma is even more damaging than external discrimination because it leads people to withdraw, stay silent, and avoid seeking the help they need.

As deeply social creatures, humans have evolved an acute sensitivity to how others perceive them. Usually, this helps us navigate society and make better choices, but in the context of mental health, it often works against us. Anticipating judgment and rejection, people become reluctant to openly discuss their struggles—not because their fears are exaggerated, but precisely because they're realistic. Overcoming these internal doubts requires immense effort and energy, which mental illness often significantly diminishes (we'll explore this further in the coming chapters). Even when someone finds the strength to push past their inner hesitations, they still face external barriers—stigma from family, friends, colleagues, and the broader community.

This combination—internal fears reinforced by genuine societal discrimination—is precisely why many delay seeking help or avoid it altogether. It's easy for some to say, "Who cares what others think? Just do what's best for you." But not everyone has that privilege. In many cultures, social acceptance isn't simply desirable—it's essential, deeply tied to personal identity and opportunities. Being supported and respected by your community can determine your sense of worth and your future, making stigma far more than just another opinion to brush aside.

Perhaps the hardest part is how stigma feeds itself. When people don't seek help, their experiences remain hidden, reinforcing misconceptions. Without visibility, the myths about mental illness—that depression signals weakness, anxiety means overreacting, or bipolar disorder indicates unreliability—persist unchallenged, embedding stigma even deeper into our collective consciousness.

That's why stigma is so hard to dismantle. It runs deeper than just personal biases, rooted instead in culture, traditions, and beliefs passed down over generations. Reinforced by institutions, media portrayals, and even our everyday language, stigma doesn't simply fade when we recognize it. Social movements, educational campaigns, and public dialogue can help shift perceptions—particularly when influential figures lead the conversation—but substantial change typically takes decades, emerging slowly and in small increments.

It's not always clear where stigma originates, but one possible explanation is our innate fear of the unknown. This fear can drive society's reluctance to confront conditions that feel confusing or frightening—phenomena lacking straightforward explanations or clear solutions. When faced with such uncertainty, people tend to react in one of several predictable ways. Some attempt to minimize or downplay the problem, making it appear insignificant and unworthy of attention. Others seek simple, understandable explanations, often lacking scientific or rational backing, to restore a sense of control. Still others tie these phenomena to more powerful forces, framing them in religious terms, for example, or as something forbidden, dangerous, and best left unmentioned. These responses are common and understandable from a social psychology perspective, as they help individuals regain a sense of control. Yet collectively, these very reactions strengthen stigma's grip. And unfortunately, its power grows at an alarming rate.

Given how slowly cultural attitudes evolve, there must be another path toward progress. Historically, objective evidence has proven most effective at shifting deeply entrenched beliefs—especially when new scientific data or measurable outcomes emerge, fundamentally reshaping our understanding of entire disorders.

Take multiple sclerosis, for example. For decades, it was poorly understood and frequently misdiagnosed. Patients—often young adults in their 20s and 30s—presented with strange, fluctuating symptoms like fatigue, numbness, or vision problems, but without any visible signs of illness. And because there was no definitive test, many were dismissed or misdiagnosed with conditions like hysteria or conversion disorder. Women in particular—already more likely to be diagnosed with MS—were often told their symptoms were psychological, not physiological. In fact, a systematic review published in *The BMJ* found that up to 29% of patients initially diagnosed with hysteria in the 1950s were later found to have a clear neurological condition, including MS.[3]

That began to change with the introduction of magnetic resonance imaging (MRI) in the 1980s. For the first time, clinicians could see the damage—lesions in the brain and spinal cord—confirming what patients had been describing for years. With the ability to *see* the illness, MS was no longer dismissed or questioned. It became medical fact. And with that shift, the stigma surrounding it began to unravel—not because people became more empathetic, but because there was finally undeniable proof.

A similar transformation happened with epilepsy. For centuries, epilepsy was surrounded by fear, myth, and superstition. In ancient cultures, seizures were often interpreted as signs of possession, divine punishment, or madness. Even into the twentieth century, people with epilepsy were routinely stigmatized—denied employment, excluded from education, institutionalized, and in some places, even prohibited from marrying. The condition was feared not just because of its symptoms, but because it was poorly understood and impossible to prove without witness. That changed with the development of electroencephalography (EEG) in the 1920s, which allowed scientists to observe abnormal electrical activity in the brain during seizures. For the first time, epilepsy could be *seen*. It had a biological basis, a measurable pattern, and a place in medical science. This didn't erase all stigma overnight, but it marked a critical shift—from mystical to medical, from shame to science. Visibility, once again, brought legitimacy.

One of psychiatry's most persistent ambitions has been to find objective markers—measurable, replicable indicators that could definitively confirm the presence of a disorder. Ideally, these would be as clear and consistent as those we have in other areas of medicine: brain scans, genetic signatures, biological signals—something tangible and reliable that clearly distinguishes genuine illness from subjective feelings or personal narratives. Decades of research, multiple promising hypotheses, and countless approaches have been dedicated to finding such markers, yet we still have no definitive results. There remains no simple test, no universal biomarker, no clear biological indicator that reliably applies across different patients and situations.

This absence of objective evidence creates enormous problems. When a condition lacks visible, proven markers, it inevitably becomes subject to doubt and suspicion. People begin to question its legitimacy—is it a genuine medical issue, or merely an emotional overreaction, a sign of personal weakness, or burnout mistakenly labeled as illness? Such uncertainty not only reinforces stigma but amplifies it. This is a critical point that I'll revisit frequently throughout the book, as it influences nearly every aspect of psychiatry—from patient experiences and clinical decisions to societal attitudes and the broader pace of scientific progress. In Chapter 3, we'll explore in greater detail why psychiatry continues to lack these objective markers, examining closely the scientific challenges and underlying reasons behind this persistent gap in knowledge.

Right now, Maria has nothing to hold onto except her own feeling that something isn't right—and even that, she constantly questions, trying to understand the nature of her condition. A quiet internal dialogue persists: one part of her recognizes that these changes she's experiencing are new, unusual, and perhaps deserving of attention, while another voice quickly casts doubt—what if this is just temporary, a passing phase that will soon disappear?

Her mind involuntarily plays out various scenarios. What might happen if she gathers the courage to see a doctor? Would she feel embarrassed for wasting the doctor's time—and her own? And what if it turns out that she truly isn't well, and she receives an actual diagnosis? The thought is terrifying. What will people think of her then? Will her parents support her, or will they quietly judge her—see her as ungrateful, or dramatic? Will her partner stick around, or start to pull away, unsure how to handle her mood swings? What about work? Would her colleagues still trust her, or would they start quietly excluding her from the projects that matter? What if things get worse, and she ends up in a mental health facility? Would that become part of her identity forever? She keeps replaying these scenarios in her mind—the kind of scenarios many of us have quietly imagined. The questions persist, circling endlessly and amplifying her anxiety, each loop pushing her further from the possibility of seeking help.

This is the subtle but destructive power of stigma. It transforms natural uncertainty into deep-seated fear, stretching moments of hesitation into prolonged silence. It convinces people like Maria to delay just a little longer—until symptoms become impossible to ignore, until pain grows too intense, and until the chance for timely help slips away. Not because they don't wish to be helped, but because stigma has conditioned them to believe that needing support is something shameful.

Recognizing the Invisible Changes

After pushing through her internal doubts and overcoming the initial resistance caused by stigma, Maria finally allows herself to consider that something might genuinely be wrong. This acknowledgment, simply accepting the possibility of illness, was only the first step. Now she faces an even more challenging task, one frequently clouded by uncertainty—carefully assessing what exactly has changed and understanding the magnitude of these changes. She begins to question herself, wondering precisely what feels different, how significant these shifts really are, and when they started occurring, knowing all too well that such introspection rarely yields straightforward answers.

Changes in mental health typically develop slowly and subtly, making them notoriously difficult to recognize. Additionally, these shifts often alter the way our minds function, distorting the very perception we rely on to evaluate reality. Maria inevitably faces a wave of uncertainty as she tries to interpret behaviors that trouble her—behaviors that might serve as genuine indicators of an underlying issue, or alternatively, may simply be characteristics she's never paid close attention to before. Her perception becomes unreliable, clouded by stress, mood fluctuations, or whatever emotional haze she finds herself in that day. She repeatedly returns to the same unsettling questions: "Am I actually more irritable than usual, or have I always been this way? Am I really binge eating, or is this just how I've always coped with stress? Am I withdrawing socially, or am I simply tired because of my workload and new projects? Has my sleep gotten worse, or was it never particularly good?"

Answering these questions honestly requires a high degree of self-awareness—an exceptional level of introspection that's more often an exception than the rule. To achieve that kind of clarity, a person needs substantial mental resources, not to mention sufficient time and space to turn attention inward. But today's pace of life, particularly in busy cities, rarely permits such reflection. Most people remain caught in an endless cycle of work–home–work, too preoccupied even to notice obvious signs—basic physical cues like hunger or lack of sleep—let alone more subtle signals indicating deeper mental changes.

Even if someone manages to recognize these signals, evaluating their meaning and importance is often complicated. With physical or more visible changes, the process tends to be simpler and more straightforward. For instance, if you gain weight, a scale provides clear feedback; if your heart rate increases, your watch or health tracker immediately alerts you. But shifts in mood, changes in thinking, or subtle differences in how you perceive your surroundings aren't easy to measure or confirm objectively. There's no clear signal or measurable indicator. Instead, you're left interpreting these changes through the same subjective lens that's already influenced by the state you're trying to assess.

Another barrier to objectively evaluating our own state is the absence of a clear, established baseline—some fixed understanding of our personal "normal" that could serve as a reference point. It's similar to the marks parents draw on a doorframe to track their child's growth, or knowing your baseline blood pressure so you can quickly recognize any deviations. Many of us regularly measure ourselves in some way—whether by consistently weighing ourselves or using wearable devices to track various health metrics—and this helps us develop a clear, personalized understanding of what's typical for us. For example, my own standard is walking about 7,000 steps daily; this doesn't necessarily reflect a universal norm, but it accurately represents my lifestyle and physical habits. When it comes to emotional states or cognitive abilities like attention or memory, however, we lack these regular, objective measurement tools. Currently, there are few solutions available that consistently track how we usually feel, think, or behave across multiple dimensions. Without these tools, we have no reliable way of comparing our current state against a known baseline.

Maria doesn't have concrete records showing how many hours per week she typically enjoyed working, how often she laughed with friends, or how much energy she generally had. Without a clear reference point, she struggles to determine how much things have truly changed. If she knew she previously felt happy around twenty hours a week and noticed a clear reduction, this would provide strong evidence of an issue—but that kind of information simply doesn't exist for her, nor for most people.

Unfortunately, our mood and perception of the world are inherently fluid, heavily influenced by external factors and closely tied to our individual personalities and behavioral patterns. This variability makes it difficult to confidently judge whether something is truly unusual or simply a normal variation, even within our own lives. You've probably experienced moments when you've shared your feelings with someone else, asking if they've ever felt the same—an attempt to calibrate yourself against others and understand what's unique or typical for you.

One practical step toward clarity is seeking feedback from someone outside yourself—someone who knows you well and cares enough to notice subtle shifts in your behavior. This might be your parents, partner, friends, or colleagues. Perhaps they've already observed changes and are trying to gently point out their concerns. Yet even here, another barrier often emerges: your willingness to accept their input is filtered through your trust in that person, your relationship dynamics, previous experiences, and current emotional state. Let's be honest—when was the last time you genuinely welcomed someone close to you suggesting something might be wrong?

Most of us react to such feedback defensively, with irritation or even withdrawal. On top of that, the observations of others may themselves be distorted by their own stress, moods, expectations, or changing relationships. Even if their perception is accurate, you may simply not believe them—or may prefer not to hear it.

Thus, recognizing there might be a problem—pushing past internal hesitation and social stigma—is only the initial step. The next challenge, which is often even greater, lies in gathering reliable evidence of meaningful change.

In the absence of clear measures or baselines, Maria remains stuck with vague impressions and uncertain guesses, forced to evaluate her condition through perceptions already influenced by mood and doubt. Without objective measurement tools or well-defined reference points, clarity is nearly impossible. This represents the second major barrier: we simply haven't created effective tools to help people accurately recognize when something has changed. Without seeing those changes clearly, it becomes much harder to take appropriate action.

The Search for Answers in a Misinformed World

Eventually, perhaps even without fully realizing it, Maria begins to search for answers, predictably turning first to the internet, and it is precisely at this point that the situation becomes increasingly complex. Online, she encounters an overwhelming array of resources promising to help her gain a deeper understanding of herself. Among these resources are numerous self-assessment quizzes, asking her to recall how she has felt over the preceding weeks, despite her difficulty remembering even what she ate the previous day. Additionally, she comes across a variety of mental health blogs, TikTok influencers, and Instagram therapists—some offering seemingly genuine insights, others appearing superficial or deliberately crafted solely to capture attention. Amid this extensive and often contradictory information, Maria also encounters more authoritative resources, such as books, academic papers, and professional advice. However, which of these numerous sources Maria ultimately chooses to trust or internalize frequently depends heavily on her current emotional state, her capacity to maintain attention, and her willingness—or reluctance—to fully acknowledge the potential implications of what she might discover.

Instagram and TikTok alone host over ten million posts tagged #mentalhealth. In some respects, this is a positive development, as social media normalizes discussions around mental health, enabling people to become more open about these issues and speak more freely, potentially even addressing stigma-related challenges. Nevertheless, the reliability of such content frequently remains questionable, and for vulnerable individuals actively seeking guidance, credibility becomes critically important.

This online landscape is also a breeding ground for what researchers call **neuromyths**—widespread but inaccurate beliefs about brain function and mental health.[4,5] These misconceptions typically sound scientific and authoritative, making them easy to spread, especially on platforms optimized for quick and straightforward content delivery. Initially, the term was used to describe common misunderstandings in neuroscience, which typically arose due to insufficient research or hypotheses that emerged but remained unverified. However, even after many of these beliefs have been disproven, neuromyths continue to persist not only among the general public but also among educators and healthcare providers. Familiar examples include claims that humans use just 10% of their brains, that teaching methods should be matched strictly to so-called "visual" or "auditory" learning styles, or that individuals are inherently "left-brained" or "right-brained." The term neuromyth is also appropriate beyond pure neuroscience; for example, in psychiatry, since most scientific psychiatric theories are directly tied to the mechanisms of the brain and central nervous system. Over the years of psychiatric research, numerous misconceptions have emerged, many of which have either been disproven or at least shown to have had insufficient scientific grounds. Examples include oversimplifications such as depression resulting purely from "low serotonin," dopamine being the exclusive driver of motivation or addiction, or the misconception that the "entire brain lights up" during manic episodes in bipolar disorder.

The central issue with neuromyths lies in their inherently deceptive nature; they often sound scientifically credible or contain elements of truth, which enables them to effortlessly embed themselves into public consciousness and be perceived as accurate. With the widespread adoption of social media, the dissemination of false or partially accurate information has reached unprecedented proportions. This is partly due to the very format in which information is delivered, as videos and posts primarily aim to capture and retain viewers' attention. Consequently, the content on such platforms is often significantly simplified to be easily understandable by a broad audience, emotionally colored (sometimes excessively so) to engage viewers, and heavily shortened due to constraints of text and video formats supported by these platforms. Moreover, this content is frequently created not by professional therapists or psychiatrists but by individuals without expertise in mental health. Such creators either share their personal experiences, which, given the nature of mental illnesses, are often not relevant to other patients, or use publicly available sources, simply paraphrasing or replicating information from one another without additional verification or rigorous fact-checking.

When such statements are repeatedly circulated and echoed by various pseudo-experts, they become deeply entrenched in users' perceptions, becoming exceedingly difficult to correct or disprove. In the context of mental health, this issue becomes particularly acute, as such misinformation may lead to incorrect self-diagnosis, delays in seeking necessary care, or even the outright refusal of treatment, potentially exacerbating existing conditions or, paradoxically, increasing mental distress due to the misleading content encountered on social media.

There are still relatively few studies on this topic, partly because the phenomenon of information dissemination via social media is itself relatively new, and partly due to the difficulty in establishing clear criteria for what constitutes accurate information and what should be classified as misinformation. Nevertheless, even preliminary data offer some insight into the general quality of such content. For instance, one study analyzed YouTube content about schizophrenia intended for a Spanish-speaking audience.[6] Despite YouTube typically attracting a more attentive audience and generally providing more detailed information compared to other platforms, even there only 39% of content cited at least one scientific publication. The same study also noted that although videos created by healthcare professionals were significantly more accurate and informative, they generally received fewer views and interactions compared to non-professional content. Considering the basic logic of how recommendation algorithms on such platforms operate, it can be assumed that scientifically validated videos would appear less frequently in users' recommendations compared to more popular but less reliable materials.

Similar results regarding content quality were demonstrated by an analysis of YouTube videos related to ADHD (attention-deficit/hyperactivity disorder). Among approximately 159 videos appearing first in search results for relevant queries, 39% contained misleading information, while only 5% provided useful information on ADHD.[7] These figures deteriorate further when it comes to entertainment-driven platforms with shorter content formats, such as TikTok. For instance, an analysis of the 100 most-viewed TikTok videos about ADHD, with an average view count of 2.8 million per video and an average share count of roughly 31,000, revealed that approximately 52% of the information presented was misleading. This study also supports the hypothesis that the most popular videos were typically not created by healthcare professionals but rather originated from individuals simply sharing their personal experiences.[8]

Of course, these indicators can vary significantly depending on the topic, country, or specific disorder in question, yet general trends reflecting average content quality remain relatively consistent. For instance, a comprehensive analysis of 1,000 of the most-viewed TikTok videos on various mental disorders, covering 3 different languages and created across several countries, found that only about 21% of the content was supported by any scientific references.[9] Typically, misinformation appeared as overly simplistic self-diagnosis criteria—for example, suggesting that simple forgetfulness automatically indicates ADHD—or misleading statements promoting supposed remedies through dietary supplements. In mental health content, misleading claims often presented mental illness merely as an attitude problem or advocated replacing therapy entirely with positive thinking, thereby minimizing the severity of genuine mental health conditions. Videos discussing personality disorders frequently depicted borderline or narcissistic traits inaccurately or in a stigmatizing manner, typically devoid of any clinical grounding. Content on suicide occasionally romanticized suicidal thoughts or portrayed recovery without professional support as universally achievable. Regarding psychotic disorders, hallucinations were sometimes misleadingly represented as spiritual enlightenment or experiences easily controlled by sheer willpower. Finally, misinformation related to treatment often involved promotion of unproven therapies or discouragement of psychiatric medication use through claims like "antidepressants worsen your condition" or "therapy is just a scam."

And it is even difficult to imagine how such content might influence an already discouraged and confused patient who doesn't know where to seek help, and who, in search of answers, encounters these kinds of statements widely disseminated across the internet due to their large number of views and shares. Moreover, given how recommendation algorithms function—suggesting videos similar to those previously viewed, liked, or saved—there is a real risk that patients like Maria might simply become trapped in a rabbit hole of misinformation, unable to find their way out.

Another common resource individuals like Maria often turn to in their search for answers is self-help literature. Compared to the chaotic and overwhelming environment of TikTok or Instagram, books typically provide a sense of stability and depth, offering readers a calmer, more structured, and deliberate approach. Their thoughtful tone, coherent structure, and formal presentation inherently create an impression of greater credibility and reliability compared to posts circulating on social media.

Indeed, in many cases, this impression holds true. Some self-help books have been demonstrated to effectively assist individuals in managing anxiety, depression, or stress. Research on "bibliotherapy"—the practice of guided self-help reading—suggests it can significantly alleviate symptoms, particularly in mild to moderate cases. Certain studies have even reported outcomes comparable to those achieved through traditional therapy, especially in situations where therapy is unavailable, when the books focus on specific problems and provide actionable strategies rooted in evidence-based methods such as cognitive-behavioral therapy (CBT).[10,11] Unsurprisingly, more than 85% of psychotherapists report recommending self-help literature to their clients at some stage.[12]

Nevertheless, this does not imply that all self-help books are inherently safe or beneficial. The self-help market is enormous, with thousands of new titles published annually, yet the majority never undergo scientific evaluation. According to estimates from researchers who have examined the self-help book industry, only around 5% of these books are supported by any peer-reviewed evidence.[13] As a result, readers are largely left to their own judgment in determining which books provide sound, evidence-based advice and which merely represent polished personal opinions. Consequently, readers must find the motivation and energy to thoroughly evaluate each book before making a choice, as neither popularity nor high sales figures necessarily guarantee the quality of content or the usefulness of the advice provided. For instance, in a review of 50 bestselling self-help titles addressing anxiety, depression, and trauma, researchers found that while certain books did align with validated clinical methodologies, others presented recommendations that were not only unsupported by scientific evidence but potentially harmful.[14]

For readers like Maria, this distinction often remains unclear. Many books appear scientific or include popular psychological terminology, yet they lack genuine clinical rigor. Moreover, when a book promises profound transformation—such as "heal your trauma in 30 days" or "banish anxiety forever"—it can create unrealistic expectations. If the advice ultimately proves ineffective, readers may not attribute the failure to the book, but instead blame themselves. Psychologists refer to this phenomenon as false hope syndrome, wherein individuals internalize feelings of inadequacy and failure after following methods that were fundamentally flawed from the outset.[15] Moreover, the consequences can extend beyond mere disappointment or unmet expectations. Approximately 12% to 24% of readers report experiencing adverse effects from using self-help books, including heightened confusion, increased anxiety, or worsening of symptoms; additionally, nearly one in five therapists have observed clients harmed by low-quality self-help materials.[16]

Another factor that significantly impacts the credibility of self-help books is the qualification of the author. While many books are written by licensed psychologists or therapists, a substantial number are authored by individuals without clinical expertise. Indeed, several best-selling authors in this genre have no formal clinical training at all, often relying solely on personal anecdotes, persuasive charisma, or "mindset coaching" techniques to promote their advice. Studies confirm that self-help literature authored by qualified professionals generally offers more accurate and beneficial content compared to those by untrained individuals; however, credentials alone do not always guarantee quality.[14]

In summary, self-help books can either serve as valuable tools or lead readers astray. When they are scientifically validated and authored by qualified specialists, these books can effectively supplement therapy or provide crucial support for those without access to professional mental healthcare. Yet, in an unregulated market saturated with exaggerated claims and limited oversight, readers must remain vigilant. Although books might appear to offer a safe avenue for personal exploration, the reality is that, particularly in the context of mental health, not all self-help materials are equally reliable or beneficial.

In her pursuit of clarity, Maria finds herself entangled in a maze of conflicting information. What initially began as a quiet, manageable concern swiftly escalates into profound confusion, complicating an already emotionally demanding situation. Rather than guiding her toward meaningful progress, this overwhelming barrage of contradictory content—misleading posts, oversimplified symptom checklists, neuromyths, and overly confident social media therapists—serves only to heighten Maria's anxiety and deepen her self-doubt. Consequently, individuals like Maria often experience substantial delays in seeking legitimate professional assistance, with some never obtaining appropriate care at all. Research indicates that only around one-third of those struggling with depression or anxiety ultimately pursue clinical treatment; the remainder frequently find themselves trapped, attempting to navigate their difficulties alone.[17,18]

There are three reasons why this happens so often:

- First, neuromyths and emotionally charged content can amplify distress. Instead of offering clarity, they fuel worry by presenting vague or exaggerated descriptions that feel personal but offer no real path forward.
- Second, misinformation leads to misdiagnosis. Once someone internalizes a label they've picked up online, it can shape how they talk about their symptoms, what they believe will help, and even what kind of treatment they're willing to accept.
- And third, once a self-diagnosis feels convincing, the urgency to seek professional care often disappears. It creates the illusion of understanding—without the support that might actually make a difference.

That Evening in Tribeca

Looking back at that evening in Tribeca, I can now see clearly how all the themes discussed in this chapter surfaced simultaneously.

First came the internal barrier. I convinced myself I was being open and sincere by attending the meeting and sharing my experience, despite feeling deep down that I probably wasn't in the right condition for it. I chose to go anyway—partly due to fear of missing an important opportunity, partly because admitting I needed rest seemed more difficult than simply pushing myself forward, and partly because I had no reliable way to objectively evaluate my condition and justify staying home. Internal stigma also quietly played its role, manifesting subtly as an inner voice telling me to keep going.

Then came the external reaction. I openly shared my personal story: my long history with depression, years spent on medication, and my recent decision to stop taking it. At the time, it felt like important and relevant context about myself and my work. Yet almost immediately afterward, I felt something subtle but noticeable—a slight distancing, as if revealing these experiences had changed how I was perceived professionally. This external stigma is exactly what many people fear when openly discussing their mental health, often leading them to stay silent.

Next came the assumptions. The person I met with that evening was not a practicing clinician. This was only our second meeting, and she didn't have detailed knowledge of my medical history, my background, or my typical baseline state. Yet she quickly offered firm advice about my condition, implicitly suggesting a diagnosis and even recommending treatment. Moments like this highlight a broader issue: without objective tools or clear reference points, assessments easily become subjective, even those coming from well-intentioned individuals.

Finally, there was the advice itself: "SSRIs are like an inhaler—they just increase your serotonin." It sounded confident and reassuring, yet this was a clear example of a neuromyth—an oversimplified idea I'd heard many times before. Hearing it from an experienced professional in the mental health industry genuinely surprised me; I'd expected a more nuanced perspective. Later in Chapter 3, we'll briefly discuss where this neuromyth originated and why it continues to persist despite lacking scientific support.

When I reflect on psychiatry, I often think of the famous line from the TV series *House*: "Everybody lies." In psychiatry, people do not intentionally hide their truth, but the truth itself remains unclear. We lack reliable tools to objectively measure, define, or confirm our experiences. As a result, we often doubt our own symptoms or dismiss the experiences of others, settling for simplified explanations that feel easier to manage.

In the next chapter, we'll explore how this fundamental uncertainty directly shapes interactions between patients and clinicians, profoundly influencing the diagnostic process itself.

2 | Diagnostic Roulette

The door opened, and the doctor looked at Maria with visible surprise. She stood on crutches and offered a half-apologetic smile.

"Well… it's a long story. I broke my foot last week. Nice to meet you."

She stepped into the room—it looked like something out of a Woody Allen movie: a soft couch where patients were expected to lie down and stare at the ceiling, a low coffee table that seemed to serve no purpose at all, and a single armchair for the doctor—perfectly placed for asking questions in a calm, measured voice.

Soft jazz played in the background—supposedly to soothe the nerves and, perhaps, to muffle conversations so they wouldn't be overheard through the thin walls.

"So, what brings you here?"

Maria exhaled. She didn't want to sound ungrateful. She tried to hide her exhaustion behind a polite tone and an artificial smile.

"I've been treated for depression for the past three years," she said. "And I don't like how it's going."

"Can you tell me more?"

Another sigh.

"Well… where should I start…"

She was tired. A little annoyed. She had no idea where to begin.

She'd told this story so many times that the pain had already been sanded down into something numb, almost scripted—like she was performing a half-hearted stand-up routine.

Why am I even here today? It's a good day. I don't feel depressed at all. It feels kind of stupid—wasting money and time like this.

But she knows it doesn't last. The bad days always return. The spiral always comes back. And if she really wants help, she has to do this—one more time.

This is her third psychiatrist.

She has to start all over again.

* * *

Seeking Help: Who Answers First?

Having finally overcome her stigma, acknowledged that she genuinely felt unwell, and grown thoroughly confused by the whirlwind of online advice, Maria decided it was time to see a doctor. One evening, after yet another overwhelming day, she sat down on her couch, opened her laptop, and started calling clinics, one by one, hoping to find a psychiatrist. She wasn't sure exactly what kind of specialist she needed, what qualifications were important, or even how much experience they should have; she simply knew she needed professional help. Any help. She opened an online medical directory, entered her zip code, and began making calls. But every clinic gave her the same response: "Sorry, we're not accepting new patients." Maria continued scrolling through websites—trusted hospital networks, private practices with welcoming photos, individual doctors with professional-looking profiles. Some didn't answer the phone at all. Others said the earliest appointment would be in two months. After a week of frustration, she finally gave up and scheduled an appointment with a general practitioner instead.

Many people follow exactly this route, and often it makes sense as a first step. Regardless of the symptoms you're experiencing, it's common practice to first consult a general practitioner. Usually, it's the GP who conducts the initial evaluation and decides which specialist you might need. There's a reason for this: mood fluctuations, changes in appetite, or sleep disturbances can signal a variety of issues beyond psychiatry—vitamin deficiencies, hormonal imbalances, or thyroid disorders, to name a few. Instead of attempting self-diagnosis, it's practical to start with a GP who can view your symptoms in a broader medical context.

The second reason relates to safety—internal and emotional safety. Going to a general practitioner often feels safer, since usually it's someone you've already seen before and developed at least some trust toward. It also helps you temporarily avoid confronting the uncomfortable possibility that your symptoms might reflect a mental health issue. It gives you additional time to hope that your problem might resolve itself, perhaps with minimal adjustments.

Third, as in Maria's case, there's the issue of access. The number of psychiatrists continues to decline, creating shortages in many regions. While the situation varies significantly by region, in many parts of the United States, the wait time to see a psychiatrist can be as long as six months[1]—an alarmingly long period. Such delays become especially critical when a person's condition is severe, since even a few days of waiting can drastically affect their state. Psychiatry, just like other medical specialties, depends heavily on timely intervention, and delayed care often makes the situation significantly worse.

And finally, there's the financial aspect. Visiting a general practitioner usually costs less—it's a more affordable option. On top of that, insurance coverage often becomes a deciding factor, since not all insurance plans fully cover mental healthcare, and some only partially. As a result, many people initially see their GP, describe what's bothering them, and expect the doctor to evaluate their condition and, if necessary, refer them to the appropriate specialist. At first glance, this approach seems entirely harmless and even logical: the GP assesses your situation and sends you onward to the right professional if needed.

But in reality, things rarely work this way. Consider this statistic: around 80% of antidepressants are prescribed by general practitioners.[2] In practice, this means patients briefly describe their symptoms during a standard 15- to 20-minute appointment[3] and often leave with a prescription. To illustrate why this is concerning, imagine applying the same logic in other medical situations. Suppose you find a suspicious lump and suspect cancer—you visit your GP, and after just fifteen minutes of conversation, they immediately begin treatment. Or you arrive with a broken leg, and fifteen minutes later you're already leaving the office with a cast and crutches. Clearly, that would be absurd.

Yet somehow, when it comes to mental health, this approach has become standard practice. A general practitioner, often with minimal specialized psychiatric training, prescribes medication that directly impacts brain chemistry—based solely on what the patient manages to convey in one brief conversation. Within those same fifteen minutes, the doctor is expected to thoroughly evaluate the patient's condition, rule out other medical causes, listen to their personal story, gauge how significantly their current state deviates from their usual baseline, review relevant family medical history, and select the most suitable medication.

To be clear, I fully recognize that receiving help from any trained medical professional is far better than receiving none at all, and I don't intend to blame general practitioners personally. They do not control appointment lengths or the structure of the healthcare system itself. However, the reality remains that a genuinely thorough psychiatric evaluation—the kind required for accurate diagnosis and effective treatment—simply cannot happen within these limited constraints, even for psychiatrists with decades of experience.

Here's why.

At the Psychiatrist's Office

An ideal psychiatric assessment should be deep and thorough—detailed enough to construct a full and coherent picture of the patient's complaints, psychiatric and medical history, and all relevant risk factors. The American Psychiatric Association (APA) has outlined clear clinical guidelines[4] to structure this evaluation across all major domains. The goal is straightforward: to determine whether psychiatric care is needed, to arrive at an accurate diagnosis, and to define a treatment plan that will support the patient moving forward.

What Brings You Here Today?

The first step in the evaluation is to understand why the patient has come to see a psychiatrist. At this stage, the clinician is expected to identify the main complaint, establish how long it has been present, and—as the APA guidelines suggest—explore what the patient hopes to achieve through treatment, and to do so in "sufficient detail." This is where the classic question comes in: "What brings you in today?" And this is when the patient is expected to articulate their concerns and describe what they are going through.

But we already know how complex that can be. Articulating one's experience requires a certain level of self-awareness, but more importantly, the ability to evaluate one's current state in relation to how things used to be. In the context of psychiatric illness, however, this kind of comparison becomes profoundly unreliable. Mental disorders affect not only perception of the external world, but also one's sense of self. And when this internal frame of reference shifts, the task of describing what exactly is "wrong" becomes increasingly elusive.

A significant part of the difficulty lies in how mental illness interferes with emotional granularity—the ability to distinguish and precisely label emotional states. Individuals with higher emotional differentiation typically demonstrate greater success in regulating their emotions in daily life, whereas those with lower granularity tend to express emotions in vague, generalized terms, frequently relying on broad descriptors like "bad," "tired," or "overwhelmed."[5] Given that emotional clarity is often impaired in psychiatric conditions, it is unsurprising that patients not only struggle to identify what they feel but also question whether their descriptions accurately reflect their experiences.[6]

There is also the matter of language itself—emotional vocabulary is highly individual. The same word may carry significantly different meanings from one person to another. "Tired," for example, can describe emotional burnout, chronic physiological fatigue, or simply a low-energy day. "Depressed" might refer to clinical anhedonia, a temporary sense of emptiness, or a reaction to disappointment.

Multiple studies conducted across diverse demographic groups, including both adults and children, have demonstrated that interpretations of emotional terms can vary significantly.[7–9] In such studies, participants are typically asked to categorize various emotional words into basic groups like "happy," "sad," or "angry," and a notable percentage of responses show substantial variability, heavily influenced by individual background and personal associations. Additionally, research has indicated that when new categories are introduced, participants often re-categorize words, further increasing instability and demonstrating the flexible, context-dependent nature of emotional language. Thus, what initially appear to be familiar terms become unstable categories—meanings shift subtly depending on each individual's personal experience and context. Consequently, when one patient describes feeling "overwhelmed," it is highly likely that they mean something quite different from another patient using the same term.

The guidelines suggest that clinicians should also take into account collateral information from family members or close contacts. But those accounts can be just as unreliable—shaped not only by their own interpretation of the patient's words, but also by expectations, projections, and personal judgments. Our internal experiences often don't match how others perceive us. In fact, for many patients, those closest to them are the ones who misunderstand them most.

So, the clinician ultimately has to rely entirely on the patient's own account—no matter how incomplete, subjective, or imprecise it might be. The evaluation depends exclusively on the patient's ability to put their experience into words, even though words alone rarely capture the full complexity of mental states. An additional layer of uncertainty arises from the clinician's interpretation itself—the subtle nuances they notice, the context they add, and the ways their own professional background, biases, and experience inevitably shape their understanding of the patient's story.

Uncovering the Clinical History

Once the initial complaint is clarified, the psychiatrist needs to understand how the current condition developed, how long it has persisted, what events or factors might have contributed to it, and what preceded it. To do this, they collect a broader history that includes psychiatric, medical, social, and family background. While structurally this process might appear systematic, in practice, it largely depends on the patient's memory, their willingness to share details, and the natural dynamics of the conversation.

The first step is capturing the history of the present illness. Ideally, the psychiatrist tries to establish when the symptoms began, what circumstances might have triggered them, how they evolved over time, and whether the person tried managing things independently or sought professional help. In reality, though, most people don't closely track these details as they happen. Instead, they adapt, postpone action, or reinterpret their experiences. By the time they finally see a psychiatrist, weeks, months, or sometimes even years have passed, making it difficult to pinpoint precisely how everything started. The illness itself further complicates this process: depression can impair memory, anxiety fragments concentration, and psychosis distorts perception of reality. Even when patients try their best to provide specifics, they often rely on intuitively significant markers—such as a breakup, relocation, or new job—that might not fully correspond to clinical insights. Ultimately, the psychiatrist must build their assessment from whatever the patient can recall, even though it's often incomplete.

Next, the psychiatrist gathers information about the patient's past psychiatric history, asking about previous diagnoses, hospitalizations, or treatments. But this approach presumes the person has actually received formal care in the past. In reality, many people experience prolonged psychological distress without ever identifying it as such or seeking professional help. Others may have briefly seen a provider once or twice, without clear diagnosis or consistent follow-up. Even if medication was prescribed at some point, patients often remain unsure about the exact reason, and clear records of these treatments are rarely available. Patients' descriptions of their past psychiatric experiences can therefore be vague and generalized: "I took something for sleep," or "They said it could be anxiety." Some patients forget what medication they took; others never knew precisely what it was.

Clarifying substance use often proves even more complicated. Typically, psychiatric assessments include questions about alcohol, drugs, and medications taken without prescription or beyond their intended use. Yet patients frequently hesitate to give straightforward answers. People may minimize their use due to fear of judgment or because they simply don't view casual or socially acceptable consumption as relevant to their current issues. Even when openly discussed, it remains challenging to differentiate clearly between occasional recreational use, dependency, or self-medication attempts. Additionally, when there are potential legal or employment consequences, patients tend to become even more cautious, sometimes omitting significant parts of their history entirely.

Medical history might seem straightforward at first glance, but it has its own significant limitations. Patients frequently leave out conditions they didn't fully understand or those that never seemed urgent enough to mention. Hormonal and neurological issues in particular often remain unreported because patients may not recognize their connection to mood and cognitive function. Similarly, medication histories are frequently incomplete, as prescriptions get adjusted, treatments end, and the reasons behind these changes gradually fade from memory. When asked about previous medications, it's common for patients to respond vaguely: "They gave me something for nerves, but I don't recall its name."

From medical history, psychiatrists typically move toward developmental, psychosocial, and cultural backgrounds, including early life experiences, education, relationships, and social roles. Here the psychiatrist tries to understand how a patient learned to process and respond to life events. Childhood memories seldom unfold neatly or chronologically; over time, patients reinterpret their experiences, gradually reshaping memories until events once experienced as chaotic become recalled as ordinary or unimportant. Cultural context further complicates this picture—emotional struggles might remain unnamed, minimized, or described differently based on family or community norms about what's acceptable to feel or discuss openly. By the time someone seeks psychiatric help, their story has often been reshaped multiple times, edited both consciously and unconsciously.

Occupational and legal histories require especially careful navigation, as patients may hesitate to discuss job losses, workplace conflicts, or prior legal difficulties. People often choose not to share these details, either doubting their relevance or worrying that disclosure might negatively affect their treatment. Over time, many learn how to frame their personal histories in ways that limit discomfort or avoid inviting further questions, leaving potentially significant pieces of their background partially hidden or completely unaddressed.

Family history generally concludes the psychiatrist's inquiry, focusing on psychiatric diagnoses, substance use, or major medical conditions among close relatives. But often patients simply don't have accurate information to provide. Families frequently avoid openly discussing mental illness, sometimes actively concealing it. Even when issues were present, they might have been described vaguely or reframed as something entirely different. A patient may have grown up sensing something was wrong without ever receiving clear language to describe or understand it. By adulthood, these family silences have woven themselves into the patient's history, existing as notable gaps in information rather than concrete facts.

Out of this complex mixture—fragmented memories, forgotten details, emotionally charged moments, information reshaped by shame or cultural expectations, and simple gaps in knowledge—the psychiatrist must attempt to construct a coherent story. They need to interpret what the patient is able to express, notice what remains unsaid, and piece these incomplete elements together into something resembling a clear, structured narrative.

In one study, researchers compared how psychiatric patients described their own medication history with what was actually listed in their clinical records. Out of 219 people, 162 had at least one significant discrepancy—in many cases, medications were omitted entirely, misnamed, or remembered with the wrong duration or dose.[10] And this was just one aspect of the medical history. In a real diagnostic setting, the psychiatrist is working not only with a list of drugs, but with timelines, emotional shifts, family background, substance use, and events that span decades. All of it filtered through what the person remembers—and what they feel ready to share.

Even if the patient's account were perfectly clear, the clinician listening to it still plays a crucial role. Psychiatric assessment relies heavily on conversation, making the clinician's mental state and attention level particularly influential. Numerous studies have shown that personal conflicts at home, excessive administrative workload, time pressure, or professional burnout significantly increase the likelihood of diagnostic errors.[11,12] Moreover, this exhaustion may negatively impact the emotional quality of communication, making psychiatrists more irritable and less empathetic and compassionate toward patients.[13] In some cases, this mental exhaustion leads to **decision fatigue**—a state where clinicians skip essential assessment steps, overlook critical information, or oversimplify their conclusions, all of which contribute to a higher frequency of mistakes.[14]

Ultimately, psychiatry doesn't assess illness directly. Rather, it assesses illness as reflected through multiple layers of distortion. The first layer is the patient's mind, shaped by symptoms, memory gaps, shame, or learned avoidance. The second includes the perspectives of people around the patient—family, partners, coworkers—whose observations are often partial, subjective, or emotionally charged. The final layer involves the clinician, whose interpretations and judgments are filtered through their own mental fatigue, time constraints, and unconscious biases.

Given all these overlapping sources of distortion, a key question arises: how much of the original signal actually survives by the end of this complex process? And how much confidence can we reasonably place in the final interpretation?

Examination Relying on Doctor's Inner Scale

After the patient's history has been gathered, the assessment transitions into a more direct and observational stage—the examination. According to APA guidelines, this typically includes three core elements: a review of systems, a basic physical evaluation, and a mental status examination. Each provides the clinician with an immediate impression of the patient's current condition, shifting the focus from the patient's narrative toward real-time observation.

Some aspects of this examination appear relatively straightforward. For instance, a physical exam allows clinicians to identify visible symptoms—like a rash, tremor, or injury—that might require input from another specialist. Provided the psychiatrist has sufficient training, recognizing the need for referral based on these tangible signs is typically uncomplicated.

The review of systems adds another dimension. Here, the psychiatrist asks about aspects such as sleep, appetite, energy levels, pain, and other bodily functions that can reflect overall well-being. Sleep provides a clear example: most people can offer at least a rough estimate of their sleeping habits, including bedtime, frequency of night awakenings, and how rested they feel upon waking. These details aren't precise metrics, yet they are generally accessible, familiar, and understood. That shared understanding significantly enhances clarity.

This highlights how having a clear, objective reference—an external ground truth—can positively shift the diagnostic dynamic. Recently, wearable devices have started transforming how clinicians interpret self-reported sleep. Smart watches, rings, and sensors provide continuous monitoring—not just subjective estimates but concrete patterns, rhythms, and irregularities tracked over extended periods. Such tools enable patients and psychiatrists to discuss sleep using the same tangible data, rather than depending solely on how someone feels or describes their experience on a given day.

In contrast, appetite assessments still rely exclusively on the patient's self-observation. No real-time, objective tool currently exists to track hunger or eating patterns reliably. Patients must therefore judge and communicate changes based entirely on their internal reference of what's "normal" for them, a comparison often difficult to make clearly or consistently.

The mental status examination introduces yet another layer of complexity. The psychiatrist closely observes the patient's speech patterns, the pace of their thinking, shifts or flatness in their emotional tone, and the consistency or fragmentation of their thoughts. In clear-cut cases—such as acute psychosis—the difference from typical functioning can be stark and obvious. But when symptoms are more subtle, distinguishing between personality traits and clinical symptoms becomes challenging. The clinician faces questions like: Does this patient normally speak at this pace? Is their scattered thinking usual or new? Are they emotionally distant today, or is that simply how they express themselves?

To accurately answer such questions, psychiatrists would ideally have detailed knowledge of a patient's baseline—their usual way of thinking, speaking, and behaving. Without this baseline, the evaluation inevitably involves guesswork. On an initial visit, psychiatrists lack context; there is no established timeline or prior point of reference. The best they can do is listen closely and attempt to discern whether what they're observing feels clinically significant or merely unfamiliar.

Ultimately, the psychiatrist must rely on their own accumulated experience. Over years of practice, clinicians develop a personal, internalized baseline—a sense of how people generally think, speak, and behave when healthy, and how these patterns typically shift in illness. Although informal and unwritten, this internal standard guides their clinical judgment. The more varied cases psychiatrists have encountered, the sharper and more accurate their internal reference becomes, allowing them to more reliably notice when something doesn't quite fit.

The Challenge of Assessing the Risk of Suicide

One of the most critical—and sensitive—parts of psychiatric evaluation is assessing a patient's risk of suicide. According to APA guidelines, psychiatrists must directly explore suicidal thoughts, plans, previous attempts, and protective factors, trying to judge whether immediate intervention is necessary.[4] But here, perhaps more than anywhere else, psychiatry confronts an uncomfortable reality: suicidal thoughts are deeply private, often fiercely guarded. Patients may hide or minimize these feelings—not just due to fear or shame, but because they genuinely want to avoid hospitalization, extra monitoring, or simply being viewed differently.

Psychiatrists depend heavily on information patients choose to disclose, often relying on subtle behavioral cues and clinical intuition to guide their assessments. However, even experienced clinicians frequently miss critical warning signs. Historical data indicates that approximately 25–30% of individuals who died by suicide had contact with a mental health professional in the year preceding their death, with roughly half seeing their clinician within a week of their suicide.[15] Furthermore, around 80% of those individuals were assessed by professionals as having a low suicide risk, with most explicitly denying suicidal thoughts.[16,17] These assessments were neither rushed nor negligent; rather, they highlight the inherent challenges psychiatrists encounter when trying to uncover hidden intentions, particularly when patients appear calm, respond convincingly, and effectively mask their distress during seemingly ordinary conversations.

This data underscores a subtle but significant limitation intrinsic to psychiatric practice, directly tied to the complexities of human interaction. It emphasizes the challenges clinicians encounter when interpreting silences, omissions, or detecting intentions patients may never explicitly express. Thus, accurately assessing suicide risk involves more than asking appropriate questions; clinicians must also be attuned to and accurately interpret responses that may remain partially or entirely unspoken.

Reducing Life to Diagnostic Criteria

By this stage, after an extensive conversation, careful observation, and a thorough exploration of medical, social, and personal backgrounds, the psychiatrist should ideally have enough information to move confidently toward a diagnosis. But as we've discussed, the information at hand is far from perfect, largely because it depends heavily on patient self-reporting. Even setting aside issues like faulty memory or subjective perception, the task of assembling all these fragmented and partial insights into a clear, accurate diagnosis is inherently challenging. Symptoms themselves are inherently fluid, often shifting over time or blending in ways that complicate clear distinctions. Determining where one disorder ends and another starts—or separating clinically meaningful symptoms from ordinary emotional fluctuations—is an inherently complicated task. Yet psychiatrists are expected to take this ambiguous mixture of information and form a clear, consistent diagnosis. To make this complex process clearer, psychiatrists usually rely on diagnostic manuals—structured guidebooks that clearly outline each disorder based on lists of symptoms. In the United States, the main reference is the *Diagnostic and Statistical Manual of Mental Disorders*, known simply as DSM.[18] The current version, DSM-V, was recently updated in 2022 as DSM-V-TR (Text Revision). Published by the American Psychiatric Association (APA), the DSM started in the 1950s as a short booklet meant mostly to collect data on psychiatric disorders. Over the years, it became more detailed and influential. A major turning point happened in 1980 with DSM-III, when psychiatry shifted from vague narrative descriptions to specific checklists of symptoms. This change aimed to make diagnoses more consistent—so that two psychiatrists looking at the same patient would, ideally, reach the same conclusion.[19]

This marked a significant turning point. Mental health conditions are by nature complex, and applying fixed diagnostic categories to the nuanced reality of human suffering has always been challenging. By trying to organize and standardize this messy reality, DSM has made it possible to clearly name and recognize mental health conditions. As a result, millions of people have found validation, treatment, and support they otherwise might not have received. Recognizing the limitations of DSM—like those I'll discuss shortly—doesn't diminish its value. Instead, it helps us appreciate exactly where we stand in our understanding of mental disorders and shows us what needs improvement going forward.

While DSM is primarily used in the United States, its impact stretches worldwide, shaping how researchers and clinicians in many other countries understand and diagnose mental illness. Even places that rely mainly on different classification systems—like the International Classification of Diseases (ICD), published by the World Health Organization—are still influenced by DSM. Its definitions and criteria often set the tone globally. So, as we dig deeper into the DSM's limitations, it's important to remember that similar issues affect almost all psychiatric manuals around the world. The criticisms we'll explore are not just problems with the DSM—they reflect deeper challenges shared by psychiatry internationally.

But if we look beneath this structured surface, DSM reveals a serious limitation. DSM-V and DSM-V-TR criteria are created by committees of experts—around 200 psychiatrists and psychologists who carefully review studies, debate, and finally vote on each diagnosis and its defining symptoms. While these experts are undoubtedly knowledgeable, it raises an obvious question: can 200 specialists truly represent the reality of nearly one billion people living with mental disorders worldwide? And can such a small group—even the most experienced—fully understand, evaluate, and integrate all the complexity and variety of human mental health?

One clear example of this limitation is **sample size**—the number of participants included in a research study. Many diagnostic decisions, influencing treatment plans for millions, rely on studies involving surprisingly few people—often just a few hundred participants.[20,21] Take the introduction of Disruptive Mood Dysregulation Disorder (DMDD) in DSM-V as an example. This diagnosis was supposed to help children with severe irritability and emotional outbursts, but the initial evidence behind it was minimal. Early studies had small sample sizes, were retrospective in nature, and far from representative of all the children who would later receive this diagnosis in real clinical practice.[22] Yet the decisions based on this limited data now affect how countless children and families understand their challenges, receive treatment, and navigate their lives.

This issue underscores a fundamental challenge inherent in psychiatric practice. Psychiatry, more than most areas of medicine, deals with highly personal experiences that vary widely from one individual to another. Each patient's life story, genetics, culture, environment, and coping strategies make them unique. Trying to generalize from small research samples to hundreds of millions of people creates an unavoidable distortion.

Another important issue stemming from limited data is that diagnostic criteria often aren't generalizable. **Generalizability** refers to how well findings from research studies can be applied to larger, more diverse groups beyond those originally studied. Simply put, most psychiatric research is conducted on specific groups—often college students, volunteers from academic medical centers, or individuals living near major research universities. Scientists themselves joke that the best-studied people on the planet probably live in Cambridge, Massachusetts—home to Harvard, MIT, and countless other institutions constantly recruiting research participants. But what about everyone else? Entire populations—people from different cultural backgrounds, races, ethnicities, socioeconomic groups, or even geographic areas—are often underrepresented or completely absent from these studies.

This lack of representation isn't trivial. It means that diagnostic criteria, treatment guidelines, and even our basic understanding of mental illness might not fit everyone equally. For instance, studies show African American patients in the United States often receive diagnoses of schizophrenia at much higher rates than White patients with similar symptoms.[23] At first glance, this looks like bias or prejudice in clinical practice. But beneath that is a deeper problem: researchers and clinicians might simply lack accurate data on how mental disorders present differently across various groups. DSM-V has tried addressing this by introducing tools like the Cultural Formulation Interview, but critics argue these efforts remain limited and superficial.[24] Without adequate research representing diverse populations, clinicians are left applying criteria that might not truly reflect how symptoms manifest across different cultural or socioeconomic contexts. It's not necessarily intentional bias—it's a blind spot caused by uneven research and inadequate data.

The issue of **reliability**—how consistently psychiatrists agree on the same diagnosis when evaluating identical cases—is another important piece of this discussion. To check how reliable DSM-V criteria were in real-life practice, researchers ran special studies known as "field trials." They included over 2,200 patients evaluated independently by nearly 280 psychiatrists across 11 clinics and hospitals in the United States and Canada.[21,25] Each patient was assessed separately by two different clinicians, both using the exact same DSM-V checklists. Then researchers measured how often these psychiatrists agreed on the diagnosis.

The results were mixed. For certain disorders, reliability was relatively high; for example, clinician agreement was strong for conditions such as post-traumatic stress disorder (PTSD) and autism spectrum disorder. However, reliability was considerably lower for several common psychiatric diagnoses, with clinicians often failing to reach consensus despite using identical diagnostic criteria. For instance, major diagnoses such as major depressive disorder and generalized anxiety disorder showed only modest reliability, with average kappa scores (a statistical measure of agreement) ranging between 0.20 and 0.39. Moreover, some newly proposed diagnostic categories, such as Mixed Anxiety-Depressive Disorder, exhibited even lower reliability, with kappa scores below 0.20—a level described by researchers as "unacceptable," indicating that clinicians rarely agreed on these diagnoses.[25]

To put this plainly, if you visit two different psychiatrists, both using the same diagnostic criteria, the chance that they'll agree on a diagnosis like depression is roughly one in four. For generalized anxiety, the agreement drops to about one in five. In practical terms, this means your diagnosis can depend significantly on which psychiatrist you happen to see—and that directly affects your treatment options, your medications, your insurance coverage, and how you and your family understand your condition.

A deeper issue underlying all these problems—small sample sizes, limited generalizability, inconsistent diagnoses—is what's known as **validity**. Validity means whether diagnostic categories actually reflect real and distinct disorders, or if they're just convenient groupings of similar symptoms. Psychiatry, as we've seen repeatedly, historically relies almost entirely on subjective reports—patients describing their experiences, clinicians interpreting these descriptions, and accounts from family members or close friends. But as we've discussed, people's descriptions are rarely precise: the same words can mean different things to different people, memories become distorted, and emotional states are experienced and expressed uniquely.

Because of this, critics argue that DSM diagnoses might not always correspond to clear, meaningful categories. Instead, they may bundle together different underlying conditions simply because they look similar on the surface. This creates serious questions about the validity of psychiatric diagnoses—whether the categories we've built are capturing something genuinely distinct or just grouping together symptoms in convenient but superficial ways.

Of course, criticizing this symptom-based approach is much simpler than replacing it with something better. Psychiatry hasn't yet managed to move beyond subjective reports and descriptions because, as we'll see in the following chapters, identifying objective criteria or reliable biological indicators isn't straightforward. Why this challenge has persisted—and what it will take to overcome it—will be a major focus moving forward.

All these points might feel like criticism aimed squarely at the DSM—but that's not quite accurate. In fact, the DSM initiative has done exactly what was realistically possible given the current state of psychiatric knowledge and research methods. Everything we've discussed here—concerns about validity, reliability, limited data, and generalizability—isn't exclusive to DSM-V. The same limitations apply equally to other major diagnostic manuals used worldwide. And if we're being truly honest, these challenges are inherent to psychiatry as a whole. Recognizing these issues clearly and openly isn't about undermining psychiatry or DSM—it's about seeing clearly where we stand now, so we know exactly what to tackle next.

The Failings of the Diagnostic Process

A thorough psychiatric evaluation involves several interconnected steps, each carrying its own uncertainty: clarifying the reason for the visit, analyzing patient history, conducting physical and mental examinations, and assessing immediate risks. Throughout each stage, psychiatrists face significant challenges stemming from the lack of objective measurements, incomplete or unreliable historical information, and the absence of a clear, quantifiable baseline. Moreover, due to its inherently subjective nature, the assessment is vulnerable to distortion at multiple levels—when patients attempt to interpret their emotional states, when they try to translate these feelings into words, when clinicians interpret what they've heard, and finally when clinicians attempt to match these descriptions to established diagnostic criteria. Thus, even after an hour or more of careful, meticulous evaluation by a highly trained psychiatrist using standardized manuals like the DSM, considerable uncertainty remains in arriving at precise diagnoses—diagnoses that are essential for making effective treatment decisions.

And if even psychiatrists—specialists who spend considerable time with each patient—regularly struggle to diagnose mental disorders accurately, how realistic is it to expect general practitioners to identify the right diagnosis and medication within a brief 15-minute appointment? Yet general practitioners have become the primary prescribers of antidepressants. Patients, on their end, often have no real choice—psychiatric care is inaccessible, unavailable, or simply feels too intimidating. General practitioners themselves have little choice either: they're expected to provide immediate help, even without sufficient resources, guidance, or specialized training. Psychiatrists, in turn, do what they can despite operating within a field where, let's be honest, we fundamentally don't know enough. Everyone involved—patients, general practitioners, psychiatrists—is doing their best with limited knowledge, limited resources, and limited choices. Unfortunately, that often means prescribing medicine that is statistically likely to not work, something we'll talk about in the next chapter.

3 | Treatment, Pharma, and the Brain

A long, dimly lit corridor. Dirty-yellow walls. Dark, uncomfortable leather chairs lined up along the wall. Maria sits nervously in one of them outside the door, anxiously shuffling papers in her trembling hands. She whispers quietly, rehearsing her speech over and over. She's on edge, terrified. Behind that door lies a power capable of changing her life completely. They could kill her. They could kill her husband. Maria exhales deeply, struggling to compose herself. Her legs shake involuntarily, her heart pounds against her chest. She pushes through the overwhelming fear, returning to her practiced words: "You can do this. You must do this. Otherwise...."

The door opens suddenly. An older, heavy-set woman in a floral Soviet-era dress stares straight through Maria, her voice icy, devoid of warmth or emotion: "They're waiting for you. Go in."

Fighting the weakness in her legs, Maria steps through the anteroom and finds herself in a large office. White walls paneled with dark wood, the unusual arched ceiling giving the impression of an underground bunker. Directly across from the entrance stands a massive wooden desk covered with green felt, scattered with documents. Behind it sits him—authority incarnate, fear itself, the terror of an entire generation, the man who instilled dread into millions. He carefully examines the papers without lifting his gaze, and in his low, commanding voice says, "Ready? Begin."

Maria swallows hard, forcing a breath through her constricted chest, projecting as much confidence as possible: "Comrade Stalin, my research indicates that the current condition of the Soviet educational system is deplorable and urgently requires immediate reforms...."

Stalin slowly lifts his eyes from the papers and fixes them on Maria. "Deplorable, you say?"

Maria feels herself drowning under his gaze—eyes that have already determined her fate, and that of her husband.

Maria jolts awake, gasping, heart racing violently. She's in New York. It's 2023. Her husband sleeps quietly beside her. Their bed is soaked through, her whole body drenched in cold sweat.

"Damn antidepressants," she mutters, catching her breath.

* * *

Treatment and Magic Pills

Maria, like countless other patients, had already tried multiple antidepressants, each time hoping they would finally improve her condition and help her function better. Yet each new medication brought unexpected surprises, such as her quite colorful and detailed vivid nightmares. Although some of these drugs partially alleviated some of her symptoms—reducing anxiety or dampening negative emotions—they also introduced peculiar side effects that worsened other aspects of her depression, such as increased appetite, vivid nightmares, or excessive nighttime sweating.

Maria's experience is far from unique. You've likely heard the common anecdote, often shared ironically among patients newly prescribed antidepressants, highlighting that one of the primary side effects listed is suicidal ideation. Ironically, a medication intended to enhance mental well-being can potentially lead to life-threatening outcomes. Her experience reflects the frustrating trial-and-error journey many patients endure in the search for effective medication.

After psychiatrists somehow manage to summarize complex, subjective diagnostic indicators, their next step is determining treatment and prescribing medication. In theory, this process seems straightforward: take the prescribed pills for a set period, and recovery should follow. Yet in reality, things rarely unfold so simply. Consider the numbers behind the most prevalent mental disorder—major depressive disorder (MDD). Typically, the most frequently prescribed medications—the standard first-line treatment psychiatrists use for MDD—are selective serotonin reuptake inhibitors (SSRIs), drugs designed to increase serotonin levels in the brain by blocking its reabsorption. In simple words, drugs designed to increase the levels of serotonin in your brain. Serotonin is a neurotransmitter, a chemical messenger involved in regulating mood, emotions, sleep, and appetite—simplistically speaking, increased serotonin levels are believed to improve mood, promote emotional stability, and alleviate symptoms of depression and anxiety.

Unfortunately, despite their widespread use and seemingly straightforward mechanism of action, these medications yield modest results: only about 30% of patients achieve remission with their initial antidepressant treatment. As a patient, you essentially have a one-in-three chance that the prescribed medication will be effective and improve your condition—not very encouraging, is it? This remission rate extends beyond theoretical data from clinical trials or laboratory settings, as extensive real-world patient records also support these findings. Specifically, large-scale analyses from insurance databases covering more than 3.6 million individuals and healthcare records comprising over 10 million antidepressant treatment episodes consistently confirm that only about one-third of patients achieve full symptom resolution in actual clinical practice.[1]

Because it's difficult to predict whether a medication will actually help, psychiatrists usually recommend frequent follow-up visits—often every two weeks in the early stages of treatment. During these visits, psychiatrists assess the medication's effectiveness, monitor side effects, and promptly decide whether adjustments to the treatment plan are necessary. But the uncomfortable reality is that each subsequent medication tends to be even less effective than the previous one. Real-world studies consistently show declining remission rates: approximately 28–30% of patients achieve remission with their first medication, but this rate drops sharply to about 21% with the second antidepressant, further declines to around 16% by the third attempt, and reaches a mere 7–10% by the fourth medication trial.[2,3] This means each unsuccessful antidepressant trial reduces a patient's likelihood of responding to subsequent treatments by approximately 20–30%. Simply put, every ineffective medication trial decreases the chances of recovery.

There are several biological and psychological explanations for these diminishing returns, such as receptor desensitization due to prolonged antidepressant use, changes in neurotransmitter availability, reduced neuroplasticity, and decreasing placebo responses following repeated treatment failures. But, let's be honest: patients generally don't care about the precise biological or psychological mechanisms—they simply want to feel better. Instead, they confront the harsh reality of navigating an exhausting, prolonged trial-and-error process. Patients must regularly visit their psychiatrists, incurring significant financial and logistical burdens. They repeatedly try different medications, each potentially introducing new side effects and unpredictably altering their physical and emotional states. In most cases, this treatment process lasts over a year, and for approximately 44% of patients, it extends beyond five years,[4] with an average annual cost exceeding $10,000.[5,6] Such prolonged, costly, and inefficient treatment highlights just how burdensome the current approach is for patients struggling with depression. Perhaps most discouragingly, all this effort provides no guarantee of success—in fact, each additional medication trial further reduces the likelihood of achieving remission. So no surprise, many patients choose to withdraw from the treatment process, which of course can be dangerous, but it often feels like there is no choice.

Ultimately, despite these lengthy, costly, and exhausting attempts at finding the right antidepressant, outcomes remain disappointing. Only about 50% of patients eventually reach remission at some point during treatment.[2] Yet for most of these patients, the relief is temporary; approximately 50–80% experience relapse within a year,[7] meaning their depressive symptoms inevitably return. Even more challenging, around 30% of all patients are eventually classified as having **treatment-resistant depression (TRD)**.[8] Clinically, TRD is officially defined as a depressive episode that fails to achieve adequate improvement despite at least two appropriately dosed antidepressant treatments of sufficient duration.[9] Simply put, standard medications don't help these patients, regardless of how many different pills they try. For them, conventional antidepressants offer little hope, rendering the trial-and-error approach not just inefficient, but ultimately futile.

Unfortunately, these disappointing outcomes are not limited to depression. Similarly poor results are seen across various psychiatric disorders. For instance, approximately one-third of schizophrenia patients are classified as treatment-resistant, failing to achieve meaningful symptom relief despite multiple attempts with standard antipsychotics.[10] Likewise, in bipolar disorder, treatment-resistant episodes occur frequently, with about 25–33% of patients showing minimal or no response to conventional mood stabilizers or antipsychotics despite extensive trials.[11,12] These parallels highlight a critical issue: the current psychiatric approach—characterized by trial-and-error medication regimens, prolonged uncertainty, high costs, and diminishing returns—is consistently inadequate across various mental health conditions.

These troubling statistics inevitably lead us to a critical question: do we truly understand what we're treating? Do we genuinely know how to treat it effectively, or if it can even be cured? And perhaps most importantly, how is it possible that medications that pass clinical trials yield such disheartening real-world outcomes? These figures clearly illustrate a profound gap between our theoretical assumptions about mental disorders and the harsh reality patients face—a gap that calls into question the very foundations of modern psychiatry and our attempts to heal the human mind. And I am not the only one asking these questions—they have recently resurfaced within psychiatric circles, fueled by provocative new critiques challenging the fundamental rationale behind antidepressants. One influential example is a landmark review by Moncrieff and colleagues,[13] which systematically examined decades of research underlying the serotonin hypothesis—the cornerstone belief that depression primarily results from serotonin deficiency—and found remarkably little empirical evidence supporting it. Their analysis revealed significant inconsistencies and methodological weaknesses in studies measuring serotonin levels, receptor functions, and related biological processes. This stark conclusion calls into question the scientific foundation of SSRIs, which have become the most widely prescribed class of antidepressants worldwide.

But how accurate or fair is this critique? Could there be more complexity behind these seemingly straightforward conclusions? Perhaps the serotonin hypothesis is overly simplified, or it may represent only one part of a multifaceted biological picture we haven't yet fully unraveled. Are the problems highlighted by Moncrieff's team genuine failures in the theory itself, or do they instead reflect broader methodological issues or even biases within the research process? To address these crucial questions, we need to carefully examine how antidepressants are actually developed, tested, and approved. By unpacking this process, we may gain a clearer understanding of the true challenges behind creating effective psychiatric medications.

The Struggles in Drug Development

Most medications psychiatrists prescribe today were discovered decades ago, often by chance or originally intended for entirely different purposes. For example, chlorpromazine, now widely known as Thorazine, was first synthesized in 1951 as an anesthetic aid. Unexpectedly, it showed remarkable effectiveness in managing schizophrenia symptoms—reducing agitation, hallucinations, and delusions—and is still commonly used for schizophrenia, acute psychosis, and severe behavioral disturbances.[14] Similarly, imipramine (Tofranil) was initially developed in the 1950s as a potential antipsychotic. Although ineffective against psychosis, it significantly alleviated depressive symptoms, becoming one of the earliest antidepressants. Today, psychiatrists continue prescribing imipramine mainly for major depressive disorder, anxiety, and nocturnal enuresis (bedwetting).[15] However, early clinical trials for these medications lacked modern rigor, often missing standardized assessments, randomized designs, and structured methodologies essential for accurately evaluating efficacy.

SSRIs were also developed decades ago but through a more deliberate, hypothesis-driven approach. Researchers based their development on the theory that insufficient serotonin contributes to major depressive disorder. Over time, clinical trial standards improved significantly, enabling more structured and rigorous testing of these drugs. For example, fluoxetine, introduced in 1987, underwent trials using standardized symptom rating scales to measure outcomes quantitatively.[16] Sertraline, approved in 1991, was evaluated in placebo-controlled studies carefully designed to assess efficacy and safety systematically.[17,18] Escitalopram, approved in 2002 as a refined form of the earlier antidepressant citalopram, represented a significant advancement, benefiting from extensive double-blind, placebo-controlled trials demonstrating improved efficacy and tolerability compared to earlier medications.[19,20]

In the 1990s, regulatory and methodological changes significantly raised the standards for clinical trials. The FDA introduced stringent requirements, including mandatory randomized controlled designs, larger sample sizes, clearly defined endpoints, and strict blinding protocols to minimize bias and enhance reliability. Modern clinical trials, exemplified by those evaluating escitalopram, now feature precise patient inclusion criteria, comprehensive safety assessments, and detailed statistical analysis plans, resulting in greatly improved scientific rigor. However, this increased complexity raises a critical question: have stringent modern trial standards inadvertently slowed innovation in psychiatric drug development?[21]

Indeed, escitalopram remains the most recent significant psychiatric medication breakthrough, introduced nearly two decades ago. Remarkably, despite rapid technological advancements and a deeper understanding of psychiatric conditions over the past twenty years, no equally transformative medications have emerged, highlighting stagnation in the field. Some experts suggest that escalating complexity, costs, and regulatory demands in modern clinical trials might unintentionally discourage innovation and limit the development of new psychiatric treatments.[22] But for me, this raises a different question: Would the psychiatric medications approved decades ago even pass today's rigorous standards? Perhaps these heightened requirements reveal deeper flaws—not only in how we develop treatments but in our fundamental understanding of psychiatric disorders themselves.

Pharma Struggles Too

Due to several historical controversies, it has become almost automatic to blame pharmaceutical companies when treatments don't work or cause harm. Given high-profile cases like the development and marketing of OxyContin, such skepticism makes sense. However, when it comes to psychiatric medications, I'd suggest avoiding overly harsh criticism. Pharmaceutical companies are businesses, after all—and like all businesses, their survival depends on creating products that genuinely help their customers—in this case, patients. Yet developing new psychiatric medications is uniquely challenging, even for large pharma corporations with their extensive resources, access to top specialists, cutting-edge technologies, and considerable budgets. To truly understand why these companies struggle to create effective psychiatric drugs, we need to look closely at the drug development process itself. This process begins long before a medication ever reaches patients, starting with the discovery and development of a promising molecule.

Pre-clinical Phase

The pre-clinical phase, though often invisible to the public, sets the foundation for every new drug. During this phase, researchers identify and validate therapeutic targets—specific biological processes, receptors, enzymes, or genetic pathways believed to influence psychiatric conditions. Once a promising target is identified, scientists screen thousands of chemical compounds using computational methods, laboratory cell tests, and animal models to find a molecule that effectively interacts with this target.

The goal at this stage isn't just to select a molecule that hits the intended target. Researchers must also evaluate numerous parameters that will affect the drug's safety and effectiveness. These parameters include pharmacokinetics (how the drug moves through the body), pharmacodynamics (how the drug impacts biological functions), and potential toxicity. Typically, testing is done in **animal models**—usually rodents or primates—which are genetically engineered or chemically induced to mimic psychiatric symptoms like anxiety, depression, schizophrenia, or cognitive impairment. Only when a molecule demonstrates clear biological effectiveness, a favorable safety profile, and a well-understood mechanism of action can it move forward into clinical trials involving human subjects.[23]

Despite technological advances, psychiatric drug discovery faces deep challenges right from this early pre-clinical stage. One major issue is the limitation of animal models, which struggle to accurately represent human psychiatric disorders. Mental illnesses involve complex cognitive, emotional, and social aspects that are extremely difficult to replicate in animals. For instance, rodents cannot realistically express human feelings like worthlessness, guilt, or existential despair seen in depression, nor do they adequately capture symptoms like hallucinations or delusions common in schizophrenia.[24] Despite the general similarity in brain structure between rodents and humans, there remain—surprisingly—some significant differences. Psychiatric conditions involve intricate interactions among various brain regions, far more complicated than we often pretend when using simplified animal models. After all, as impressive as rodents are at learning (sometimes even better than certain humans), it's still a stretch to imagine them experiencing existential despair or intense feelings of guilt.

Another major issue, which we briefly touched on when discussing SSRIs and the serotonin hypothesis, is the lack of clear **biological targets**. Because we still don't fully understand the true nature of psychiatric conditions, it becomes incredibly challenging to pinpoint specific biological targets that can reliably improve psychiatric symptoms. Unlike diseases such as diabetes or hypertension, psychiatric disorders typically lack well-defined biological markers. The underlying biological mechanisms behind most psychiatric conditions remain largely unknown, which complicates identifying and validating drug targets. Researchers often rely on speculative theories rather than solid biological evidence, increasing the risk of chasing ineffective or incorrect therapeutic pathways.[25] This uncertainty is one of the key reasons why, despite two decades of research, there have been almost no groundbreaking advances or fundamentally new psychiatric medications.

Another big challenge in pre-clinical psychiatric research is the so-called "**reproducibility crisis**." Simply put, this means that findings from one laboratory often can't be consistently replicated by other researchers, making it difficult to trust the results. You might hear about a study claiming some exciting new discovery—maybe a compound dramatically reducing depression-like behavior in rodents—but when another team tries to repeat the experiment, the results don't match up. This happens for several reasons, including studies with small sample sizes, inconsistent testing methods across labs, and a tendency for scientists to report only their most promising findings (while quietly shelving the less impressive results). Taken together, these issues significantly weaken confidence in pre-clinical studies and make it even harder to identify genuinely promising new psychiatric treatments.[26]

To summarize, for a drug candidate to be considered successful at the pre-clinical stage—and therefore ready to advance into clinical trials involving human patients—it must meet several important criteria. First, it needs to consistently show biological efficacy across multiple animal studies, meaning the drug reliably produces beneficial effects in animal models designed to mimic psychiatric conditions. Second, extensive toxicological evaluations must confirm the compound is safe, with minimal risk of serious side effects or toxicity. Third, scientists must thoroughly understand how the drug behaves in the body—its pharmacokinetics (how it's absorbed, distributed, metabolized, and eliminated) and pharmacodynamics (the specific biological changes it produces). Finally, ideally, the drug should offer clear advantages compared to existing medications, such as improved effectiveness, fewer or milder side effects, or perhaps even a new mechanism of action that could help patients who haven't responded well to current treatments.

If—and only if—a candidate drug meets all these criteria, it moves forward into the next crucial step: clinical trials.

Clinical Trials

Once a drug candidate successfully passes the rigorous checks of pre-clinical testing, the next critical step is clinical trials—studies involving human participants. The primary goal of these trials is to confirm that the medication is safe and effective for use in humans. Typically, clinical testing is structured into three key stages known as Phase I, Phase II, and Phase III trials, each designed with its own specific purpose and methods.

Phase I. Testing if the Drug Is Safe

Phase I is the first stage of testing in humans and primarily focuses on evaluating the drug's safety. Usually, Phase I studies involve a relatively small group—around 20 to 100 participants. These participants are typically healthy volunteers rather than patients with the targeted psychiatric condition. The main goal at this stage is to establish the safety profile of the new medication, identifying potential side effects and determining how the drug is absorbed, metabolized, and eliminated by the body. In other words, before checking whether the drug actually improves psychiatric symptoms, researchers must first ensure it doesn't harm those who take it.

While Phase I typically has the highest success rates among clinical trial stages across many therapeutic areas, psychiatric drugs face notably greater challenges. Psychiatric drug candidates demonstrate lower success rates even at this early phase compared to medications for other conditions. In fact, recent analyses indicate that only about 52.7% of psychiatric drug candidates successfully complete Phase I and move forward to Phase II—markedly lower than the general average of around 65–70% for other therapeutic categories.[27] This difference highlights the unique difficulties in psychiatric drug development, stemming from complexities in how psychiatric medications interact with the human brain and the inherently subjective nature of psychiatric symptoms. Still, despite these additional hurdles, Phase I trials remain crucial, providing essential data that forms the foundation for subsequent stages of clinical testing.

Phase II and Phase III. Testing if the Drug Is Effective
Once the safety of a new medication has been established in healthy volunteers, clinical testing moves forward to better reflect real-world conditions. These so-called **late-stage clinical trials—Phase II and Phase III**—are conducted on patients who actually have the condition the medication aims to treat. Phase II and Phase III trials have quite similar designs, so we'll discuss them together. However, they differ significantly in terms of their primary objectives and the number of participants involved.

The main goal of Phase II is to confirm that the medication effectively treats the target condition. Since this is the first time the drug is tested in patients with the disease, these trials typically enroll a relatively small number of participants, usually between 100 and 250 individuals. This sample size is carefully selected: it's large enough to provide statistically meaningful results—that is, ensuring the observed benefits aren't just due to random chance—but still small enough to avoid excessive financial and resource losses if the medication ultimately proves ineffective.

Phase III trials, however, aim to demonstrate that the beneficial effects seen in Phase II trials consistently hold up when tested in much larger and more diverse groups of patients. While 100–250 people might be sufficient to suggest efficacy, such a group often doesn't fully represent the broader patient population found in everyday clinical settings. Therefore, Phase III trials enroll significantly larger groups, typically ranging from several hundred to thousands of participants. Their goal is to ensure the medication works reliably across a wide spectrum of patients who differ by age, sex, ethnicity, medical history, and severity of the disease, thereby closely mimicking the complexity and variability of real-world populations.

Moreover, Phase III trials serve several additional critical purposes beyond confirming efficacy. They provide robust evidence regarding the drug's safety in larger populations, carefully track adverse reactions or rare side effects, and help determine the optimal dosing regimen for the final approved product. Importantly, regulatory agencies such as the FDA typically require results from **at least two successful Phase III trials** demonstrating consistent and statistically significant efficacy and safety before considering approval for widespread clinical use.

Apart from their differences, Phase II and Phase III clinical trials share significant similarities in their overall design. First, both phases have clearly defined inclusion and exclusion criteria. These criteria serve to eliminate external factors that might influence the trial's outcomes—such as concurrent use of other medications—and minimize potential risks, including adverse events or trial failure. Additionally, careful patient selection enhances the likelihood of detecting genuine therapeutic effects by reducing variability in patient responses.

Second, clinical trials employ clearly defined **endpoints**. An endpoint is typically a quantifiable measure or scale that objectively evaluates a patient's condition before and after treatment. By translating symptoms or conditions into numerical values, researchers can measure treatment-induced changes in a standardized way, providing clear evidence of the medication's effectiveness.

Third, a crucial component of these trials is the use of a **control group**, intended to distinguish genuine treatment effects from the so-called **placebo effect**. The placebo effect refers to the improvement of symptoms experienced by patients due to their expectations or beliefs about receiving treatment, rather than from the direct physiological action of the treatment itself. To clearly separate these psychological improvements from the actual therapeutic benefits, clinical trials use a randomized, double-blind approach. In such studies, patients are randomly assigned either to a group receiving the real treatment or to a control group receiving an inactive intervention (placebo or sham procedure). Neither the patients nor the researchers know who is receiving the real or inactive treatment, ensuring unbiased assessment of the treatment's true efficacy.

But while the structure of these trials appears solid in theory—carefully chosen patients, objective endpoints, strict control groups—this is exactly where psychiatric drug development begins to break down. In practice, the overwhelming majority of psychiatric drug candidates never make it to market. Only 7.3% of all compounds that enter clinical development for psychiatric conditions ultimately receive regulatory approval—meaning that more than 92% fail somewhere along the way, despite years of research, substantial financial investment, and promising early-stage data.[27] Crucially, most of these failures occur during the late stages of development, especially in Phase II and Phase III trials, where the medication must demonstrate actual clinical benefit in patients. On average, only about 27% of psychiatric drugs advance beyond Phase II—the lowest success rate among all major therapeutic areas.[27]

Patient Selection One of the first and most fundamental challenges in Phase II and Phase III psychiatric trials lies in patient selection. Since these trials evaluate whether the drug actually helps people with the condition, they must enroll participants who have been properly diagnosed. And here, the entire process typically hinges on the use of DSM-V diagnostic criteria, which we already examined in detail in Chapter 2. As we discussed, one of the core issues with DSM-V is its poor diagnostic reliability—even two experienced psychiatrists may arrive at entirely different diagnoses when evaluating the same patient.

But beyond inconsistent agreement between clinicians, there's a deeper problem: the symptom profiles of different psychiatric conditions often overlap significantly. This means that patients included in clinical trials may either have been misdiagnosed or may simultaneously meet criteria for multiple conditions. In both cases, this undermines the precision of the study population. For example, in major depressive disorder (MDD), it has been shown that nearly 70% of patients diagnosed with MDD also meet diagnostic criteria for at least one other psychiatric disorder.[28] As a result, many clinical trials end up testing drugs on mixed or poorly defined patient groups—making it extremely difficult to isolate whether a medication is truly effective for the intended condition.

The Endpoints The second major reason behind the high failure rates in psychiatric trials lies in how treatment success is measured. In most psychiatric studies, endpoints are not lab values, brain scans, or molecular markers—like, for example, blood glucose levels in diabetes or tumor size reduction in oncology. Instead, psychiatric trials rely on **questionnaires** filled out by clinicians, based on symptoms patients report or that are observed during interviews. These questionnaires attempt to translate a person's internal emotional state into a single number—a **total score**.

Let's take depression as an example. In trials for major depressive disorder, the two most commonly used tools are the **Hamilton Depression Rating Scale (HAM-D)** and the **Montgomery–Åsberg Depression Rating Scale (MADRS)**. Both are widely used, considered "gold standards," and have been around for decades. The HAM-D, developed in 1960, includes between 17 and 29 items, depending on the version, and covers a broad range of symptoms—mood, anxiety, guilt, insomnia, weight loss, somatic discomfort.[29] Some of the questions may sound like this: *"Do you feel hopeless about the future?," "How is your sleep?,"* or *"Have you had any thoughts of death?"* The clinician interviews the patient and then assigns a number for each item—usually from 0 to 4—based on their interpretation of what was said and how it was said. The MADRS, introduced in 1979, was designed to be more sensitive to change during treatment. It contains only 10 items and focuses more narrowly on core psychological symptoms—sadness, inner tension, pessimistic thoughts, and inability to feel pleasure. Each item is scored from 0 to 6. For example, the "reported sadness" item includes anchor points ranging from *"No sadness" (0)* to *"Extreme despondency" (6)*.[30]

All of the items are then combined into a single total score, and that score determines everything—from how severe the depression is, to whether a treatment is considered effective. For example, in the HAM-D, scores below 7 are considered remission, 8–13 indicate mild depression, 14–18 moderate, and anything above 19 is categorized as severe. In the MADRS, similar ranges apply, though with slightly different thresholds.

And while this may look systematic on the surface, it's worth pausing for a moment. Because really—how exactly do you quantify something like *"sadness"* or *"emotional tension"* on a scale from 0 to 6? Is the patient sad enough? Or not quite yet? A bit more sadness and maybe they'd qualify as a 5. Or perhaps they're still a 4. A single-point difference can move a patient from "moderate depression" to "mild"—or the other way around. And yes, that shift can define not only the patient's condition but the trial's outcome.

Clinical trials typically rely on two key benchmarks to evaluate treatment success. The first is **response**, defined as a reduction of at least 50% in the total score compared to baseline. So if a patient starts at 14, they need to reach 7. If they start at 20, they need to fall to 10. On paper, that seems logical. But in practice, it means patients with more severe symptoms must demonstrate larger absolute improvements to be counted as "responders."

The second benchmark is **remission**, which refers to achieving a score low enough to be considered "not clinically depressed." For HAM-D, that means a score of 7 or less; for MADRS, 10 or less. And here's where the logic gets shaky again: if someone scores an 8 on HAM-D, they're still officially depressed. But drop just one point—to 7—and they're now considered in remission. One point—on a subjective, interview-based scale—marks the boundary between being ill and being well.

To be fair, final trial outcomes usually involve more nuanced statistical analysis, which can adjust for some of these edge cases. But the underlying issue remains: when your primary measure of treatment success is this unstable, the entire system rests on a fragile foundation.

At first glance, it would seem logical that the very tools we use to measure treatment success should reflect the same framework we use to define depression itself. After all, if we're measuring whether someone is getting better, that measurement should align with how we define being ill. Yet despite this apparent logic, neither HAM-D nor MADRS was built on the diagnostic criteria used in the DSM-V. Both were developed independently—HAM-D in the early 1960s, before the DSM even attempted formal operational definitions, and MADRS in the late 1970s, with a focus on sensitivity to treatment response rather than diagnostic precision. As a result, the symptoms they assess only partially overlap with the official criteria for major depressive disorder.

Neither HAM-D nor MADRS captures the full set of symptoms described in DSM-V. For example, MADRS does not include items assessing psychomotor agitation or retardation, both of which are explicitly listed in the DSM as diagnostic criteria. It also lacks any mention of feelings of worthlessness, and doesn't distinguish between insomnia and hypersomnia—despite the DSM considering both equally valid indicators of depression. In contrast, HAM-D does include both agitation and retardation, but treats them as separate symptoms that both add points to the total score. This means that two patients—one visibly slowed down, the other visibly agitated—can end up with identical severity scores, despite presenting with diametrically opposite forms of motor disturbance. It's like running a clinical trial for a drug that's meant to regulate body temperature, and giving the same "improvement" points for both hypothermia and fever, as long as the thermometer moves far enough from baseline.

Not surprisingly, this kind of ambiguity has a direct impact on trial outcomes. Even well-trained clinicians can assign different scores to the same patient. Two psychiatrists might conduct identical interviews, use the same rating scale, and still arrive at different conclusions—not because either one made a mistake, but because the language and structure of the tools leave room for interpretation.

So the logical question becomes: do these tools at least agree with each other? Somewhat. Studies comparing HAM-D and MADRS show moderate to high correlations, typically in the range of 0.76 to 0.88.[31-37] That may sound comforting, but the agreement is far from perfect. In some trials, a medication shows clear improvement on MADRS but fails to meet the threshold on HAM-D—or the other way around. And when the entire fate of a drug hinges on crossing a numerical cutoff, even a one-point disagreement can make the difference between a drug moving forward or being shelved indefinitely.

Placebo Effect The subjectivity and inherent instability of questionnaires used as endpoints in psychiatric clinical trials significantly contribute to another major issue: the unusually high placebo response rates, directly influencing trial effectiveness. Specifically, in Phase II and III trials, placebo responses are frequently documented at extremely elevated levels, sometimes making it virtually impossible for an active drug to demonstrate clear superiority over placebo. For example, revisiting major depressive disorder (MDD), approximately 30–40% of participants experience substantial improvement after taking an inert pill—one that is specifically designed to produce no pharmacological effect—yet achieve mental health improvements comparable to those who receive effective medication.[38] These figures represent averages; in certain trials, the placebo effect is even more pronounced, with about half of participants in placebo groups reporting significant improvement.[39,40] In studies involving children and adolescents, placebo response rates climb even higher, reaching up to 60%. To better grasp the magnitude of these numbers, we can compare them with placebo responses in other medical fields. In oncology trials, placebo response rates typically range between 1 and 4%,[41] while in cardiovascular trials, they hover around 15%.[42] Thus, although placebo effects are observed across various medical conditions, they rarely approach a scenario where nearly half of the patients significantly improve. This stark contrast underscores the unique challenges psychiatric research faces, where subjective assessments and patient expectations dramatically shape outcomes.

Unfortunately, this issue is not limited to depression, which, as previously discussed, poses numerous diagnostic challenges, but also extends to seemingly more objectively diagnosable mental disorders such as schizophrenia. Intuitively, one might assume it would be considerably more difficult to err in diagnosing or assessing the severity of schizophrenia, given its distinct symptomatology. Yet even here, the figures are surprising: placebo response rates in schizophrenia trials average around 30% and can occasionally rise to 41%.[38] But what do these numbers imply for the actual efficacy of psychiatric medications, especially considering that the most commonly prescribed first-line antidepressants exhibit efficacy rates of approximately 30%? Could this support the theory that existing antidepressants might be functioning predominantly through placebo effects? More critically, how does such a substantial placebo effect impact drug development? Could this phenomenon help explain the noticeable shortage of novel and effective medications in psychiatry, as new drugs consistently struggle to show meaningful improvements over placebo groups in rigorously designed modern trials? Ultimately, one must question whether developing a psychiatric medication capable of substantially outperforming such powerful placebo effects is even feasible under current clinical methodologies.

If you have been following the full clinical trial process closely, it becomes clear how such striking placebo response rates can emerge. Given that we continue to rely on scales based on the relative assessments made by clinicians or patients themselves, outcomes can easily be influenced by seemingly trivial factors. For example, a sunny day or traffic congestion encountered on the way to the psychiatrist's office could substantially affect survey results following treatment administration. Similarly, behavioral patterns or interpersonal dynamics may strongly impact outcomes: patients might attempt to make a positive impression on their psychiatrist by reporting improvement, driven by feelings of guilt or gratitude for the attention they received. In some cases, this very attention—especially with elderly patients—plays a significant therapeutic role. Elderly individuals might exhibit depressive-like symptoms primarily due to loneliness, and simply becoming involved in a structured project and engaging in regular social interaction can noticeably improve their overall emotional state. There are numerous plausible explanations for the placebo effect, ranging from patient expectations of recovery to the relatively short duration of some trials. Yet, regardless of its causes, the phenomenon itself raises profoundly uncomfortable questions: What kind of illness improves substantially from external factors such as positive expectations or rapport with the clinician? How should we interpret medications prescribed to millions, whose efficacy is statistically indistinguishable from placebo? Moreover, is there genuinely any chance to develop truly effective psychiatric treatments under these circumstances? With these challenging questions in mind, we now approach a central issue underlying psychiatric research: heterogeneity.

Heterogeneity To clearly understand the concept of heterogeneity, let's first consider an example outside of psychiatry. Imagine you visit a doctor and describe the following symptoms: fever, nasal congestion, cough, and body aches. Notice that nearly all these symptoms, except perhaps body aches, are objectively measurable—fever can be quantified with a thermometer, nasal congestion and coughing can be directly observed. Almost every one of us has experienced this set of symptoms, yet we intuitively understand these symptoms alone are insufficient—they require a precise diagnosis to guide treatment. In fact, the range of diagnoses consistent with this symptom cluster is extensive: it could indicate the common cold, influenza, COVID-19, bacterial infection, pneumonia, bronchitis, sinusitis, or even more severe conditions such as tuberculosis, certain autoimmune disorders, or allergic reactions. Clearly, symptoms alone, despite being objectively measurable, do not define a specific disease. Instead, they reflect a wide spectrum of conditions, each with fundamentally different underlying causes, disease courses, and optimal treatment strategies.

Returning to our example of symptoms such as fever, nasal congestion, cough, and body aches, various diagnostic tests can identify or exclude specific underlying diseases. For instance, a COVID-19 test—typically a PCR or rapid antigen test—detects viral genetic material or viral proteins, confirming or excluding a SARS-CoV-2 infection. Similarly, a flu test, also based on viral antigen detection, can identify influenza virus types. Chest radiography (X-ray imaging) or fluorography can reveal characteristic lung changes or inflammation, thus confirming or ruling out pneumonia or tuberculosis. Blood tests, including complete blood counts (CBC), can differentiate bacterial infections (often indicated by elevated white blood cells and specific markers like procalcitonin) from viral infections. Allergy panels or specific antibody tests (IgE levels) can pinpoint allergic reactions or autoimmune responses as underlying causes. Each of these diagnostic procedures provides biological and objective data that clarify the precise disease behind symptoms that otherwise appear nearly identical.

This is precisely where the concept of **heterogeneity** comes into play. In medicine, heterogeneity is defined as the existence of multiple distinct biological mechanisms or processes that can result in very similar clinical symptoms or disease presentations, complicating diagnosis and treatment strategies.[43] In simpler terms, heterogeneity means that although patients may exhibit identical or nearly identical symptoms, these symptoms may be caused by entirely different underlying problems or biological factors. In other words, even when conditions look similar from the outside, their internal causes can vary dramatically, requiring completely different treatments tailored specifically to those underlying causes.

Now, let's return to mental disorders and explore what happens there, using depression as our primary example. If we consult the DSM-V to diagnose major depressive disorder, a patient must exhibit at least five out of nine possible symptoms during the same two-week period, with at least one symptom being either depressed mood or loss of interest or pleasure. These symptoms include:

- Depressed mood most of the day, nearly every day (e.g., feeling sad, empty, or hopeless).
- Markedly diminished interest or pleasure in all or almost all activities most of the day, nearly every day.
- Significant weight loss or weight gain (when not dieting), or decrease/increase in appetite nearly every day.

- Insomnia or hypersomnia (excessive sleeping) nearly every day.
- Psychomotor agitation (restlessness, inability to sit still, pacing) or psychomotor retardation (slowed speech, thinking, and body movements) nearly every day.
- Fatigue or loss of energy nearly every day.
- Feelings of worthlessness or excessive, inappropriate guilt nearly every day.
- Difficulty concentrating or indecisiveness nearly every day.
- Recurrent thoughts of death or suicidal ideation (thoughts or plans to commit suicide).

These symptoms can vary significantly in their intensity and may manifest in dramatically different forms. For instance, psychomotor agitation and psychomotor retardation—two entirely opposite behavioral states reflecting drastically different alterations in psychomotor functioning—are nonetheless classified as a single diagnostic criterion within MDD.[44] Thus, a patient who reports experiencing a depressed mood, feelings of guilt, significant weight loss, insomnia, and difficulty concentrating would most likely receive the exact same diagnosis—major depressive disorder—as another patient who presents with an almost entirely opposite clinical picture: pervasive indifference and loss of interest in previously enjoyed activities, constant fatigue, increased sleep, increased appetite, and noticeable psychomotor retardation, characterized by slowed reactions and movements. Despite these striking differences in clinical presentation, both patients would meet the DSM-V criteria for the same diagnosis, illustrating vividly the profound heterogeneity within psychiatric disorders.

If we approach this purely as a combinatorial problem—ignoring for a moment the fact that each individual symptom can manifest in varying degrees of intensity—the nine diagnostic criteria listed in the DSM-V yield approximately 227 possible symptom combinations, each of which could still result in the same singular diagnosis of major depressive disorder. However, even this substantial number significantly underestimates the true complexity of clinical reality. Certain studies have delved deeper into this diagnostic complexity, finding that the number of unique symptomatic profiles among depressed patients can exceed 1,000 distinct combinations.[45] This striking figure underscores the profound heterogeneity inherent in depression, raising critical questions about whether we are truly dealing with a single disorder or an extensive spectrum of fundamentally distinct conditions grouped under a common diagnostic label.

If we carefully reconsider all the statistics we've thoroughly analyzed in previous chapters—from the sheer number of affected individuals and rates of misdiagnosis, to the inefficiency of current treatments and persistent difficulties in developing new effective medications—the hypothesis of heterogeneity emerges as a logical and rational explanation for these ongoing challenges. Imagine, for instance, treating pneumonia and general bacterial infections identically, without accounting for their distinct biological origins; the resulting outcomes would undoubtedly be disappointing.

Now, let's propose a scenario in which the symptom cluster we currently label "depression" actually encompasses a relatively modest number of distinct disorders—say, five. Under these conditions, how might the outcome of a clinical trial appear? Suppose researchers test a novel antidepressant medication that demonstrates an extraordinary 100% efficacy (admittedly impossible in real life) in just one of these five depression subtypes. However, if we ignore these subtypes and continue recruiting trial participants based solely on their shared symptom profile, the observed efficacy of the drug would naturally be reduced to approximately 20%. Furthermore, factoring in additional complicating elements—such as inaccurate patient selection potentially including individuals without genuine depressive disorders, subjective and unstable assessment scales, and the exceptionally high placebo effect—our hypothetical medication would have virtually no chance of demonstrating meaningful clinical benefit.

Can we genuinely say that this hypothetical medication was ineffective? According to the results of our imaginary clinical trial—yes, it was an utter failure. However, in reality, this same medication could potentially help one-fifth of all depression sufferers, translating into tens of millions of individuals globally. It works, but only for a specific subtype of the disorder.

If we embrace the concept of heterogeneity in mental illnesses and recognize that each psychiatric diagnosis likely represents merely a common denominator for a range of distinct conditions, many statistics previously viewed as alarming or incomprehensible begin to take on a different meaning. For example, existing antidepressants, often criticized for their relatively low efficacy, may in fact be effective—but only within certain patient subgroups. These medications might be specifically addressing one particular subtype within the broader spectrum of depression, and within that subtype, they might indeed demonstrate substantial efficacy.

Experienced psychiatrists who have observed hundreds of patients intuitively understand the profound heterogeneity within psychiatric disorders. Through careful clinical observation and internal analytical judgment, they notice significant differences among patients sharing the same diagnosis and accordingly strive to select the most suitable treatments. They closely track how patients respond differently to identical medications and monitor specific side effects—such as Maria's vivid dreams or nightmares—as crucial indicators for adjusting therapy. However, no widely accepted paradigm yet exists to systematically guide this nuanced process. As a result, identifying appropriate treatments still requires months of trial and error, during which therapeutic effectiveness gradually diminishes due to incorrect initial medication choices, altered brain chemistry from prior interventions, and psychological factors such as discouragement and despair arising from repeated treatment failures.

Reflecting on this complexity naturally prompts a critical question: if psychiatric disorders genuinely exhibit such significant heterogeneity, why haven't we identified specific biological characteristics that could enable more precise diagnoses, more effective drug development, and ultimately personalized treatments that consistently work? Yet, as you may anticipate from the preceding discussion, addressing this fundamental issue also involves considerable challenges.

Persistent Challenges of Psychiatric Research

Paradoxically, the expectation for new discoveries, fresh perspectives on mental disorders, and detailed efforts to understand their biological underpinnings falls largely upon academia. Academic researchers are precisely those individuals who rigorously dedicate their careers to specialized topics, meticulously analyzing historical data, formulating new hypotheses, and conducting systematic studies to validate these theories. Indeed, these scholars constitute one of the key driving forces behind medical progress. It is therefore entirely reasonable to ask whether any particular studies or research initiatives currently underway could finally clarify the biological nature of mental illnesses.

The idea that mental disorders are heterogeneous and that we must identify distinct subtypes is not new. And of course it has triggered and initiated multiple different research initiatives to understand the structure and actual biological underpinnings of psychiatric disorders. One significant initiative aimed at addressing this psychiatric heterogeneity was the Research Domain Criteria (RDoC) project, proposed in 2009 by the U.S. National Institute of Mental Health (NIMH) under the leadership of its director at the time, Thomas R. Insel.[46] The concept central to this initiative, known as a biomarker, refers to a measurable biological indicator—such as genetic mutations, specific biochemical substances, physiological patterns, or brain-imaging signals—that can objectively identify a particular medical state, condition, or disease subtype.[47] In simpler terms, a biomarker provides a concrete, measurable way to accurately determine exactly what subtype of illness a patient has, allowing clinicians to deliver precise diagnoses and tailored treatments. Essentially, what researchers and clinicians strive to find is precisely this type of reliable biomarker for psychiatric conditions.

The RDoC was aimed to fundamentally transform psychiatric research by shifting the focus away from traditional diagnostic categories based on observable symptoms toward a deeper understanding of underlying biological mechanisms. Recognizing the significant heterogeneity and overlap among mental disorders defined by traditional classification systems like DSM, RDoC proposed a dimensional framework grounded in neuroscience. Instead of grouping disorders by symptom clusters, RDoC emphasized investigating specific functional domains, such as negative and positive valence systems (responsible for processing reward, punishment, and emotional states), cognitive systems (memory, attention, perception), social processing systems, arousal and regulatory systems (sleep and circadian rhythms), and sensorimotor systems (motor control and sensory processing).

At the heart of RDoC was the concept of studying brain systems—networks of interconnected brain regions and pathways that coordinate specific functions and behaviors. Brain systems were chosen as the primary investigative targets because they provide measurable biological markers and can be objectively assessed through various methods, including genetics, neuroimaging, electrophysiology, behavioral tasks, and physiological monitoring. For instance, abnormalities in brain circuits responsible for reward processing and motivation could underlie conditions traditionally diagnosed as depression or addiction, while disruptions in cognitive control systems could be involved in disorders like schizophrenia or ADHD. By studying these systems directly, RDoC intended to clarify the specific biological pathways contributing to psychiatric symptoms, allowing researchers and clinicians to differentiate disorders more precisely at the level of underlying neurobiology rather than external symptom presentation.

The NIMH envisioned RDoC as a foundational research framework, guiding scientists worldwide to organize and design their studies differently from conventional clinical diagnostic criteria. Rather than focusing research solely on patients diagnosed according to DSM categories, researchers were encouraged to recruit participants based on measurable biological and behavioral traits corresponding to particular RDoC-defined dimensions. This approach was anticipated to reveal novel patterns linking biological abnormalities to specific symptoms and cognitive deficits, thus facilitating the development of biomarkers and new targeted treatments. Over time, it was expected that discoveries derived from RDoC-based research would inform revised diagnostic classifications and personalized therapeutic interventions.

Unfortunately, as of today, this approach has not produced significant breakthroughs, nor have its results been translated into clinical practice. For research findings to move successfully from laboratory experiments into real-world clinical practice, they must meet several essential criteria, such as reliability, replicability, and generalizability. **Reliability** refers to the consistency and stability of measurements or findings across repeated tests under similar conditions. In simpler terms, reliability means if the same test is performed multiple times, it should consistently produce the same or very similar results. **Replicability** means that an experiment or study, when conducted independently by other researchers using the same methodology, should yield similar outcomes. Practically, this means different scientists conducting the same study independently should arrive at the same conclusions, reinforcing trust in the findings. Finally, **generalizability** refers to the extent to which findings from a specific study can accurately apply to broader populations or situations beyond the original research context. In everyday terms, generalizability means the results of a study should not only hold true for a small group in one research setting, but also be applicable to a larger and more diverse group of people in different contexts or environments.

Unfortunately, most psychiatric research today fails to meet these critical criteria, primarily due to the inherent complexities of mental disorders themselves. For example, consider studies not framed by comprehensive frameworks like RDoC, but instead focused on uncovering biological factors related to psychiatric conditions. A significant issue immediately arises regarding population size in these studies. Psychiatric research involving neurophysiological measures—such as magnetic resonance imaging (MRI)—typically includes relatively small samples. Recent analyses indicate that clinical MRI studies conducted between 2020 and 2023 had a median sample size of approximately 75 participants, and over 90% of these studies involved fewer than 350 participants.[48] Given the large and diverse populations affected by psychiatric disorders, such small sample sizes severely limit generalizability, making it challenging to translate findings effectively to broader patient populations. Yet, even if sample sizes were adequate, another significant challenge remains: the lack of stable and consistent results. Due to the substantial heterogeneity within psychiatric diagnoses, patients recruited based solely on diagnostic labels evaluated through subjective questionnaires are likely to represent numerous distinct biological subtypes. As discussed earlier, estimates suggest hundreds of unique symptom profiles for depression alone, dramatically decreasing the likelihood of obtaining statistically significant (i.e., results not attributable to chance and robust enough to indicate true effects) and reproducible findings. Consequently, even if a study yields intriguing results, independently replicating these findings with the same experimental design—let alone with minor modifications—becomes nearly impossible. Thus, stable and widely validated biomarkers have remained elusive in psychiatric research.

Even adopting structured frameworks like RDoC does not fully resolve these challenges. Although RDoC studies investigate clearly defined biological systems rather than diagnostic labels alone, they still rely on relatively small participant groups, making it difficult to obtain reliable and consistent outcomes. Furthermore, another significant challenge arises when attempting to integrate findings across diverse research areas into a unified clinical approach that aligns with existing diagnostic norms. This complexity further hinders the practical application of research results in real-world clinical settings. Ultimately, academia faces a profound barrier: the intrinsic heterogeneity of psychiatric disorders combined with an overreliance on symptom-based classifications consistently prevents studies from meeting the fundamental criteria of reliability, replicability, and generalizability, thereby obstructing the accurate depiction of mental disorders.

However, even if we imagine an ideal scenario in which we successfully identify distinct clinical subtypes of psychiatric disorders and selectively recruit patients belonging exclusively to each subtype, we still encounter formidable logistical challenges. Estimates suggest that depression alone might encompass at least 200 distinct subtypes, and when considering hypotheses linking specific symptoms to various neural networks, this number potentially increases to over 1,000 unique symptom profiles.[45] Identifying reliable biomarkers for each subtype would require conducting multiple rigorous studies for each subgroup, each with sufficiently large samples to ensure statistically significant findings, and then independently reproducing these findings several times. Under optimistic assumptions, accurately characterizing each subtype would necessitate enrolling at least 1,000 highly specific patients per subtype across multiple studies. Aggregating these requirements reveals an extraordinary scope: using a traditional research approach to comprehensively understand depression alone would require thousands of studies involving potentially millions of participants. Clearly, such a task is nearly impossible to accomplish in practice.

Such a research strategy exemplifies the "bottom-up" approach, which has proven effective in various biomedical fields but encounters significant limitations in psychiatry. The bottom-up approach in biomedical research involves identifying fundamental biological components—such as specific genes, molecules, or neural circuits—and systematically examining how their individual interactions give rise to complex biological behaviors or conditions.[49] In practical terms, researchers start by proposing a specific biological hypothesis, recruit a targeted cohort of patients exhibiting relevant symptoms, and conduct focused studies to test their assumptions. Promising initial findings then progress to larger-scale studies for validation, ultimately aiming to inform precise diagnostic tools or targeted therapeutic interventions. While this structured, step-by-step methodology has driven significant progress in many medical fields, psychiatry's intrinsic challenges—such as subjective symptom evaluation, the absence of definitive biological markers, and profound disorder heterogeneity—limit its effectiveness in the study of mental illnesses.

Despite extensive efforts, significant resources, and the systematic application of rigorous methodologies, even academic research has so far been unable to unravel the complexity of psychiatric disorders. The fundamental barriers lie in the intrinsic heterogeneity of these conditions and the persistent lack of sufficient, reliable data. The diagnostic categories currently in use—built primarily upon observable symptoms—do not adequately capture the diverse and multifaceted biological processes underlying these disorders. As a result, attempts to translate laboratory findings into clear, actionable insights often fall short, and genuinely personalized treatments remain elusive.

Ultimately, the core issue may be that mental disorders are structurally far more complex than previously anticipated. Unlike many physical illnesses, psychiatric disorders do not appear to stem from singular, easily identifiable biological causes. Instead, they likely involve dynamic interactions among multiple genetic, neurochemical, physiological, environmental, and psychological factors, each contributing uniquely to individual cases. Until research strategies and technologies evolve sufficiently to handle this intricate web of causation, our understanding of mental disorders—and consequently our ability to treat them effectively—will remain severely limited, highlighting the urgent need for innovative approaches beyond traditional frameworks.

The Core Question Behind Psychiatry's Limitations

In the end, we face a troubling reality: Like Maria, more than a billion individuals worldwide have been diagnosed with psychiatric disorders based solely on their symptomatic profiles, and they continuously struggle to find treatments that genuinely alleviate their suffering. Like Maria, many patients, discouraged by ineffective medications and frustrated by prolonged trial-and-error processes, often abandon treatment altogether. Despite decades of dedicated efforts—ranging from increasing public awareness and improving diagnostic accuracy to tirelessly pursuing the development of new medications—progress remains fragmented and insufficient. Ultimately, all these multifaceted problems lead us back to one fundamental, unanswered question:

> What exactly are mental disorders? Where do they originate, and what genuinely defines them?

The sooner we acknowledge that the alarming statistics, limited effectiveness of treatments, and failures of clinical research largely stem from our fundamental misunderstanding of psychiatric illnesses, the sooner we can redirect resources effectively. Rather than prematurely assigning blame to clinicians, pharmaceutical companies, or research institutions, we must recognize that our collective inability to grasp the true biological nature of these disorders is at the core of current challenges. As a consequence, we continue to perpetuate myths about the origins of mental illnesses and their appropriate treatments, further obscuring our understanding. Our most urgent task, therefore, is not merely refining existing classifications or incrementally improving medications, but fundamentally rethinking our approach—identifying precisely which illnesses lie behind these unbearable symptoms.

The critical questions remain:

> What conditions are genuinely hidden beneath the masks of psychiatric symptoms, and where do they truly come from?

With this chapter, we've completed our exploration of the patient journey, allowing us to understand the psychiatric field step-by-step. Along the way, we've touched upon deeper systemic issues, including the complexities of pharmaceutical drug development and the limitations inherent in academic research. Together, these insights have helped us clarify the obstacles patients face as they seek effective treatment and recovery. Before moving on to analyze potential solutions, let's step back once more and consider the psychiatric field as a whole—examining additional challenges and barriers that might arise in the quest for answers and innovation. That broader perspective will be the focus of the next chapter.

4

Psychiatry as a System

It was under Miami's blazing sun in 2015 when I was not yet an entrepreneur and my only personal connection to psychiatry was through my diagnosis. Despite the beautiful weather, my attention was fully absorbed by the final pages of Ken Kesey's *One Flew Over the Cuckoo's Nest*, where the passionately rebellious McMurphy was ultimately subdued by the psychiatric system and destroyed through lobotomy. This story, as old as the world itself, shows a hero who tries to shatter established boundaries but is crushed against the immovable rock of existing rules and relationships.

Is this tragic sacrifice really the only way to shift a monolithic system, or could there be another path? A system, after all, is inherently dynamic—a network formed by various nodes and centers that can evolve, be transformed, and shifted, but only if approached appropriately. For some reason, philosophical lessons from school came to my mind, and I recalled Aristotle's categorization of people's relationship with the state. He split them into three classes depending on their virtue, but most importantly, their role and relationship with the state—patient and diligent craftsmen and workers who create the foundations through labor, passionate and brave warriors and defenders who protect the system, and wise, balanced philosophers who govern and guide the state.

Back then, sitting at my school desk, I reflected sadly that my personality would place me among warriors, somewhat similar to McMurphy. But now, one thought haunted me: this perspective could apply to any system beyond the state. After all, one can relate to any system in three ways. One can exist within a system, unquestioningly living by its rules, perhaps uncomfortably but completely absorbed by its internal issues, unknowingly reinforcing its status quo and strength. Alternatively, one can be like McMurphy, observing the system's imperfections and trying to influence, disrupt, and change it through fiery rebellion—an approach likely to end in defeat, as the deeply entrenched system is far stronger and will most likely revert to its previous state once the irritant is removed.

Perhaps, if many such rebels united, the system could indeed shift, but alone, as the saying goes, one is not enough to win the war. However, the third option is to understand the system intimately, study it, and then gently influence its direction by playing by its own rules—not trying to directly oppose the system but instead guiding it toward change through its own laws and structures.

Suddenly, I realized my lips had started to go numb, and chills had spread across my body. As the sun sank toward the horizon, it was time to set aside all this philosophy and return to my daily tasks, saving these thoughts about systems for another moment of mind-wandering.

Years later, having forgotten these insights, I found myself attempting direct confrontation. Now a startup founder, like countless other innovators, I presented alarming statistics about psychiatric illnesses to investors, hoping to illustrate the dire state of psychiatry and convince them that innovation could transform the world. Yet my passionate pleas were met with rejections and setbacks. Then one day, a simple phrase took me back to that afternoon in Miami: "The problem is so vast, it no longer seems to belong to anyone."

Indeed, psychiatry has become so entrenched as a system that it's unclear whose responsibility it is, or how to move it. Innovators like me, driven by inner fire, often crash and burn in our attempts to change what we dislike about the system. Perhaps instead, we should simply pause, learn the system's rules, and figure out how to play—and win. Maybe real innovation begins not with rebellion, but with calm observation and understanding.

* * *

Defining the System

In previous chapters, we examined the journey a patient undertakes, from recognizing subtle changes in their mental state to seeking professional help and treatment. This patient-centric approach allowed us to identify existing shortcomings in psychiatry that significantly hinder patient recovery. We were even able to touch upon some of the underlying reasons behind these persistent issues, highlighting critical gaps that urgently require innovation.

The patient journey we've reviewed can be visualized as a straight line, with clearly defined stages or nodes along the path: self-assessment, initial diagnosis, and the treatment process (see Figure 4.1). Each of these nodes is filled with various obstacles and issues that complicate the patient's progress toward their ultimate goal—relief and recovery. However, patients do not exist in isolation, and the challenges they encounter are not standalone issues; rather, these problems arise because patients are connected to multiple institutions, each of which is interconnected with others. In other words, patients are integral components of a larger system, and they often occupy multiple roles within this system simultaneously. The same individuals struggling with mental disorders and searching for effective treatment—or even giving up on that search—may also work as employees at pharmaceutical companies, serve as contributors in research institutions, or influence policy decisions. The cumulative influence of all patients creates a force powerful enough to establish, sustain, or shift the existing ecosystem. For instance, a substantial number of patients can overload healthcare providers, leading to

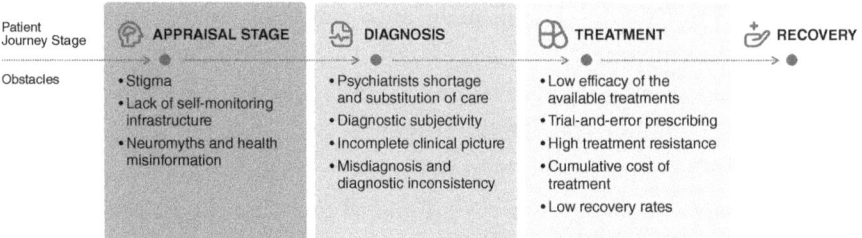

Figure 4.1 Linear patient journey, with defined stages and problems occurring at every stage.

longer waiting periods, lower treatment response rates, prolonged treatment durations, and increased demand for constant medical support, ultimately preventing clinicians from addressing the needs of additional patients. Furthermore, widespread disability related to mental disorders can cause significant economic consequences, impacting workforce productivity and financial stability across all major institutions within the psychiatric system.

My point is that although reviewing the patient journey has allowed us to identify significant gaps and gain deeper insights, and perhaps even inspired you to envision possible solutions, these steps alone do not guarantee that such solutions will be successfully integrated into real-world practice. To introduce meaningful, sustainable innovation—especially ideas involving advanced technologies such as AI and Big Data—we must first understand psychiatry as an interconnected whole, recognizing the complex relationships among all stakeholders and institutions within this ecosystem. In this chapter, I invite you to integrate all that we've previously discussed into a cohesive framework and examine psychiatry from another perspective—as if stepping back and viewing the entire system from above.

What exactly is a **system**? In its simplest form, a system is a structure composed of individual components—stakeholders—each fulfilling its own distinct role while continuously interacting with the others. Collectively, these components form an integrated whole designed to achieve a common objective. Every time I use the word "system," I picture a crystal lattice: a precisely organized structure in which each atom occupies its own defined position, connected to its neighbors through specific physical interactions—such as ionic or covalent bonds. Together, these atomic interactions form a coherent and stable structure with unique physical properties. Just as individual atoms in a crystal lattice contribute to the material's overall strength, flexibility, and conductivity, the components within any complex system collectively determine its overall behavior, enabling the system to function effectively for its intended purpose.

The psychiatric system resembles such a crystal lattice, composed of distinct players, many of whom we've already explored in previous chapters. Each stakeholder pursues specific goals and executes their designated functions, but together, they share a broader common objective: improving the lives of individuals struggling with mental disorders. Until now, however, we've primarily examined this system from the perspective of only one player—the patient. Indeed, patients are integral to the system, driven by the personal goal of feeling better. They fulfill their role by consulting physicians, describing symptoms, and adhering to prescribed treatments.

The primary goal of innovation is typically not to disrupt the system, as it may seem from the outside, but to shift how it operates, improving its ability to achieve the collective aim. Imagine attempting to alter the properties of a crystalline material—to change it from a solid to a liquid state, for example. Influencing a single atom alone would rarely suffice to trigger such a fundamental transition; rather, you would need to affect the interactions among multiple atoms, altering their collective structure and thereby changing the state of the entire material. Similarly, implementing meaningful innovation in psychiatry requires a comprehensive understanding of the complex interactions among all the players within the psychiatric system.

To give an example, one seemingly straightforward idea that might come to mind is replacing the questionnaires currently used in clinical trials with a more objective measurement tool. At first glance, this appears simple—but as soon as you attempt to implement it, you will find yourself needing to engage with multiple players within the system. First, you would require sufficient data, meaning you would need to license datasets from existing sources or somehow collect them yourself to develop reliable new metrics. Subsequently, you'd have to collaborate closely with research institutions to validate that your proposed measurement tools are both stable and scientifically sound. You'd then be required to gain regulatory approval, without which your new tools can't be integrated into clinical practice. After that, you'd need to train healthcare professionals on how to properly use your measurement system, ensuring pharmaceutical companies can effectively adopt and implement it in their clinical trials. Only after overcoming all these hurdles might your solution finally reach real-world application. Each of these interactions represents a potential risk that could lead to failure, transforming what initially seemed like a straightforward task into an unattainable goal. Without a proactive understanding of who influences your solution's implementation, how they grant approval, what motivates their decisions, and how they interact with each other, you risk becoming like that lone fighter exhausted by endlessly running from atom to atom, attempting to move the entire structure.

On the other hand, thoroughly analyzing the entire system can reveal additional gaps and hidden issues, uncovering new opportunities for further innovation. It can also facilitate strategic integration of your solution by leveraging these identified gaps, enabling a well-planned and impactful approach. This reminds me of playing Sudoku: At the start, you identify the cells whose conditions are clear and simple enough that filling them incorrectly is nearly impossible. Only after confidently solving these easier cells do you gradually progress toward finding answers for the remaining, more complex ones.

Stakeholders and Their Roles in the Psychiatric Ecosystem

Although we've briefly introduced the major stakeholders within psychiatry earlier, it's worth revisiting them here to understand what drives their decisions and actions. Even the most familiar entities have distinct objectives and priorities that often differ subtly within the shared goal of enhancing mental healthcare. Appreciating these differences helps explain why some innovations are quickly embraced while others struggle to gain traction, revealing both barriers and hidden opportunities for meaningful change.

> **Patients** are at the heart of this system, driven by their fundamental desire for improved health, enhanced quality of life, and relief from symptoms. Their active involvement—recognizing mental health issues, seeking professional assistance, and following recommended treatments—is crucial for the overall effectiveness of the psychiatric care system. Without patient engagement, no innovation, however promising, can fully succeed.

Clinics, hospitals, and healthcare providers form the operational core of psychiatric care. Doctors, including general practitioners and psychiatrists, assess patients, provide diagnoses, recommend evidence-based treatments, and track patient outcomes. Their primary motivation is the delivery of effective and timely care within real-world constraints, such as limited resources and increasing patient loads. Successful healthcare providers help minimize clinical risks, reduce burdens on society, and improve patient outcomes through careful, informed clinical decisions.

Pharmaceutical companies develop, manufacture, and distribute medications central to psychiatric treatment. Driven largely by commercial objectives, their role involves translating scientific research into viable therapeutic products, and they invest heavily in clinical research and shape treatment standards. Effective pharma companies expand treatment possibilities, improving patient outcomes and reducing the long-term economic and social impact of inadequately treated mental health disorders.

Academic institutions and research centers serve as critical engines of innovation, as they investigate the underlying biological, psychological, and social factors that influence psychiatric conditions. Universities, laboratories, and independent research facilities generate new insights, develop theoretical models, and rigorously test clinical hypotheses. Motivated by the pursuit of knowledge, professional recognition, and the potential real-world impact of their findings, academia continuously pushes the boundaries of our understanding, ensuring that clinical practice remains current and evidence-based.

Professional associations, like the American Psychiatric Association, establish and uphold the standards of psychiatric care, transforming scientific evidence into clear, practical guidelines. Their motivation lies in maintaining credibility, consistency, and quality of care, to safeguard public trust and ensure patient safety. By defining and disseminating best practices, these associations facilitate seamless collaboration among healthcare providers, researchers, and regulators, supporting continual improvement across the psychiatric ecosystem.

Regulatory agencies, such as the FDA, act as essential gatekeepers, meticulously reviewing new psychiatric treatments, diagnostic tools, and technologies. Their mission revolves around protecting public health by enforcing rigorous safety, efficacy, and quality standards. Regulators play a critical role in guiding clinical research design, overseeing product manufacturing, and continually monitoring safety post-approval. Effective regulation ensures patient trust in available treatments and safeguards the integrity and dependability of psychiatric care.

Governments shape psychiatric care through policy decisions, funding allocations, insurance regulations, and broader public health initiatives. Driven by objectives like societal stability, economic productivity, and public welfare, governments aim to promote population mental health, reduce healthcare costs, and address interconnected social issues such as homelessness and disability. By strategically supporting psychiatric care, governments help integrate mental health services within the wider healthcare system, enabling early intervention and resilience at both the individual and community levels.

Insurance companies play a crucial financial role, enabling widespread access to psychiatric care by managing the financial risks associated with mental health treatments. Through risk pooling, price negotiation, and reimbursement strategies, insurers aim to facilitate access to affordable healthcare while maintaining financial stability and profitability. When effective, insurance companies help ensure predictable, reliable access to mental health services, benefiting patients directly and enhancing the stability of the healthcare system overall.

Clearly identifying each player and understanding their unique roles is only the starting point. However, this initial task allows innovators to identify who within the system could potentially become an ally and support the innovation. It also helps determine an integration strategy, as the goal of introducing new technology is usually not only to shift the system but also to become part of it. This integration can be achieved in two primary ways: either by assuming the role of an independent player, which requires substantial resources and significant influence within the system, or by merging with one of the existing stakeholders. To properly evaluate the potential for successful integration, it is also important to observe how these players interact while pursuing their individual objectives.

When players actively engage and collaborate across the system, an even more intriguing phenomenon occurs: the system itself develops its own inherent logic, organization, and overarching purpose. In other words, the interplay between different stakeholders creates a dynamic structure, guided not merely by individual motives but also by shared interests and mutual dependencies. This insight is critical for anyone seeking to introduce a new technology or innovation into the psychiatric ecosystem. Successful integration into this complex system depends greatly on recognizing that achieving your objectives is deeply intertwined with engaging other players effectively. To enlist their active participation, it's crucial to ensure that supporting your goal simultaneously advances theirs. Only when mutual benefit is clear can your innovation or goal become fully embraced, enabling it to thrive within the system.

Complex Network of Interactions Within the Psychiatric System

Because each player's success depends on effective collaboration with others, the psychiatric ecosystem naturally develops into an intricate web of ongoing interactions. This network of relationships, continually shifting and evolving, determines how the overall system functions and adapts over time. Before attempting to integrate and establish new relationships within this system, it is beneficial to first understand which connections already exist and how they are reinforced by each player's individual interests. Of course, fully capturing every single interaction is nearly impossible; many connections are hidden, informal, or unique to specific contexts, such as certain types of disorders. Nevertheless, even a general awareness of these relationships can significantly help you optimize your approach when introducing new innovations.

To provide a foundational understanding of these interactions, Figure 4.2 illustrates the primary connections among various stakeholders. This visual representation aims to clarify the main direct and indirect dependencies and relationships within the ecosystem. It is important to emphasize that this depiction is deliberately high-level and approximate; it does not capture the full complexity or depth of these relationships but instead provides a general

	Patients	Clinics and Hospitals	Professional Associations	Regulators	Academic Institutions	Pharma Companies	Insurance Companies
Patients		Request for care, payment, clinical data, feedback	Patient experiences, advocacy needs, feedback on care standards	Safety data, adverse event reports, real-world treatment outcomes	Research participation, biological and clinical data	Medication consumption (market demand), clinical efficacy data	Premium payments, claims information, personal health data, treatment history
Clinics and Hospitals	Medical services, diagnosis, treatment, prescriptions, monitoring, patient education, care coordination		Clinical practice data, adherence to guidelines, insights on standards effectiveness	Compliance data, quality metrics, reporting of safety and adverse events	Clinical research sites, access to patients for studies, clinical data, collaboration	Clinical trial sites, patient enrollment, clinical trial data, efficacy and safety data	Billing data, claims submissions, patient utilization data, documentation for reimbursement
Professional Associations	Public educational materials, resources for understanding disorders and treatments	Clinical guidelines, diagnostic criteria, professional training, certification courses		Expert recommendations, standards of practice, data for regulatory decision-making	Framework for research, collaboration, dissemination of scientific knowledge	Guidelines influencing drug use, clinical standards for evaluating medication efficacy	Clinical guidelines informing coverage decisions, treatment standards for reimbursement
Regulators	Approval of safe and effective medications/devices, drug safety information, public health advisories	Approval and safety information on drugs, medical devices; guidelines for safe use, monitoring and reporting of adverse events	Regulatory frameworks, standards enforcement, policy guidance		Ethical guidelines, research oversight, clinical trial regulations	Drug approval, clinical trial oversight, safety monitoring, guidelines	Drug/device approval decisions influencing coverage policies, safety and efficacy data guiding reimbursement decisions
Academic Institutions	Access to clinical trials, innovative treatments, evidence-based care	Research partnerships, clinical guidelines, evidence for best practices	Scientific evidence informing guidelines, training materials, expertise	Clinical research data, scientific expertise, evidence for regulatory decisions		Research collaboration, clinical trial design, scientific validation	Evidence on treatment efficacy, cost-effectiveness data
Pharma Companies	Medications, treatment innovations, patient education	Medications, clinical trial partnerships, treatment protocols	Clinical efficacy data, support for guideline development	Clinical trial data for approval, safety monitoring reports	Research funding, collaborative trials, scientific partnerships		Pricing information, efficacy and safety data, drug utilization data
Insurance Companies	Coverage for treatments, cost reimbursement, healthcare access	Reimbursement for services, patient referrals, payment guidelines	Data influencing guideline recommendations, reimbursement policies	Utilization and cost data, compliance reporting, policy implementation data	Data on treatment outcomes, utilization patterns, cost-effectiveness	Access to formulary coverage, market access, reimbursement guidelines	

Figure 4.2 Primary stakeholder interactions within the psychiatric ecosystem. This image provides a high-level illustration of some of the direct and indirect interactions among key stakeholders within the psychiatric system. Rows represent stakeholders who provide resources, services, or influence, while columns indicate stakeholders who receive or benefit from them.

overview of how the actions of one stakeholder can influence other participants within the psychiatric system.

However, to truly grasp how intricate and layered these interactions can be, we should consider a concrete example. Let's focus specifically on the pharmaceutical company—a key ecosystem player with clearly defined objectives and roles—and explore in detail how, to fulfill its goals, it initiates a sophisticated chain of interactions throughout the ecosystem (see Figure 4.3).

At first glance, a pharmaceutical company's objective is relatively straightforward: to develop a commercially successful medication that addresses an unmet clinical need and gains acceptance from insurers who reimburse healthcare costs. However, achieving this seemingly clear goal precipitates an extensive and nuanced series of interactions with multiple stakeholders, each driven by their own unique interests and objectives.

Initially, the pharmaceutical company must thoroughly analyze market needs. They start by gathering essential data—how many patients actively seek treatment, what current prescription patterns look like, and where existing medications fall short. To acquire this information, the pharma company interacts closely with hospitals and clinics, leveraging their valuable firsthand knowledge of patient care, treatment effectiveness, and clinical challenges. Thus, the first significant relationship emerges clearly as: **Pharma → Clinics and Hospitals**.

In parallel, pharmaceutical companies must engage with insurance providers to understand purchasing power, pricing structures, and the financial constraints involved in launching new treatments. Understanding these details is vital because insurers ultimately determine patient accessibility through reimbursement decisions. This relationship forms another key interaction: **Pharma → Insurance Companies**.

Pharmaceutical companies often partner with governmental or semi-governmental organizations that conduct large-scale epidemiological research and collect extensive health data. These groups provide insights into broader disease trends, global patient populations, and public health needs, thereby further refining pharma's market understanding. Therefore, a third critical interaction arises: **Pharma → Governmental Organizations**.

With a clear market perspective established, the pharma company transition moves into the next critical phase: discovering and developing

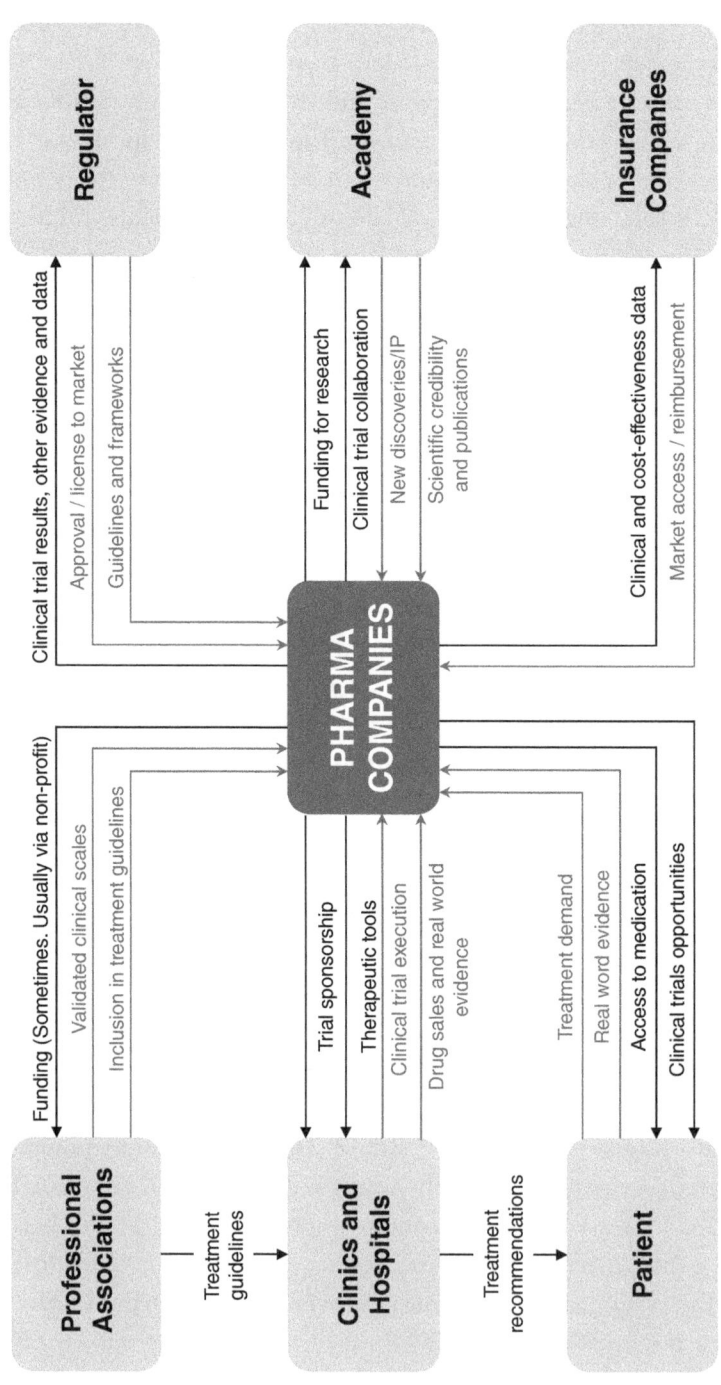

Figure 4.3 Pharmaceutical companies' interactions with different stakeholders in the psychiatric ecosystem.

promising therapeutic molecules or alternative treatment modalities. This generally involves deep collaboration with academia and research institutions. Pharmaceutical companies supply essential funding and resources, enabling research institutions to pursue targeted investigations into specific disorders. In return, academia contributes vital expertise and evidence—often through laboratory studies, animal research, and proof-of-concept experiments—that validate a molecule's potential therapeutic benefits. These collaborations usually span years, culminating in the continuous accumulation of robust scientific evidence regarding a molecule's safety, efficacy, and mechanism of action before it proceeds into clinical trials. This constitutes another significant relationship within the system: **Pharma ↔ Academia and Research Institutions**.

Once promising molecules have undergone rigorous preliminary validation, pharmaceutical companies begin clinical trials, a crucial phase explored in Chapter 3. At this stage, another essential interaction emerges between pharma companies and regulatory agencies. This relationship typically begins well before trials actually commence. Regulators provide detailed guidance and requirements for clinical trial designs, methodologies, patient selection, and outcome measures. Their ultimate goal is to ensure that trial data are scientifically robust, rigorously collected, and sufficient to justify eventual drug approval. Continuous dialogue with regulators helps pharma companies align their trials with these stringent criteria, establishing another critical relationship: **Pharma → Regulators**.

A fascinating dimension at this stage involves professional associations, such as the American Psychiatric Association (APA), responsible for developing diagnostic criteria and standardized clinical endpoints. These standards directly influence clinical trial design and patient selection processes. Occasionally, pharmaceutical companies may even influence the inclusion of new psychiatric diagnoses in official manuals. For instance, Eli Lilly actively promoted awareness and research around premenstrual dysphoric disorder (PMDD), which was initially not officially recognized, positioning their medication Sarafem—a repackaged form of Prozac—as a potential treatment. Lilly sponsored numerous studies demonstrating fluoxetine's effectiveness, helping build a compelling evidence base for PMDD. Eventually, this condition gained formal recognition as a distinct depressive disorder in the APA's DSM-V.[1]

Public discourse often labels these efforts "**medicalization**," defined as reframing human experiences and conditions into medical terms requiring clinical diagnosis and treatment.[2] While "medicalization" typically carries negative connotations—often implying commercial interests aimed at extending drug profitability—the reality is more nuanced. Psychiatry frequently addresses highly heterogeneous disorders. Defining and recognizing specific patient subgroups based on symptom clusters or treatment responsiveness can have genuine clinical importance. When medications exhibit unique effectiveness for clearly defined groups, officially recognizing these groups through diagnostic guidelines is essential. This necessitates extensive interactions and cooperation between pharma companies and other players in the psychiatric ecosystem to gather sufficient evidence and advocate successfully for these diagnostic distinctions: **Pharma → Professional Associations**.

To ensure clinical trial data truly reflect real-world scenarios, pharmaceutical companies establish close partnerships with clinics and hospitals. These healthcare institutions receive detailed clinical protocols, comprehensive training, specialized equipment, and ongoing support. As a result, hospitals can conduct high-quality clinical research within their regular care environments. Additionally, pharma companies engage directly with patients, offering them opportunities to participate in clinical trials. Through these trials, patients gain early access to potentially life-changing experimental medications that are not yet broadly available. This mutually beneficial relationship allows pharmaceutical companies to gather essential real-world data, hospitals to strengthen clinical research capabilities, and patients to benefit from innovative therapies. Thus, another clear relationship emerges: **Pharma → Clinics and Hospitals → Patients**.

Following successful clinical trials, pharmaceutical companies submit extensive data packages to regulators, formally seeking market approval. Regulators undertake detailed evaluations, carefully examining safety profiles, clinical effectiveness, potential side effects, trial methodologies, and the overall value the medication offers. At the same time, pharmaceutical companies independently engage insurance companies, negotiating reimbursement terms and demonstrating both clinical effectiveness and economic justification for the new treatment. Securing insurance coverage is vital to ensure patients can access these newly approved medications. These parallel interactions are crucial for bringing innovation to the market: **Pharma → Regulators and Pharma → Insurance Companies**.

However, approval and insurance coverage alone aren't sufficient for widespread adoption. Pharmaceutical companies must also actively engage healthcare providers—clinics, hospitals, and individual physicians—to educate them about the new medication. This includes sharing detailed clinical data, appropriate patient selection criteria, safety profiles, and clear usage guidelines. Equally critical is collaboration with professional associations, which integrate validated medications into formal treatment guidelines. Once these associations officially recommend a treatment, broad clinical acceptance generally follows, ultimately benefiting patients. These final critical relationships facilitate widespread clinical adoption and patient benefits: **Pharma → Clinics and Hospitals and Pharma → Professional Associations → Treatment Guidelines**.

At first glance, developing a new psychiatric medication might appear to be a clearly structured process. However, as we've explored, this seemingly linear task rapidly expands into a multidimensional challenge, drawing pharmaceutical companies into complex interactions with virtually every other player in the psychiatric ecosystem. Hospitals, insurers, regulators, research institutions, governmental bodies, professional associations, and patients—all distinct and independent entities—find themselves intricately linked, each playing a vital role in achieving the overarching goal of delivering effective treatment. This vivid example demonstrates precisely how systems function, integrating diverse and sometimes divergent interests into a cohesive and coordinated effort. If we were to examine other players within this ecosystem in similar detail, we'd undoubtedly reveal equally intricate patterns of interdependence, as each participant pursues their unique objectives by engaging and influencing the entire network.

What does this mean for innovators in psychiatry? It underscores a critical insight: When you introduce any new idea or innovation, you inevitably impact multiple players across the ecosystem. It's not enough to align your innovation with just one participant—you must carefully build relationships and communicate value to all stakeholders involved. Each player has their own motivations, goals, and sensitivities to risk, and if your innovation introduces complexities or conflicts with their interests, they may reject or obstruct your idea. The more players you successfully engage and secure support from, the greater the likelihood your innovation will gain a lasting foothold in the system.

Understanding the ecosystem at such a detailed level also uncovers entirely new innovation opportunities. Every small interaction among the players presents the potential for optimization and improvement. Consider, for example, the use of AI to streamline the preparation of FDA submission documents. While this might not seem directly transformative or inspiring at first glance, it represents an incremental innovation that can significantly reduce the time it takes to bring a new treatment to patients. Opportunities like these, while subtle, enhance critical parts of the larger process. We'll explore the broad range of innovative potentials and pathways more deeply later, in the third part of this book.

The Missing Player in Psychiatry: Diagnostics

As discussed in Chapter 3, the very definition and classification of psychiatric disorders has historically been based exclusively on subjective assessments of symptoms. The resulting heterogeneity of these disorders has, to date, prevented the identification of stable and reproducible biological markers—for example, brain-based indicators—that could be widely accepted and integrated effectively into diagnostic procedures or drug development processes. The nature of psychiatric disorder classification, based on self-reported symptoms or observable but non-measurable changes in behavior, creates a significant distinction between psychiatry and other medical fields, where diagnoses rely at least partially—if not entirely—on measurable biological indicators such as rashes, body temperature, or blood composition. This ultimately results in the absence of specialized diagnostic tool providers and diagnostic laboratories as a distinct class of players within the psychiatric system.

In oncology and other fields grounded in clear biological indicators, diagnostic companies occupy a significant, well-established position within the healthcare ecosystem, influencing key decisions across multiple levels simultaneously. Rather than just supplying tools, these providers become vital participants that directly shape how diseases are understood, diagnosed, and treated. Their presence creates an environment in which hospitals and clinics can move beyond subjective judgment toward precise, data-driven clinical strategies, enhancing treatment accuracy and outcomes.

For pharmaceutical companies, integrating advanced diagnostics early in drug development clarifies mechanisms of action, identifies patient subgroups, and reduces uncertainty around clinical trials. This predictability not only streamlines trial design but also accelerates the regulatory approval process, as regulatory bodies such as the FDA increasingly rely on clearly validated biomarkers and diagnostic criteria to set official guidelines and standards. Furthermore, insurers leverage these precise diagnostic measures to optimize resource allocation, ensuring that treatments reach the patients most likely to benefit from them. In this way, diagnostic tools both enhance clinical outcomes and allow for the introduction of refined financial and reimbursement models, making healthcare spending more targeted, efficient, and sustainable.

Professional associations similarly integrate these validated diagnostic methods into their clinical guidelines, standardizing best practices and promoting consistency in patient care. By clearly defining essential diagnostic tests for various stages of treatment, they elevate overall clinical quality and reliability across healthcare settings. At the same time, academia and research institutions rely on diagnostic data to deepen their understanding of diseases at a fundamental level, uncovering new potential pathways for both innovative treatments and more effective diagnostics.

Diagnostic tools and laboratories typically hold a central and stable position within healthcare systems, sustained by robust interactions with every major stakeholder. As we've explored, diagnostic providers do not merely pursue their own commercial goals through equipment manufacturing and tool development; they also play a critical role in helping all other stakeholders improve the efficiency and effectiveness of their tasks, decisions, and responsibilities.

But what happens when such an integral player is entirely absent from the psychiatric ecosystem? How does the lack of these traditionally vital diagnostic providers impact psychiatry as a whole?

The most significant impact of diagnostic providers typically comes from their role in generating and accumulating extensive real-world data, which then becomes foundational for the entire healthcare ecosystem. These data inform everything from diagnostic precision and clinical decision-making to drug development and personalized treatment strategies. However, psychiatry's current structural configuration and historical development have trapped it in a complex Catch-22 situation. On the one hand, introducing objective diagnostics into a mature system like psychiatry demands substantial real-world datasets from which accurate and reliable diagnostic tools can be built. On the other hand, the absence of such robust data is itself a direct result of the lack of routine, objective diagnostic procedures within the psychiatric care pathway.

As discussed in Chapter 3, one major limitation of academic psychiatric research is precisely this lack of access to sufficiently large and representative datasets. Research institutions tend to rely on relatively small-scale data collected through painstaking individual efforts. However, due to the extreme heterogeneity of psychiatric disorders, effective diagnostic methods require much greater data volumes—and these datasets must reflect realistic clinical populations.

By contrast, in other medical fields, substantial and representative datasets emerge naturally as byproducts of routine clinical practice and diagnostics. Consider oncology again: Routine procedures, like MRI scans used for simple tumor localization or biopsies intended to confirm cancer types, have steadily accumulated over the years. Eventually, these large-scale, real-world datasets enabled researchers to identify tumor subtypes, predict treatment response, and create precise diagnostic tools. Moreover, these same datasets have become foundational for advanced genetic studies, uncovering stable genetic markers associated with specific cancer types, thus further enriching diagnostic methods and therapeutic targeting.

In psychiatry, however, relying exclusively on symptom-based diagnoses—combined with the almost total lack of routine biological data—creates a fundamental barrier that hinders meaningful progress. Without a steady stream of measurable and objective data, psychiatry struggles to move beyond subjective groupings of symptoms and toward precise, reliable biomarkers. As a result, the entire psychiatric ecosystem remains constrained, deprived of the essential foundation required for genuine innovation and long-term advancement.

Another consequence of psychiatry's lack of specialized diagnostic providers, which may seem controversial or debatable—and I acknowledge this fully, yet still consider it important to highlight—is the absence of routine mental health screenings that could prevent or at least detect disorders at earlier stages. Although the U.S. Preventive Services Task Force (USPSTF) has recommended routine mental health screening for adults under 65, these guidelines are far from consistently implemented, resulting in uneven application across primary care settings.[3] Even in countries like Germany, where the healthcare system mandates regular health check-ups, psychiatric evaluations are generally not included, with assessments conducted only if there's an explicit concern or request. This gap often leads people to seek psychiatric care only after their conditions have advanced significantly. Yet beyond the obvious issues of delayed diagnosis and treatment, there's an even deeper, systemic problem: without regular mental health screenings, psychiatry lacks the essential data on healthy individuals. In other fields of medicine, routine diagnostic tests produce rich datasets covering both affected and unaffected groups, creating robust normative baselines that are crucial for medical progress.

I want to clarify that I fully recognize the role played by diagnostic questionnaires and the organizations developing and implementing them within psychiatry. As discussed in Chapter 3, these tools undoubtedly offer a valuable way to quantify symptoms and provide structure to assessments. However, despite their usefulness, they remain heavily dependent on subjective interpretations—both the clinician's judgment and the patient's self-perception—and, importantly, they aren't applied routinely in every patient evaluation, but only when clinicians specifically choose to use them. As a result, questionnaires alone cannot fully address the core problem identified earlier: the absence of systematic, objective data collection from the broader population. While questionnaires certainly help structure symptom evaluation, they don't produce the comprehensive and detailed normative data necessary for substantial scientific and clinical advancement.

Starred Problem: Breaking the Stagnation

In the first part of this book, we've examined psychiatry from multiple angles, assessed the magnitude of its challenges, established cause-and-effect relationships, and evaluated the complexity involved in integrating new solutions into an established healthcare system. To clearly frame the challenge ahead, let's restate the conditions explicitly.

We have:
- Psychiatric disorders characterized by significant heterogeneity, with unclear underlying biology—in other words, a fundamental lack of understanding regarding what mental disorders truly represent biologically;
- An absence of long-term accumulated biological data reflecting real-world clinical populations; and
- An established, complex psychiatric ecosystem comprising multiple interconnected stakeholders that are highly resistant to change.

Consequently, we face:
- A large and growing number of diagnosed patients whose conditions have uncertain biological origins;
- A significant stagnation in therapeutic advancements, including limited progress in medication development and persistently low treatment efficacy; and
- An accumulating societal burden, encompassing extensive economic impacts, increased healthcare expenditures, productivity losses, ongoing social stigma, cultural misunderstandings, and pervasive misinformation about mental illness.

The task is:

Under the described constraints, leveraging available technological tools and emerging innovations, to develop and successfully implement practical solutions capable of addressing these systemic issues, and ensuring these innovations are effectively integrated and accepted within this resistant and established healthcare system.

Well, I wish us good luck. But in all seriousness, if this were an easy task, someone else would have addressed it long before our conversation even began. The challenge ahead is undeniably complex, demanding not just one but numerous innovations and varied strategic approaches, all backed by substantial and sustained effort. Yet, despite the intricacies, this problem is neither unsolvable nor hopeless. With collective insight, creativity, and perhaps a bit of intellectual courage, we have every reason to believe progress is attainable.

While this book does not provide a ready-made solution—no single volume realistically could—my goal is to lay a strong foundation for understanding the critical dynamics involved, and to provide fertile ground for thoughtful exploration and meaningful innovation. But before we leap into possible answers (approaches we'll examine in the third part of this book), we must first understand the tools and resources at our disposal—notably, artificial intelligence. Thus, our next step must be a realistic and nuanced evaluation of artificial intelligence, including what it can truly offer, where its boundaries lie, and exactly what conditions and data we must have in place to fully leverage its transformative power in tackling psychiatry's most profound challenges. And this is precisely the focus of the second part of this book.

PART II
Artificial Intelligence

5 | The Fundamentals of AI

There were about 150 people in the hall. A blend of excitement and anxiety made it hard to fully take in the moment: faces in the audience blurred into an indistinct mass, time seemed to accelerate, my cheeks burned, and my palms became sweaty. Seeking a connection with the audience, I deliberately searched for eye contact, carefully studying each face I encountered. Gentle nods and quiet smiles reassured me that I had captured their attention. Gradually, a rare and almost magical sense of unity emerged, as if every word I spoke resonated deeply within them. I hadn't experienced inspiration like this in a long time. Speaking for the first time not to investors or innovators, but to people who lived psychiatry every day—doctors, psychiatrists, psychologists, mental health counselors—I poured absolutely everything I had into those ninety minutes. I spoke about the depth of the crisis in psychiatry, the extraordinary possibilities of artificial intelligence, efforts that we should make to build new innovations, and painted visions of a future we could achieve if we successfully integrated these new technologies into the complicated psychiatric world.

When the question-and-answer session began at the end of my presentation, my confidence grew even stronger. People eagerly raised their hands, some quickly scribbling notes in their notebooks, others taking pictures of my slides. My heart was beating faster than usual as I stepped down from the stage. Smiling broadly, still riding an emotional high, I walked toward the organizer. I was eager to hear his impressions, to confirm that the talk had truly met his expectations.

Yet as I approached, an unsettling feeling began to stir within me. The organizer avoided my gaze, nervously shuffling papers on the table, his shoulders tense as though weighed down by troubling thoughts. Eventually, he raised his head and cast a hesitant, uncertain glance in my direction. Carefully, as if afraid of hurting my feelings, he began to speak:

"It seemed the audience found it interesting," he said softly, pausing as he chose his words. "But we'll only know for sure once we see the survey results. To be honest, our main goal today was to reassure them that artificial intelligence isn't going to take their jobs away. I really hope that message came through…"

* * *

Everyone's Talking AI

Heated discussions about **Artificial Intelligence (AI)** have moved from the periphery of technical circles into the very center of public conversation. Over the past decade, the term "AI" has migrated from academic journals and specialized conferences to mainstream headlines and everyday discussions. Sometimes conversations about artificial intelligence come up in the most unexpected situations, like with taxi drivers or in hair salons; a couple of weeks ago, my colleague's five-year-old daughter approached him saying, "Dad, could you please install AI on my tablet?" The best reflection of how interest in and mentions of artificial intelligence have grown is, as usual, statistics from Google queries—searches for "artificial intelligence" have more than doubled in the last ten years, with a particularly sharp rise following the introduction of advanced generative models, namely ChatGPT, in 2022 and 2023.[1,2]

Of course, this rising interest in artificial intelligence has not come from nowhere: the incredible progress occurring in this area has led artificial intelligence to become part of solutions for a wide range of industries—in medicine, design, architecture, and finance. In the startup and investment spheres, the word "AI" has almost become mandatory, and nearly every team working toward developing innovative products adds these two magic letters to all their materials and presentations.

But, as with all areas where interest has grown very quickly, the consequence is a growing gap between media headlines and the perception of artificial intelligence they create, and the actual understanding of what artificial intelligence is. In most cases, the perception and understanding of AI are filled with misconceptions and misunderstandings. Surveys show that while 90% of people report familiarity with the term, only about a third can accurately describe what AI actually is or how it works.[3]

This disconnect creates fertile ground for myths and anxieties. On one hand, some attribute almost magical capabilities to any automated system, conflating simple rule-based software with genuine machine intelligence. On the other, popular narratives often veer toward dystopian scenarios, imagining AI as an autonomous force poised to surpass or even threaten humanity. Of course, these myths and fears are far from reality; yes, technological progress in AI is astonishing and absolutely impressive, but nevertheless, it remains limited—today, AI is neither a panacea nor an out-of-control frightening force, but a rapidly evolving set of tools whose true potential and limitations are still being discovered.

In this chapter, I certainly cannot explain what artificial intelligence is in detail, dispel all myths, or dive with you into the detailed architecture of all existing models, but my goal is different: it is important for you to form a high-level understanding of what AI generally represents, what tasks it can solve, and what is needed to make its use in your solutions possible. If we want to use artificial intelligence as a tool to address profound issues in psychiatry, it is important to have at least a basic understanding of what is under the hood of artificial intelligence, how the models produce the results they show, how to properly evaluate and use them, and what limitations and difficulties to expect. In my environment, there is a fairly large number of people familiar with technology, but even in these circles, I sometimes hear echoes of overestimating the capabilities of modern AI technologies, which arise from a fundamental misunderstanding of how they were formed.

Consider one of the most common criticisms leveled at generative models like ChatGPT: users frequently express frustration when these systems make errors, provide incorrect information, or fail to grasp what seems like a straightforward request. Such disappointments typically stem from a fundamental misunderstanding of what actually drives these models—the core computational processes that govern their behavior. If users understood that ChatGPT generates responses by sequentially predicting the most statistically probable next word based on the specific context provided and learned patterns from its training data, many complaints would dissolve. The model does not think critically about available information, nor does it filter truth from falsehood, nor does it intuitively grasp user intent and emotional context.

Therefore, the goal of this chapter is to provide at least a basic understanding of what developments have allowed the creation of programs that give the impression that a machine can think and act like a human. I spent a long time thinking about which approach could best form such an understanding, and the most illuminating way to understand the algorithms that power today's AI technologies is to step back several decades, look at the moment when artificial intelligence emerged, identify the key catalyst, and examine the first algorithms that already then demonstrated mesmerizing—even somewhat frightening—results, creating an impression that the machine had gained consciousness. The relative simplicity of these examples can provide the necessary basic understanding of how human decisions can be translated into algorithmic rules, and how when a program follows these rules, it can create the illusion of a new consciousness emerging.

The Birth of Artificial Intelligence

Historically, the ability to recognize patterns, understand language, and reason through problems was seen as the exclusive domain of living minds. Scientists and engineers did not seriously consider the possibility that machines could perform these tasks until the twentieth century. The shift began with a growing awareness that the essence of intelligence—at least in its computational aspects—could be understood as the manipulation of information. This realization opened the door to the idea that, if information processing could be formalized and automated, machines might one day replicate certain aspects of human thought.

Two major technological breakthroughs provided the initial momentum for the idea of developing artificial intelligence. Unsurprisingly, both were driven by pressing technological demands arising from World War II. One of these challenges emerged within the U.S. Army in the early 1940s, stemming from the urgent need for precise artillery firing tables. Such tables indicated the exact angle and explosive charge required for artillery shells to hit targets accurately at various distances, factoring in variables such as projectile weight, muzzle velocity, air resistance, temperature, wind speed, and terrain characteristics. These tables specified the exact angle and amount of explosive charge required to hit targets at various distances, taking into account factors such as projectile weight, muzzle velocity, air resistance, temperature, wind, and terrain. To create a single table, teams of human "computers" solved thousands of differential equations using mechanical desk calculators. The process was slow and labor-intensive: for every new weapon or change in battlefield conditions, the calculations had to be repeated from scratch. As a result, the Army struggled to provide up-to-date tables fast enough for military needs. Delays in producing these tables directly affected the accuracy and effectiveness of artillery units.

This daunting workload prompted military engineers to seek an innovative solution—a machine capable of automating these complex calculations to substantially enhance speed and accuracy. It was this ambitious pursuit that led to the creation of ENIAC, the first large-scale electronic computer.[4,5] ENIAC was a colossal feat of engineering, occupying an entire room measuring approximately 30 by 50 feet and weighing close to 30 tons. Its intricate structure comprised nearly 18,000 vacuum tubes, 1,500 relays, 70,000 resistors, and 10,000 capacitors, and its operation required approximately 150 kilowatts of electricity. Managed by a dedicated team of engineers and programmers, ENIAC could perform up to 5,000 additions or 385 multiplications each second, transforming calculations that previously consumed weeks of human effort into tasks achievable within hours. For the military, this advancement drastically shortened the time needed to generate artillery firing tables, allowing teams to accomplish in less than two days tasks that formerly required a full month, with consistent accuracy maintained throughout. ENIAC was among the earliest systems demonstrating the feasibility of parallel computation—the simultaneous processing of multiple operations, a principle resembling the parallel processing that occurs within the human brain. This achievement marked one of the initial significant steps toward the development of computing power, a critical technological requirement for simulating brain-like activities. To this day, advancements in computing power remain essential for continued progress in the field of artificial intelligence.

At the same time, across the Atlantic, British mathematician Alan Turing and his colleagues at Bletchley Park were confronting a different critical challenge: deciphering encrypted communications used by the German military during World War II. Many readers may recall these events from their portrayal in the film *The Imitation Game*. To tackle the sophisticated Enigma code, Turing's team constructed electromechanical machines, the device known as the Bombe. This apparatus systematically cycled through thousands of possible cipher configurations, rapidly identifying the correct encryption settings at speeds unattainable by human cryptographers.[6,7]

The Bombe operated by methodically evaluating letter combinations, logical relationships, and linguistic patterns encoded within intercepted messages, handling abstract symbols rather than merely numerical calculations. Symbolic processing, the capability to interpret and manipulate letters, words, and logical instructions, represents a fundamental component of human cognitive activity, underpinning language comprehension, reasoning, and problem-solving. Turing's innovation provided tangible evidence that machines could indeed manage symbolic information. This realization opened the intriguing possibility that computers might one day emulate cognitive functions traditionally seen as uniquely human.

These two technological breakthroughs, ENIAC and Bombe, addressed two major obstacles standing in the way of realizing the idea of artificial intelligence: the ability to perform a large number of **parallel computations**, and the ability to translate operations requiring human consciousness into a clear, algorithmic sequence that a machine could replicate. As a result, by the mid-1950s, these groundbreaking innovations had sparked increasing curiosity within scientific circles, prompting researchers to explore more systematically the potential capabilities of computational machines. This growing intellectual momentum culminated during the summer of 1956 at Dartmouth College in Hanover, New Hampshire, where a visionary group of mathematicians and engineers—led by John McCarthy, Marvin Minsky, Nathaniel Rochester, and Claude Shannon—gathered to undertake an ambitious research initiative. It was at this seminal event that the term "Artificial Intelligence" was first introduced, marking the birth of a distinct field of research built around a compelling hypothesis articulated in their original proposal: "every aspect of learning or any other feature of intelligence can in principle be so precisely described that a machine can be made to simulate it."[8,9] This pivotal gathering transformed what had previously been isolated experiments and fragmented inquiries into a unified scientific discipline, one dedicated explicitly to the creation of machine intelligence capable of emulating human cognitive skills.

The First AI Algorithms

During that same historic AI gathering at Dartmouth College in 1956, Allen Newell, Herbert Simon, and Cliff Shaw introduced their groundbreaking program, the **Logic Theorist**, widely regarded as the very first artificial intelligence software. Its primary goal was to automatically prove mathematical theorems using formal logical rules and axioms drawn from Bertrand Russell and Alfred Whitehead's foundational work, *Principia Mathematica*.[10] The Logic Theorist demonstrated remarkable capabilities, successfully proving numerous mathematical theorems at a level comparable to a skilled human mathematician. The critical innovation of this program was its ability to efficiently select optimal pathways toward a solution, rather than resorting to exhaustive testing of every conceivable step. It might sound like magic; however, this decision-making did not arise randomly—the developers embedded into the program specific guidelines, "rules of thumb," following which the program was able to prioritize promising paths and streamline the process of theorem proving. These guiding principles became known as heuristics. The Logic Theorist thus provided the earliest compelling evidence that human-like logical reasoning could be effectively captured in clearly defined, programmable rules, enabling a machine to tackle complex intellectual challenges at a level equal to, and sometimes surpassing, human abilities. This was due, in part, to the machine's consistent application of logical rules, as opposed to human reasoning, which often varies and does not always follow consistent logical principles, resulting in suboptimal solutions.

The following year, Newell, Simon, and Shaw presented another program called the **General Problem Solver (GPS)**—a spinoff from Logic

Theorist—which could solve more general tasks and problems outside of the mathematical field, while still following defined logical rules and the principle of selecting the optimal next step formulated by the developers.[11] It could solve tasks such as the "Tower of Hanoi" puzzle (determining the optimal sequence of moves to relocate disks while adhering to certain rules), symbolic logic problems, and simple planning tasks like rearranging blocks into a specified configuration. GPS operated by comparing the current state of the problem with the desired goal state, then selecting actions aimed at progressively reducing the differences between the two—another human-like decision-making approach translated into mathematical rules and defined for the program.

At the same time, in 1957, another fundamental advancement in artificial intelligence was introduced by psychologist Frank Rosenblatt—a revolutionary algorithm called the **Perceptron**, one of the first machine learning algorithms.[12] The Mark I Perceptron, Rosenblatt's pioneering hardware implementation, used photodetectors to convert images into electrical signals, which were then processed by the algorithm. It was capable of performing classification tasks such as sorting input data into two categories. Specifically, it could differentiate between geometric shapes, distinguishing circles from squares, or recognizing letters, such as distinguishing "X" from "E." Some of you may immediately recognize this as an early version of an image-recognition task—and indeed, nearly 70 years ago, the first self-learning image-classification algorithm was created. Images were first converted into numerical values: each image was divided into multiple regions, and each region was assigned a numerical value corresponding to its brightness or intensity. Within the system, each of these numerical inputs was then assigned a random "weight," essentially a coefficient representing how significantly the brightness or intensity in that particular image segment contributed to the final classification.

During the learning phase, the algorithm was presented with a set of labeled images, each clearly identified as either an "X" or an "E." After evaluating each example, the algorithm adjusted its internal weights so that the sum of the products of the brightness/intensity values and their corresponding weights would meet a certain threshold. By comparing the computed sum against this threshold—if the sum was below it, one answer was given; if above, another—the algorithm could accurately classify new images into their correct categories. Thus, Rosenblatt presented the first practical algorithm capable of learning based on provided examples, autonomously adjusting its internal parameters to identify correct solutions.

One of the first practical medical AI solutions was a program developed in 1970 at Stanford University called **MYCIN**.[13,14] The primary task of this program was to assist physicians in diagnosing bacterial infections and selecting effective antibiotics based on patient-specific data and laboratory results. Like the previously described algorithms, MYCIN followed explicit logic created by programmers, structured around sets of cause-and-effect ("if-then") rules designed to mimic the decision-making process employed by experienced physicians. These causal relationships were extracted from the expertise of practicing medical professionals and subsequently translated into a set of programmable rules. For example, one rule might state: "If the patient has symptom X, and laboratory test Y is positive, then the likelihood of infection Z increases by a certain factor."

Each of these rules was assigned a numerical weight, representing a measure of confidence or reliability associated with each factor included in the analysis, reflecting the degree of certainty physicians attributed to specific clinical evidence or symptoms. By systematically combining all relevant rules and continuously updating the confidence level based on newly accumulating evidence, MYCIN could provide a probabilistic assessment of potential diagnoses that closely mirrored human clinical reasoning. This solution demonstrated that even applied medical tasks involving the processing of large volumes of complex information, such as patient diagnosis, could be effectively broken down into a logical sequence of precisely structured rules.

These four historical examples—Logic Theorist, GPS, Perceptron, and MYCIN—illustrate how complex cognitive tasks can be solved using relatively straightforward mathematical expressions and human-defined methods. Consider the significance of these achievements: these algorithms were developed nearly seven decades ago, long before the era of modern computational power, big data, and compact personal computers. Through these pioneering examples, I aim to demonstrate that many actions, decisions, and cognitive processes that at first glance appear deeply human and complex can actually be translated into clearly defined logical rules, sequential steps, and mathematical operations. Since that time, due to technological progress, availability of digitized data, and substantial computational power, the field has developed significantly, as we will explore in subsequent sections. While tasks that modern AI systems can perform have become substantially more sophisticated, the fundamental principle remains the same—transforming human decision-making into programmable algorithms. And though this may at times appear akin to a living mind, the logic underlying it represents only a small fraction of genuine human consciousness.

Modern AI Paradigms

From the inception of the term "artificial intelligence" and the emergence of new algorithms, many changes have occurred in this industry. There have been periods of absolute stagnation, as well as periods of rapid development leaps, such as the last decade. Just as with the initial formation of this field, the development of modern AI models has been tied to two main technological advances: increased computational power, a system's ability to perform numerous parallel calculations simultaneously, as well as handle large amounts of data stored in memory, and breakthroughs in algorithms and approaches to data analysis, processing, and automation of computer-level decision-making processes. Of course, current algorithms are much more complex than the earliest ones, yet those early examples effectively illustrate the operational principles of many contemporary approaches.

Several algorithmic frameworks underpin modern AI, each representing diverse approaches to learning, and each embodying distinct philosophical principles and computational methodologies designed to address specific categories of problems across various domains. Understanding the underlying logic, practical applications, and implementation requirements of these approaches provides essential insight into the current state and future trajectory of intelligent systems development.

Supervised Learning: Classification and Regression Paradigms

One of the most fundamental paradigms underlying many modern AI solutions is **Supervised Learning**. In this approach, the model utilizes **labeled training datasets**—data provided as training examples illustrating pairs of input data and the correct outcomes the model should predict—to identify mathematical relationships between the input data and the results they should produce. Similar to the previously discussed perceptron example, where the model was initially trained on various images with the user explicitly indicating what was depicted, enabling the construction of a mathematical function that helped separate two types of images into distinct categories, the underlying idea of modern supervised learning models is that patterns identified in historical data can be generalized to make accurate predictions on previously unseen examples. This algorithm primarily addresses two types of problems: **classification tasks**, where the provided input data can be sorted into specific predefined groups—as in the perceptron example, which classified drawn letters into categories like "X" or "E"; and **regression tasks**, where the algorithm predicts numerical values, such as price, temperature, or age, based on input data, instead of sorting inputs into categories.

During training, this type of algorithm sequentially optimizes its internal parameters until the number of errors in predicting the correct outcomes is minimized. In other words, the algorithm examines input–output pairs, gradually refining its understanding of the underlying relationships until it achieves satisfactory performance metrics.

Such supervised learning algorithms find wide-ranging applications across diverse global categories. For instance, classification tasks are commonly applied to email filtering systems, where models are trained on extensive collections of emails labeled either as "spam" or "non-spam," enabling them to accurately detect and segregate unwanted messages. During training, the algorithm examines various features in the email text—such as specific keywords, sender addresses, formatting styles, and hyperlinks—and identifies patterns that frequently appear in spam emails versus legitimate correspondence. By analyzing thousands or even millions of such labeled examples, the model learns to recognize which combinations of these features indicate a high probability of spam, thus automatically categorizing incoming messages effectively.

Similarly, classification models underpin image recognition technologies, trained on vast datasets of images labeled by human annotators. These annotators explicitly specify what each image depicts—for instance, whether it contains a particular object like a cat. In fact, millions of people have been participating in this labeling process for decades by completing CAPTCHA tests, selecting images of buses, traffic lights, or animals to verify their human identity. Such labeled image datasets enable supervised learning algorithms to detect visual patterns—like shapes, textures, and color combinations—that uniquely distinguish objects, thus enabling the model to classify images accurately.

Regression tasks, meanwhile, are prominently employed in predicting continuous numerical outcomes, such as those in healthcare. Here, regression models may be trained on extensive medical datasets, where each training example includes specific patient data—such as age, blood pressure readings, medical history, lab test results, and treatment types—paired with known clinical outcomes like disease progression rates or measured effectiveness of drug dosages. By analyzing these labeled patient histories, the algorithm learns to mathematically model the relationship between patient characteristics and clinical outcomes, allowing predictions of risk scores, expected disease development, or optimal medication dosages for future patients based on similar input data.

To successfully implement supervised learning models, at least the following essential factors must be carefully considered. First, the quality of labeled data: for the model to reliably predict outcomes, the provided training examples must be accurate and representative; otherwise, if these examples contain errors, for instance, the resulting model will replicate these errors. Second, the quantity of data must be sufficient and must represent the full diversity of examples, allowing the model to detect all relevant relationships and ensuring its ability to generalize effectively to new, previously unseen data and thus remain scalable. We will discuss in detail what constitutes well-labeled and sufficiently extensive datasets in Chapter 6 of this book.

Third, engineers might need to provide the model with explicit "guidance," indicating precisely which aspects of the input data it should focus on to make correct decisions—a practice known as feature engineering. For instance, in the spam-filtering example, rather than merely allowing the model to process raw text, engineers typically extract and highlight specific features such as keyword frequency, sender reputation, presence of suspicious hyperlinks, or certain formatting patterns known to be prevalent in spam emails. Such deliberate **feature selection** often determines the effectiveness of the model; hence, it is crucial that model developers possess not only knowledge in AI and data science but also a deep understanding of the specific domain to accurately identify and construct meaningful input variables.

Additionally, thorough model testing and validation is essential, and to ensure the model works correctly, it should be evaluated using **cross-validation** techniques, verifying its performance on data it has never encountered during training. Otherwise, there is a risk of **overfitting**—a situation where the model learns patterns specific only to the training data, losing the ability to generalize effectively to new, unseen examples. Typically, part of the available data is deliberately withheld as a "test set," ensuring an unbiased evaluation of the model's performance. It is even more robust if the test data come from a separate, independent source. This consideration is especially critical in our health-focused industry, where a common issue arises with models trained on datasets collected, for example, from one hospital or one type of medical device, potentially failing to perform accurately on data gathered in another hospital or using a different model of equipment. We will also discuss this challenge in the next chapter.

Finally, deploying such models often requires significant organizational and operational efforts from a company perspective. It is necessary to establish robust data-collection pipelines, consistent annotation processes, and rigorous evaluation frameworks to maintain and monitor model performance effectively over time.

As has probably become clear from the requirements for implementing these models, they have specific limitations that should be considered when working with them, such as dependence on the input data and their quality, susceptibility to overfitting, or the ability to detect only those patterns that were present in the original examples and which may be absent in new data. Another limitation is the difficulty in explaining why and based on which elements within the data the model makes a particular decision. Modern supervised learning approaches, particularly deep neural networks and ensemble methods, operate as complex "black box" systems that provide limited insight into their decision-making processes. This lack of interpretability creates significant barriers to adoption in regulated industries, safety-critical applications, and domains requiring algorithmic accountability, such as healthcare.

Unsupervised Learning: Clustering and Pattern Discovery

Another fundamental paradigm frequently used in modern AI solutions is **unsupervised learning** algorithms. As the name suggests, unlike supervised learning models, they operate without predetermined target variables—that is, without labeled data provided as examples to help establish desired relationships. The task of these models is to discover hidden structures and patterns within unlabeled datasets, specifically some frequently recurring features that allow data to be grouped into separate clusters. The underlying logic centers on the principle that meaningful relationships exist within data, which can be uncovered through mathematical analysis of similarity, proximity, and statistical distribution properties. In other words, it groups data points together so that members within each group are as similar as possible based on certain characteristics, while being distinctly different from those in other groups. The ability of these models to autonomously identify relevant patterns makes them particularly valuable for exploratory data analysis and knowledge discovery applications.

Such models are often used, for instance, to analyze consumer audiences and their interests; recommendations provided by platforms like Netflix or Spotify are built using such algorithms. At the input stage, there is information about each user's viewing history of various movies or series, or listening history for music. Among all this variety, the model identifies subgroups of individuals who have similar tastes and preferences, making it possible to select content that the user is most likely to enjoy.

Another interesting example of applying such an approach, which I had the chance to observe, involved identifying different types of drivers based on their interaction patterns with the vehicle. The goal was to identify distinct audience segments so that car dealers could communicate with customers using their language, offering personalized services and vehicles specifically suited to their needs. The model analyzed events such as the frequency of door openings, vehicle mileage on weekdays versus weekends, frequency and abruptness of braking, number of stops, and numerous other metrics. As a result, the model distinguished approximately 20 distinct driver types. For example, one separate group consisted of individuals who made several short trips on weekday mornings, frequently stopped, and regularly opened the car's rear doors. As you've probably already guessed, these turned out to be parents dropping off their children at school each morning.

Such approaches have significant potential when working with biological data, whose meaning and nature remain poorly studied and not yet fully understood. These algorithms can identify patterns and subgroups within datasets, associated, for example, with various disease types. In the context of psychiatric disorders, they potentially can decode disease heterogeneity and isolate distinct patient groups unified by similar symptom profiles.

To successfully implement unsupervised learning models in practice, several key factors and limitations must be carefully considered. First and foremost, the effectiveness of such algorithms significantly depends on the quality and structure of the data on which they will be trained. For example, if the data are incomplete, noisy, or contain many irrelevant features, the algorithm may identify meaningless or uninformative groups. Therefore, a crucial step is preliminary data processing, including normalization (scaling all features onto a common scale for comparison), selecting the most informative features, and reducing data dimensionality to a reasonable minimum. Only after completing these steps can the model effectively discover meaningful patterns. However, this preliminary processing itself requires substantial expertise. A paradox thus arises: on one hand, the main appeal of unsupervised learning lies in its capacity to independently uncover patterns hidden from human observation; yet, on the other hand, the model's effective functioning demands a good initial understanding of the data structure within which these hidden patterns may reside.

Another significant limitation lies in evaluating the quality of the obtained results. Unlike supervised learning, there is no predefined "correct answer" against which the algorithm's outputs can be verified. Consequently, assessing the discovered groups often depends on internal metrics—such as the homogeneity of groups and their clear separation from each other—but these criteria alone do not always guarantee practical relevance. This leads to another crucial challenge: interpreting the results. The identified clusters require additional analysis to confirm their practical value and ensure they are not simply coincidental groupings. For instance, if an algorithm identifies a group of patients exhibiting similar symptoms, further examination is necessary to determine if this grouping has genuine clinical relevance. Confirming the practical significance of such findings typically requires the involvement of domain specialists who possess the expertise to validate the discovered patterns.

Thus, despite the considerable potential of unsupervised learning, the successful implementation of such models demands meticulous data preparation, profound domain knowledge, and close collaboration between data analysts and domain-specific experts.

Reinforcement Learning: Decision-Making Through Trial and Error

The third essential paradigm underlying many modern AI solutions is known as **Reinforcement Learning**. This approach fundamentally differs from the previous two: it does not rely on pre-labeled datasets containing correct answers, nor does it seek hidden patterns within static datasets. Instead, reinforcement learning models learn by interacting with their surrounding environment through trial and error, receiving **rewards** or **penalties** based on their actions. This method was inspired by the way humans and animals naturally learn—by interacting with the environment, they discover which behaviors should be repeated and which should be avoided. For instance, a person who touches a hot kettle and gets burned remembers not to repeat that action, while a dog that receives a tasty treat for correctly following a command learns to repeat that behavior in the future.

Reinforcement learning algorithms always operate within a predefined set of possible actions, from which they can choose and combine various options. In this sense, they share similarities with earlier algorithms such as Logic Theorist and GPS, which also selected from predetermined sets of steps. However, unlike these earlier models, reinforcement learning algorithms have the capacity to learn independently, progressively adjusting their behavior in response to feedback from their environment. The primary goal of these models is to discover and adopt combinations of actions that maximize rewards and minimize potential penalties.

Such algorithms are commonly applied in game scenarios, where there is a limited number of possible moves and clearly defined rules for interacting with an environment that rewards or penalizes the model based on each action. One of the most renowned examples of reinforcement learning in action is **AlphaGo**,[15] an algorithm developed by DeepMind for the board game Go. Go is a strategic board game in which two players alternate placing black and white stones on a grid board. On each turn, players have a limited set of possible actions: placing a stone on an empty intersection, passing their turn, or resigning. The objective of the game is to claim more territory with one's stones than the opponent. Players receive "rewards" in the form of territory secured and opponent's stones captured, while "penalties" occur when players lose stones or territory due to poor moves. In a similar fashion, a reinforcement learning algorithm playing Go receives feedback indicating the success of each action (placing a stone), and over time learns to select combinations of moves that maximize territory and ultimately lead to victory. Despite its straightforward rules, Go is considered one of the most complex intellectual games due to the vast number of possible move combinations. AlphaGo, learning through trial and error and continuously refining its strategies, eventually managed to defeat the world's best human players.

Beyond games, reinforcement learning is actively employed in robotics—for example, training robots for autonomous movement, precise manipulations, or complex operational tasks. This approach is also extensively utilized in self-driving car systems, where algorithms learn to optimally select actions in real-world traffic conditions, seeking to avoid dangerous situations (penalties) and ensuring the safest and most comfortable rides (rewards). Indeed, reinforcement learning can be effectively applied in nearly any domain where algorithms can learn to execute human-like actions through interaction with an environment, continually adjusting behavior based on feedback.

To successfully implement reinforcement learning algorithms in practice, several key elements must be carefully considered. To provide clarity and transparency, I'll illustrate these points using the example of developing algorithms for autonomous driving, since this scenario is widely understandable.

First, a crucial step involves properly designing the environment with which the model will interact. The environment must be clearly defined and include all necessary information enabling the model to make optimal decisions. At the same time, the number of possible environmental states and available actions must remain manageable; otherwise, the computational resources required may become excessively large, making effective training virtually impossible. For example, when training autonomous driving algorithms, the environment must realistically reflect the complexity and unpredictability of actual traffic conditions, including the behavior of other vehicles, pedestrians, and roadway infrastructure characteristics. Yet, despite the need for realism, the environment must remain sufficiently simplified to allow the model to learn and make decisions within a reasonable timeframe.

Second, carefully defining the reward and punishment system (the reward function) is critically important. It is precisely through this system that the model learns to distinguish beneficial and effective actions from undesirable or dangerous ones. A poorly designed reward system can lead to unpredictable model behavior, prompting it to seek loopholes or ignore important aspects of the task. For example, if the reward structure for a self-driving car is overly simplistic or incorrectly balanced, it may either avoid risks altogether by moving unreasonably slowly or behave too aggressively on the road, endangering the safety of passengers and others.

A third significant challenge is the so-called **exploration–exploitation dilemma**. The model must continuously balance using known, effective solutions ("exploitation") with discovering new, untested strategies ("exploration"). This dilemma is particularly critical in the context of autonomous driving: excessively cautious reliance solely on proven solutions will limit the vehicle's adaptability to novel or unusual situations, while overly aggressive exploration of new strategies could lead to hazardous scenarios and unjustified risks. Therefore, addressing this dilemma requires well-thought-out algorithmic strategies ensuring safe and effective learning.

Finally, special attention must be given to ensuring the safety and reliability of reinforcement learning algorithms. Autonomous vehicles, robots, and other self-operating systems directly interact with humans and their surroundings, making it essential to incorporate safeguards against algorithmic errors. This involves rigorous testing procedures, mandatory evaluation of models across diverse scenarios, and the development of specialized emergency mechanisms and protocols capable of promptly activating in case of unexpected situations or algorithmic malfunctions.

It's worth noting that, despite these complexities, reinforcement learning algorithms also hold substantial promise for healthcare applications. Currently, reinforcement learning is actively being explored in areas such as managing sepsis treatment in intensive care units,[16] personalizing diabetes care,[17] and developing adaptive therapeutic strategies in oncology.[18] However, applying these approaches in medicine involves additional constraints related to safety and ethical standards, given that the environment here is the human body itself, and even minor errors can have serious consequences. Therefore, any medical applications of reinforcement learning require particularly careful preparation, rigorous risk assessment, and close collaboration between data analysis specialists and medical experts.

Foundational Models: Large-Scale Pre-trained Architectures

We have now covered three main paradigms commonly used in machine learning—three fundamentally distinct approaches that solve different types of problems, each utilizing specific data types and training methods. However, there is one more important topic worth addressing separately—a subject actively discussed in recent years—known as **Foundational Models**. Interest in foundational models surged dramatically following the introduction of tools such as ChatGPT, to which we've referred multiple times earlier.

Foundational models do not directly correspond to any of the previously described machine learning paradigms. Instead, they represent an approach to building versatile, pre-trained algorithms that may incorporate elements from various paradigms. For instance, a foundational model is usually first trained on enormous amounts of data, employing both supervised and unsupervised learning methods, and subsequently fine-tuned to address specific tasks. Thus, foundational models serve as a general-purpose foundation upon which solutions for a broad range of practical applications can be built. The central premise behind this approach is the idea that data collected and processed at a sufficiently large scale inherently contain fundamental structures, patterns, and relationships, which the model is capable of learning during its initial training phase. Thanks to this previously learned generalized structure, the foundational model can effectively adapt and successfully tackle narrower, more specialized tasks.

Foundation models are easiest to understand by looking at large language models (LLMs), such as ChatGPT or GPT-4.[19] These models are initially trained on massive datasets consisting of texts gathered from diverse sources, including books, articles, webpages, and other documents freely available on the internet. During this pre-training phase, the model analyzes billions of words and sentences, capturing fundamental language patterns—such as grammatical structures, semantic relationships between words, context, and even elements of world knowledge. Importantly, this initial training occurs without specific practical tasks explicitly set in advance. Instead, the model learns to solve a seemingly straightforward task: predicting the next word in a given text. Formally, this task can be viewed as supervised learning, because at each moment, the model sees a certain fragment of text (the "input") and has the correct answer—the word that comes next (the "output"). However, the key nuance here is that the training data is not manually labeled. Instead, the labeled dataset is generated automatically from arbitrary texts: the model simply takes any existing text and uses its beginning to predict the next word. This approach is thus termed **self-supervised learning**, highlighting its intermediate nature between classical supervised and unsupervised methods.

Thanks to the enormous scale of data, the model learns foundational language structures and relationships encoded within its internal parameters. This becomes a universal foundation on which specialized tasks can be efficiently solved later. For this purpose, an additional training stage called **fine-tuning** is employed. During the fine-tuning stage, the model is further trained on a much smaller dataset specifically selected for a particular task—such as medical reports, legal documents, or customer reviews. The fine-tuning process works as follows. Initially, the model already possesses general linguistic skills and knowledge acquired during the pre-training phase. Then, a smaller dataset, reflecting the specifics of the new task, is used to precisely adjust the model's internal parameters according to the nuances of the target domain. For instance, if the task involves classifying customer reviews as either positive or negative, during fine-tuning the model receives a limited set of reviews explicitly labeled as "positive" or "negative." As a result, the model learns to more accurately discern the subtleties and unique characteristics of these reviews, while retaining previously acquired general language knowledge. Consequently, even with a relatively small volume of new data, the model quickly adapts and achieves high performance.

For greater clarity, this approach can be compared to the way a person learns mathematics. Initially, one masters the foundational logic: understanding numbers, performing basic calculations, and recognizing essential rules and patterns. Once these fundamental structures and internal relationships in mathematics have been thoroughly grasped, it becomes significantly easier to tackle narrower and more specialized problems. In any case, this process is much simpler than attempting to solve such problems without first developing a fundamental understanding of the subject.

Why are foundation models particularly interesting for our goals—innovations in psychiatry? The main advantage of this approach is the ability to work effectively even when the availability of labeled data is limited.

This feature is especially relevant to psychiatry, where the processes of collecting and systematically labeling high-quality data often aren't extensive or well-established. Typically, however, there's a substantial amount of related information available, albeit without explicit labeling. Foundation models make it possible to first train a general-purpose "foundation" using these large, unlabeled datasets. Then, leveraging this accumulated knowledge, specialized tasks can be addressed effectively using significantly smaller volumes of specifically prepared data. This approach can potentially yield higher accuracy compared to traditional supervised or unsupervised learning methods, especially when these traditional methods are applied directly to smaller datasets.

All Roads Lead to Data

The goal of this chapter was to establish a foundational understanding of artificial intelligence (AI), outline the main paradigms of machine learning, describe how modern AI algorithms are constructed, and discuss the types of tasks they effectively solve. Understanding these principles enables us to realistically evaluate AI's capabilities and set appropriate expectations about its practical applications.

We began with a historical overview, demonstrating how relatively simple mathematical and logical rules can create the illusion of meaningful machine behavior, reminiscent of human thought processes. By examining early AI algorithms, we illustrated the general model-building approach: analyzing human decision-making processes, identifying key features of these processes, translating them into mathematical representations, and subsequently training models using these established rules. Next, we thoroughly explored the core methodologies underpinning modern AI: supervised learning, unsupervised learning, reinforcement learning, and the relatively recent development of foundation models. For each approach, we identified their strengths, limitations, and primary application areas, providing examples to highlight practical relevance.

Regardless of the chosen approach, the central theme and primary requirement for effective AI model performance remains consistent: data quality. Indeed, data fundamentally determine the feasibility and accuracy of AI-driven solutions. Supervised learning relies on large, accurately labeled datasets; unsupervised learning demands carefully preprocessed and structured information; and reinforcement learning necessitates a meticulously designed, safe training environment. Foundation models, while effective in scenarios with limited labeled data, require initial training on vast quantities of unlabeled data.

Consequently, data quality and management become decisive factors for the successful practical implementation of artificial intelligence technologies. This crucial topic will be the primary focus of the next chapter, where we will comprehensively discuss the principles behind collecting, preparing, and evaluating data essential for optimal AI performance.

6

It Is All About the Data

We had real gold in our hands—a dataset with carefully structured, anonymized data from thousands of patients. It had absolutely everything we were looking for at that point: brain activity recordings, patient demographics, biological sex and age, diagnosis information, filled-out questionnaires, and even details about bad habits. Everything was meticulously cleaned and organized—a data scientist's dream.

But, being perfectionists, we couldn't resist checking every single entry. We knew well that even a minor annotation error could derail the training of our model.

After a thorough examination, we indeed found several peculiar entries. Pleased with our vigilance, we approached the professor responsible for collecting the data.

"We found a few suspicious entries," we began. "We'd like to clarify some points."

"Yes, yes, of course! Let's take a look. It will help improve our dataset even further."

"For example, here we have a couple of patients listed as being more than 140 years old—they seem to have beaten the Guinness World Records."

"Hmm, that certainly looks like a typo. I'll check the original data, and my students will correct it."

"And here's another—a five-year-old child who, according to the records, smokes heavily and drinks alcohol regularly."

"Hm, clearly something's mixed up. I don't recall any such patients. We'll investigate."

"And finally, we found five patients whose biological sex changed between visits just a few months apart."

The professor smiled wryly:

"Well, we'll definitely check this too. Although, you know in this world—anything can happen."

* * *

AI's Inescapable Data Dependency

The history of artificial intelligence clearly illustrates a simple truth: algorithms drive the performance of intelligent systems, but data remain their indispensable fuel. Today, organizations adopting artificial intelligence recognize that the effectiveness and sophistication of their solutions depend not just on computational power or algorithmic elegance, but primarily on the quality, structure, and management of the data used to train these algorithms. Over time, this fundamental link between data quality and AI success has evolved beyond merely a technical consideration, becoming a strategic priority that significantly determines the success of an AI initiative.

Modern companies implementing AI face a paradoxical situation: data exist simultaneously in abundance and scarcity. Digital transformation has resulted in vast amounts of continuously generated data; however, raw data alone are not suitable for training AI models. To serve as a foundation for high-quality algorithms, data must be transformed through a complex, multi-step process involving thorough preparation, structuring, and validation. In this context, data cease to be merely a passive resource from which value is extracted and instead become a full-fledged product requiring thoughtful design, continuous improvement, and strategic management. Organizations that approach data preparation with the same meticulousness they apply to commercial product development achieve a multiplicative effect, significantly increasing returns on AI investments and establishing a foundation for sustainable competitive advantage.

Therefore, in this chapter, we will examine in detail what makes data suitable for successful AI applications. We will discuss which characteristics and attributes of data are critical for developing effective AI models, how to manage data quality and handle noise, and what methods can be employed to avoid common pitfalls and enhance the performance of machine learning algorithms.

Just a quick heads-up: the following discussion might feel overly technical at times. However, since data truly form the backbone of any AI solution—and given that many startups and innovative projects struggle precisely due to misunderstanding data availability or how to work with it—we need to dive into these tedious yet essential details.

Structured Data and Beyond

When we speak of data, we refer to an extensive variety of information types. For instance, in the context of psychiatry, data may encompass medical indicators such as DNA sequencing results or neuroimaging scans (MRI, EEG). It may also include historical records of a patient's health, such as textual descriptions of diagnoses. Additionally, data may be behavioral, reflecting information on specific individual activities—such as internet usage, social media postings, preferences in music and TV programming, or search queries. Finally, data may comprise audio and video recordings collected, for example, during telemedicine consultations. Thus, the term "data" can be defined as a "representation of facts, concepts, or instructions in a manner suitable for communication, interpretation, or processing by humans or by automatic means."[1] In other words, data may include any information suitable for analysis and informed decision-making.

One of the most essential characteristics by which data can be classified is their degree of structure. The degree of data structure refers to how well-organized and systematically arranged the information is. From an artificial intelligence perspective, this characteristic is critical because the more structured the data, the easier it is to utilize for training models. However, highly structured data are comparatively rare, and as a result, data scientists frequently need to work with less organized datasets. Generally, there are three main types of data: structured, unstructured, and semi-structured.

Structured data, as the name suggests, are characterized by strict organization and a clearly defined format. Such data fit conveniently into traditional databases, spreadsheets, and other tabular formats, where each element occupies a predetermined position and clearly relates to other elements. A typical example would be tabular data, which we frequently encounter: in these tables, all information is organized into rows and columns, where each row usually represents an individual record (for instance, a single patient), and each column corresponds to a specific attribute or measure.

However, there is an important nuance regarding structured data. Despite their convenience for analysis and processing, data are rarely collected and stored initially in such a rigidly structured format. Typically, giving data a clear and usable structure requires omitting numerous details that may be critical for capturing the complexity of real-world situations. In other words, overly simplifying data during structuring can limit a dataset's usefulness. Such simplification often reduces the data's ability to accurately reflect the complexity and subtleties inherent in real-life processes and scenarios.

The majority of data we encounter when implementing technologies is **unstructured**. This term refers to data lacking clear organization, rigid structure, or a uniform format. Examples include audio and video recordings, textual documents, and social media posts—all forms of information challenging or impossible to represent directly in tabular form.

Developing algorithms capable of effectively handling and converting unstructured data into more structured formats represents a distinct and rapidly evolving research area, which we will explore in detail in the next chapter. Processing such data requires significantly more computational resources and specialized solutions, including graphics processing units (GPUs), cloud computing platforms, and deep learning techniques—necessary due to their ability to efficiently identify complex patterns within highly variable data. As a result, analyzing unstructured data typically proves more costly and resource-intensive compared to structured data processing.

Despite these challenges, unstructured data offer unique insights into human behaviors, preferences, and experiences—insights virtually unattainable through structured data alone. For instance, analyzing social media interactions, textual documents, or other digital traces left online by patients can provide detailed and nuanced information about their emotional state. Such analysis allows us to objectively track changes in an individual's emotional condition relative to their own baseline, a critical capability since deviations from personal emotional norms are among the primary symptomatic indicators of psychiatric disorders. Thus, mastering methods for working with unstructured data opens significant opportunities for developing innovative and precise solutions in psychiatry and related fields.

When reading about unstructured data, you may have noticed that some of this data actually contains structured elements. For instance, social media posts often include clearly structured metadata, such as the identity of the user, the timestamp of the post, or the user's geographical location. These structured elements allow us to classify or analyze the otherwise unstructured content of these posts—such as texts, images, or videos—more effectively.

Indeed, this type of data is known as **semi-structured data**, characterized by a combination of strictly organized and flexible, unstructured components. Incorporating structured elements significantly simplifies data handling: it helps guide analyses more precisely, facilitates model evaluation, and improves the interpretability of results.

However, working with semi-structured data also introduces certain challenges. Models typically find structured information easier to process and may therefore overly rely on it, neglecting crucial insights contained in the unstructured portions of the data. This bias can cause models to focus excessively on secondary characteristics, potentially overlooking deeper, subtler patterns that are critical for accurate analyses. Consequently, handling semi-structured data requires additional effort in algorithm development—particularly in managing how models allocate their attention and ensuring an appropriate balance between structured and unstructured components.

Data Quality Dimensions: Representation of the Real World

Now let's discuss data quality criteria. When we speak about data quality, our primary concern is the central question: how accurately and completely do the data reflect reality, allowing us to build reliable models based on them?

This implies that data must satisfy numerous requirements related not to their structure (which we examined earlier), but rather to their content and the essential nature of the information they represent.

Accuracy and Precision

Perhaps the first and most obvious criterion that comes to mind when discussing data quality is **accuracy**. Typically, accuracy refers to the absence of errors and the degree to which data reflect the reality they describe. The more accurate the data, the more reliable the conclusions and recommendations derived from them. For example, in medical patient records, accuracy implies that diagnoses, treatment dates, and test results correctly represent the true clinical situation, free from mistakes or discrepancies.

Even a single error in a data record can significantly distort analytical outcomes. Imagine a dataset containing medication information, where drug names or dosages are incorrectly recorded or medications the patient never took appear. A model trained on such flawed data would inevitably struggle and fail to recommend appropriate treatments accurately.

The second criterion—**precision**—is less obvious but particularly critical in psychiatry. Precision refers to the consistency and stability of measurements and assessments during data collection. Even minor variations or inaccuracies in data-gathering processes can substantially impact the reliability of subsequent analyses and model predictions. In psychiatry, precision becomes especially problematic due to the inherent subjectivity of clinical assessments, which rely heavily on patient-reported symptoms. As discussed earlier in Chapters 2 and 3, different psychiatrists frequently assign different diagnoses to the same patient. Consequently, psychiatric diagnostic datasets are fundamentally subjective and inherently imprecise, significantly limiting their value for training reliable AI models.

This is one of the critical challenges faced when developing AI-based psychiatric diagnostics. Many AI studies claim high accuracy rates, stating their models can reliably predict psychiatric diagnoses based on various data types—such as brain activity combined with diagnostic labels, or blood tests correlated with clinical diagnoses. Typically, however, these impressive results can be misleading. Even when statistical performance metrics seem robust, the underlying diagnostic labels, assigned by psychiatrists, are inherently unstable and subjective.

Some strategies can help improve the stability of these data labels. For instance, having multiple psychiatrists independently evaluate the same patient and reaching a consensus can somewhat enhance the consistency of diagnoses. Another approach is relying not solely on clinical diagnoses but instead incorporating standardized questionnaires or objective scoring scales. These methods might modestly improve metric stability; nevertheless, even these improved datasets cannot fully represent an objective ground truth. Therefore, it remains essential to exercise caution and clearly recognize the limitations when working with psychiatric diagnostic data in AI model development.

Completeness and Representativeness

When developing medical solutions based on artificial intelligence, our primary goal is to ensure algorithms perform consistently well across diverse clinical scenarios. This requires AI models to effectively process data collected from various medical devices and to accurately handle patient information spanning different demographic characteristics. To reach this goal, training datasets must adhere to strict standards of completeness and representativeness.

Completeness involves more than just the volume of examples—it demands inclusion of every relevant scenario the model may encounter in actual clinical practice. For example, when training a model to determine optimal medications and dosages, the dataset should cover an extensive range of medications, dosages, and clinical contexts. Insufficient completeness can lead to biases, causing the model to favor familiar scenarios and struggle with less common cases.

Representativeness ensures training data truly reflect the diversity of the target patient population. This means datasets must accurately represent variations in gender, age, ethnicity, and socioeconomic backgrounds. Data scientists often joke that the world's most studied individuals live in Cambridge, Massachusetts, due to data-rich institutions like Harvard and MIT, enabling AI models to excel specifically within these populations. A widely cited example demonstrating the consequences of insufficient representativeness involved an AI model developed to diagnose skin conditions from smartphone images. Its accuracy significantly declined when analyzing images of patients with darker skin tones, as these images constituted only around 5–10% of the training data.[2] This case underscores why demographic diversity in datasets is crucial—not just for model performance, but also for patient safety and equitable healthcare outcomes

One practical strategy for addressing the challenges related to completeness and representativeness involves using data augmentation techniques. These methods allow researchers to generate synthetic data examples from existing real-world datasets, effectively expanding their size and helping balance representation across underrepresented groups. However, augmentation must be applied thoughtfully and with caution. The goal is to create plausible variations of existing examples rather than unrealistic distortions, which could inadvertently introduce new biases or negatively affect the accuracy and reliability of AI model training. Special care is required when working with complex or difficult-to-interpret data, as synthetic generation could produce examples significantly different from real-world scenarios. In such cases, AI models might mistakenly focus on artificial or irrelevant features of augmented examples, thereby exacerbating biases and undermining model performance. Thus, careful evaluation is essential to ensure synthetic data genuinely reflect realistic conditions, enhancing rather than hindering the robustness and fairness of AI-driven medical solutions.

Consistency and Standardization

Another critical aspect directly influencing data quality is **consistency**. Essentially, this refers to uniformity in formats and structures, allowing a model to reliably "read" information from each example. When data entries vary significantly in format, they become not just inconvenient to work with—this is a guaranteed path toward generating errors in model output. The issue of consistency becomes especially acute when integrating information from multiple sources. Imagine a situation where one clinic records dates as "day/month/year," while another uses "month-day-year." This is a simple example, yet even such minor inconsistencies can accumulate, making the task increasingly challenging for those responsible for data quality.

To address this problem, specialists often implement practices collectively known as **data governance**. In practice, this entails establishing rules requiring all participants to record information uniformly: consistent column names in tables, standardized date and time formats, and agreed-upon terminology for medications and diagnoses. To ensure these standards are not merely theoretical, companies regularly perform audits, verifying data compliance with these rules before AI models access them.

In psychiatry, however, these ideal scenarios often clash with reality. As we've previously discussed, much depends on individual clinician approaches: whether or not to use standardized questionnaires is ultimately the doctor's personal decision. Even if clinicians use these tools, there is no guarantee the results will end up in the centralized medical database. Some records may remain on paper or within a clinician's private notes, rendering them inaccessible to the model altogether.

But even when considering seemingly more "objective" data, such as neurophysiological recordings, the situation doesn't markedly improve. When working with EEG data, for instance, we encounter variations because different clinics utilize equipment with varying numbers of electrodes—some standard setups have 32 channels, while others have 64 or even 128. Additionally, not only the number of electrodes differs, but also recording durations, equipment settings, and even how events within the data are labeled. The same applies to behavioral tests, where patients are given tasks to measure memory, attention, or reaction speed. Even if the tests share the same name, nearly everything can vary between labs—from task design and stimulus display durations to the specific metrics collected and analyzed. One test might report average reaction times, another the percentage of errors, and yet another the ratio of correct responses to total attempts. Consequently, data specialists must determine how to standardize this disparate information or even develop their own standard, recalculating everything incoming into a unified framework.

Finally, consistency pertains not only to formats and structures but also to semantic meaning (**semantic consistency**). This implies that identical or closely related terms should be treated uniformly. Consider wording in psychiatric records: phrases such as "anxious state," "anxiety," and "uneasiness" can have almost identical meanings. Yet, unless carefully managed, these terms might be interpreted by an algorithm as three entirely distinct conditions. We've already highlighted how unstable psychiatric terminology can be, changing according to individual clinicians, geographic regions, and even the personal characteristics of patients. Models face this variability almost constantly. Thus, consistency becomes a challenge that is not merely technical but conceptual as well—and it remains unclear whether this issue can be fully resolved in the context of psychiatric data.

Timeliness and Relevancy

In the end, we have to keep in mind that the data we use needs to match our objectives—and this match matters in two key ways. First, there's the issue of timeliness: does the data genuinely reflect the current situation we're trying to model? Second, there's relevance itself: does the data carry signals that are genuinely helpful in solving our problems?

At first glance, this might seem so obvious that dedicating a separate paragraph could appear unnecessary. However, allow me to illustrate with examples. Consider **timeliness**: language clearly reflects the period in which it's used, and the ways people express emotions evolve significantly over time. Therefore, if we're developing solutions to assess speech and emotional valence, our data must come from contemporary sources. Less obviously, mental disorders themselves, as well as perceptions of them and their underlying causes, also evolve, influenced by societal context and external factors. Given that psychiatry fundamentally relies upon subjective symptom assessments, temporal shifts occur not only in diagnostic criteria—such as regular updates to the DSM—but also in the terminology used to describe conditions.

As for **relevance**, it's critical not only that data contain the necessary signal, but also that we're able to clearly extract this signal from numerous other irrelevant signals. Consider functional MRI (fMRI), which shows not just brain structure but also brain activity. At first glance, it seems optimal for studying psychiatric disorders. However, we must remember that the brain simultaneously manages numerous functions. Even maintaining basic physiological processes consumes roughly 60–80% of the brain's energy expenditure at rest,[3] with additional resources devoted to processing sensory stimuli, planning, memory consolidation, and other tasks. Consequently, it's extremely challenging—and often practically impossible—to isolate the fMRI activity directly linked to psychiatric symptoms from activity related to these other brain processes.

And here we face another issue, which we'll discuss in detail in the next section: how to work with data where the relevant signal is mixed with a large amount of secondary, less useful information.

Separating Signal from Noise

In machine learning, **noise** refers to random or unpredictable fluctuations in data that interfere with algorithms' ability to recognize patterns and reduce model accuracy. Unlike a useful **signal**—which contains meaningful information—noise introduces unwanted variations capable of misleading algorithms. For example, when working with audio recordings of human speech, noise may include extraneous sounds such as neighbors performing construction work, barking dogs, or background conversations, creating additional streams of information that become intertwined with the main signal. When dealing with video data, noise may arise from motion blur, distortion caused by video compression artifacts, and variations in lighting such as shadows or glare. Medical images frequently contain what's known as Gaussian noise—random fluctuations in pixel brightness, which appear as fine graininess or speckled interference within an image. The source of this noise typically relates to physical limitations of sensors and imaging equipment, such as insufficient sensor sensitivity or random signal fluctuations during data acquisition. Gaussian noise commonly occurs in images obtained via magnetic resonance imaging (MRI), X-ray imaging, and computed tomography (CT), significantly complicating the task of medical diagnostic algorithms, which rely on accurate detection of important details and structures.

The **signal-to-noise ratio (SNR)** provides a quantitative measure of data quality by comparing the level of the desired signal to the background noise. Higher SNR values indicate cleaner data, where meaningful patterns dominate, while lower values suggest significant noise interference, potentially leading to poor model performance. Therefore, separating signal from noise is a critical preprocessing step—without it, achieving accurate model predictions is nearly impossible. Unlike humans, who naturally manage attention and can easily distinguish important information from irrelevant input, an AI model perceives all incoming data as a single whole and cannot independently discern relevant signals from noise.

If we leave noise in our data, we risk not only reduced prediction accuracy but also causing the model to rely on secondary features irrelevant to our objectives. This may lead the model to identify correlations that are meaningless for our purposes, ultimately affecting the model's reliability and interpretability. To ensure that the model learns specifically from the relevant portion of the signal and predicts precisely those parameters we're interested in, it is essential to preprocess the data beforehand. Specialized preprocessing algorithms are developed precisely for this purpose: their role is to filter out noise and retain only the useful signal in the data.

For our purposes—developing psychiatry-focused algorithms based on available data such as audio and video recordings, behavioral tests, or neurophysiological signals—it is convenient to separate the problem of noise into two categories. The first category includes situations where humans can easily distinguish the useful signal from noise, as in the audio and video examples discussed earlier. For instance, when listening to an audio recording, a human can effortlessly distinguish speech from background sounds. In these cases, removing noise becomes simpler because we can rely on expert judgment to evaluate the effectiveness of preprocessing algorithms.

Several basic methods are typically employed to address noise in such tasks. Let's briefly review a few of these methods below to better understand how they function:

- **Gaussian filtering** smooths data by performing a weighted average of neighboring points, with closer values receiving greater weight according to a Gaussian function. This approach is widely used in medical imaging, for example, where it effectively removes random fine-grain noise while preserving critical anatomical details.
- **Median filtering** removes random outliers by replacing each value with the median of neighboring points. This method is particularly effective against "salt-and-pepper" noise—random white and black dots on an image. For example, when processing video recordings, median filtering can eliminate isolated corrupted pixels caused by sensor errors or transmission interference while preserving object contours and the overall integrity of the image.
- **Wavelet transforms** reduce noise by decomposing a signal into frequency-based components and selectively removing high-frequency noise. For instance, in audio restoration, wavelet-based methods efficiently eliminate background hiss from recordings without distorting the primary audio content.

- **Independent component analysis (ICA)** separates mixed signals into statistically independent sources by identifying patterns of statistical independence. For example, if multiple voices or sound sources overlap in a single audio recording, ICA automatically splits them into individual audio tracks, extracting useful signals while eliminating irrelevant background noise.
- **Data augmentation** involves intentionally adding controlled noise to training data rather than removing it. This helps models learn to ignore irrelevant interference, improving their robustness in real-world conditions. Automatic speech recognition systems, for example, are often trained using audio samples with artificially introduced background noise to enhance their performance in realistic noisy environments.

Data scientists are skilled at determining precisely which noise needs to be removed and selecting appropriate methods, and extensive professional literature covers this topic. Here, however, I'd like to focus on a different scenario—situations where even humans find it challenging or impossible to distinguish the useful signal from the noise in raw data. This issue is particularly relevant when developing AI systems that directly analyze brain-derived data, whose nature remains insufficiently understood. Examples of such data include electroencephalography (EEG) and magnetoencephalography (MEG). EEG records the brain's electrical activity using electrodes placed on the scalp, while MEG captures magnetic fields generated by neuronal electrical currents.

Both EEG and MEG provide vast amounts of data about brain function, potentially revealing insights into psychiatric disorders and the mechanisms behind drug effects. However, despite their value, these signals typically have a very low signal-to-noise ratio (SNR). EEG recordings, for example, appear as complex wave patterns, which—besides the useful signal (brain electrical activity)—contain significant extraneous interference. Sources of such interference include patient movements, eye blinks, muscle tension, technical recording errors, interference from other medical devices, and internal noise of the EEG device itself.

While obvious noise such as eye blinks or significant movements can usually be effectively reduced using the preprocessing methods described earlier, managing subtler forms of interference is more challenging. The core problem is that currently no one knows exactly what a completely "clean," noise-free brain activity signal looks like.

A logical question then arises: If no one knows what a clean brain signal actually looks like, how can we even be certain that noise exists in the data? Typically, this becomes evident through machine learning workflows. For instance, a common scenario occurs when applying unsupervised learning, specifically clustering—aiming to identify meaningful subgroups within large EEG datasets. Models often appear successful at first glance, but further analysis reveals clusters defined not by neurophysiological features, but rather by external factors such as data collection location, equipment specifics, or recording protocols. Thus, the model makes precisely the error we seek to avoid—it learns irrelevant patterns based on technical artifacts instead of true neurophysiological information.

The significance of this type of noise can be further confirmed through another approach: training a supervised learning model on labeled data to predict recording site or equipment type. Such models typically achieve very high accuracy, demonstrating that substantial technical noise indeed permeates the original dataset.

Unfortunately, effective technical solutions for these scenarios remain limited, leaving considerable room for future research and technological innovation. Nonetheless, there is one potential strategy to partially mitigate the impact of such noise—by increasing data volume. Let's examine the logic behind this approach more closely.

Noise encountered in EEG and MEG data generally falls into two categories: random and systematic. **Random noise** varies unpredictably across recordings and is not consistently linked to specific conditions or equipment. In contrast, **systematic noise** occurs repeatedly and predictably under consistent recording conditions. Random noise can typically be suppressed effectively by using sufficiently large datasets. With a large dataset, the desired signal is consistently present across most recordings, whereas random noises vary unpredictably, enabling the model to average them out and focus primarily on stable, repeating signals.

Systematic noise, however, emerges when a significant portion of data is consistently recorded in the same environment, using identical equipment or protocols. Consequently, equipment-specific characteristics might be mistaken by the model for meaningful signals. If we increase both the amount and the diversity of data—for example, by incorporating EEG recordings from various devices and laboratories—the noise previously considered systematic becomes effectively random from the model's perspective. This variability allows the model to eventually learn how to distinguish useful signals from noise that is now inconsistent and thus easier to ignore.

At this point, you might recall the beginning of this chapter and reasonably wonder: "But won't increasing data diversity negatively affect standardization and introduce new types of noise, such as labeling inconsistencies?" You're absolutely correct. This highlights another critical paradox we face when developing AI systems: how to balance the collection and structuring of data so that, on the one hand, standardization and consistency are maintained, while, on the other hand, sufficient diversity is preserved to reduce systematic noise. Achieving an optimal balance between these two competing needs is a central challenge, significantly impacting the ultimate effectiveness and reliability of psychiatric AI models.

Collecting flawless data—perfectly labeled, standardized, and evenly distributed—is an impossible task, just as eliminating all noise from data is unrealistic. Nevertheless, when developing new technologies in medical settings, it's essential to clearly define minimal data requirements and anticipate potential issues—not only to avoid development pitfalls but, crucially, to prevent harm to patients. First, invest in thoroughly understanding your data: identify the ideal qualities your data should have, recognize inherent errors, determine their accuracy in representing real-world conditions, and distinguish meaningful signals from noise. Second, always implement multi-site validation protocols, testing models using datasets from multiple locations, labs, or hospitals to uncover hidden biases early in development. Third, ensure collaboration not just with data science experts but also with specialists who have deep domain expertise. These experts will effectively evaluate your data, interpret processing outcomes, and, critically, confirm the clinical relevance and significance of the resulting models.

Privacy and Ethics: Mind the Innovation Gap

Like any technology capable of significantly transforming society, artificial intelligence has brought not only positive advancements and remarkable progress across many fields, including medicine, but has also raised critical questions concerning security, privacy, and the ethical use of personal data. Recent studies indicate growing public anxiety regarding ethical issues in AI and data privacy. According to large-scale consumer surveys, approximately 68% of global users express serious concern about the privacy of their online data, and 57% explicitly identify AI as a substantial threat to their personal privacy.[4,5] These concerns are justified: many contemporary algorithms have been trained on vast publicly available datasets, frequently without explicit consent from data owners.

The use of personal data in training AI models introduces unique privacy risks extending beyond traditional data protection concerns. During the training process, personal data can become implicitly embedded within the model itself, creating a scenario where, even if original datasets are securely stored or deleted, sensitive information might still be reconstructed or extracted through advanced analysis methods or targeted cyberattacks. Additionally, there is a growing and legitimate concern that AI systems trained on biased or skewed datasets reflecting existing social inequalities and prejudices could further amplify these inequities.

Consequently, issues of privacy and ethics become directly linked to real-world problems of algorithmic bias, misuse of data, and the potential of AI systems to perpetuate or even exacerbate existing social disparities. When AI models, trained on historically biased data, make influential decisions in critical areas such as credit approvals, hiring processes, or medical diagnoses, the implications extend far beyond technical performance, affecting fundamental societal values of equality, fairness, and human dignity.

In response to these challenges, numerous global initiatives and regulatory frameworks have emerged, aiming to ensure the responsible deployment of AI and manage its associated risks. Among the most comprehensive of these initiatives is the IEEE Global Initiative on Ethics of Autonomous and Intelligent Systems, which develops standards based on foundational principles like the "Safety First Principle" and "Safety by Design."[6,7] As part of this effort, the well-known Ethically Aligned Design platform was established, offering developers practical guidance on integrating ethical norms and human welfare considerations at the earliest stages of AI system design.

The United States has pursued its own distinct strategy through the National Institute of Standards and Technology (NIST), releasing the AI

Risk Management Framework in January 2023.[8] This voluntary framework guides organizations in building trust and transparency into AI systems throughout their entire lifecycle—from initial design and development to evaluation and deployment. A core principle of the NIST approach is the recognition that while ethical values may differ culturally, the universal need for trustworthy and reliable artificial intelligence systems remains constant.

The European Union has introduced perhaps the most ambitious regulatory framework to date—the AI Act—aiming to regulate artificial intelligence with the same thoroughness and rigor previously applied to data protection under GDPR.[9] This law classifies AI systems according to their risk level and imposes particularly stringent requirements on high-risk applications in sensitive domains, such as healthcare, the judicial system, and employment. Central to the EU's approach is the belief that AI regulation and personal data protection must not be seen as separate issues, but rather as deeply interconnected aspects of a unified regulatory framework.

On the international stage, the Organization for Economic Co-operation and Development (OECD) developed a set of ethical principles for AI, adopted by 42 countries by 2019, establishing a common foundation for global coordination.[10] Collectively, these international efforts represent an unprecedented attempt to balance the ethical responsibilities and safety concerns surrounding artificial intelligence with the need to preserve innovation and technological progress.

Despite the clear importance and genuine necessity of oversight and regulatory initiatives in artificial intelligence, an excessive focus on ethical constraints may unintentionally hinder the development of valuable, socially beneficial AI applications.

First, overly complex regulatory requirements and associated compliance costs can create substantial barriers to market entry. This issue is particularly acute for smaller companies and startups, which often lack the resources needed to fully meet new regulatory demands. Under such circumstances, AI development risks becoming concentrated in the hands of large corporations capable of managing regulatory burdens. Consequently, the diversity of innovation—which is essential for addressing a wide range of societal challenges—could suffer significantly.

Second, the emergence of organizational cultures heavily focused on risk avoidance and rigid adherence to ethical guidelines can suppress creativity and experimentation. Fear of penalties or potential ethical breaches might lead to overly cautious behaviors, limiting the willingness of teams to explore new ideas and innovative approaches. This is especially problematic in fields like healthcare, where access to high-quality data and opportunities for innovation is already limited. Introducing additional barriers under these conditions could severely delay or entirely prevent the development of critical solutions that could improve health outcomes and save lives.

The intersection of data privacy and AI ethics represents a pivotal moment in technological advancement. Society faces the challenging task of balancing fundamental human rights protection with preserving the innovative potential that drives progress. The real risk posed by excessive regulation—potentially stifling beneficial AI developments—must receive careful consideration alongside traditional ethical concerns. Regulatory frameworks should therefore not merely impose constraints, but also actively facilitate responsible innovation, enabling society to fully leverage emerging technologies.

Additionally, the unprecedented pace of artificial intelligence development creates fundamental challenges for regulatory systems. Technological advances consistently outpace regulatory adaptation, leading to situations where excessive caution delays urgently needed innovations. For example, in healthcare, where AI systems can substantially enhance diagnostic accuracy and improve patient outcomes, regulatory delays might contribute to preventable morbidity and mortality. This raises a critical question: what represents greater harm—using currently available, albeit imperfect data, or endlessly postponing solutions that could positively impact millions of lives?

It remains challenging to accurately predict how ethical and regulatory frameworks in AI will evolve. Yet, I have one request for you as innovators: approach your data responsibly and transparently, remaining consistently mindful of potential biases and their implications for the quality and fairness of the decisions you enable. Indeed, helping you navigate these very issues is the central purpose for writing this chapter.

PART
III

Innovating Psychiatry with AI

7 | Innovation Starts with Data

The large, nearly empty room in the pharma company's office. Simple black folding chairs were arranged in a wide circle. Someone quietly joked, "Startup anonymous?" A few muted chuckles broke the awkwardness. Indeed, it felt like we were about to stand up, one by one, with defeated expressions, and confess: "Hi, I'm John, and I'm an innovator."

The moderator politely invited us to briefly introduce our companies, after which we'd have the chance to question the pharma representatives about potential partnerships. We exchanged uncertain glances. It was a strange format: presenting complex medical ideas in just thirty seconds, without slides or materials—definitely not something we were used to. The turn slowly moved from one founder to another. Each mumbled something vague, while the rest strained to figure out who was doing what. The scene felt unimpressive at best.

But suddenly, the dynamic shifted. A young woman with an ambitious look and a striking accent leaned forward slightly and started talking. Her words were clear, sharp, and confident. She began pitching all the ideas everyone knew pharma desperately needed yet nobody had managed to deliver. Diagnostic biomarkers, precision treatment selection, better-designed clinical trials—one by one, she checked off every unmet industry need.

The pharma representative responded cautiously. Mindful of corporate restraint, he carefully replied: "Potentially interesting," "We'd need to look deeper." But she wouldn't back down. Like a tennis pro serving a relentless series of aces, she tossed out statistics and studies, pressing him for genuine interest. We watched closely, turning our heads from one to the other. Serve, return, serve. Then suddenly she paused. We held our breath. She glanced briefly around the circle, as if making sure every single person was paying attention. And then, looking directly at the pharma rep, she delivered the decisive strike:

"We could license our data to you."

The room fell silent. That phrase captured everyone's attention instantly. After all, it was the ultimate goal, the dream we all secretly shared—collecting enough data to have it stand alone as a valuable product. Even the pharma rep visibly straightened.

"Yes... Potentially very interesting," he conceded carefully. "Depending, of course, on specifics and conditions."

Sensing an opening, she doubled down: exclusive terms, non-exclusive options, letters of intent—she smoothly tossed around conditions, pulling all eyes toward her. What began as a collective discussion soon transformed into a private negotiation.

When our allotted time ran out, we shuffled quietly from the room, somehow feeling defeated, outplayed. Intrigued and slightly envious, I decided to find out more about her impressive dataset. Spotting one of her colleagues near the coffee machine, I casually approached.

"Impressive presentation," I started cautiously. "You guys have achieved some serious results. How did you manage to get so much data?"

The colleague smiled proudly. "We've been working nonstop for six years."

"That's incredible," I replied, genuinely impressed. "But licensing data at scale to pharma—that's next-level. How large is your dataset exactly?"

He leaned in slightly, lowering his voice as if about to share an extraordinary secret.

"Oh, it's huge," he whispered proudly. "We have a whole 165 patients."

* * *

Toward Big Data in Psychiatry

By now, we have completed all necessary steps to begin exploring the potential innovations artificial intelligence could bring to psychiatry. In the first part of this book, we comprehensively examined the systemic challenges faced by key stakeholders in the psychiatric ecosystem: patients, clinicians and healthcare facilities, pharmaceutical companies, and research institutions. We analyzed the existing structure of psychiatric care, identified risks associated with introducing new technologies, and clearly defined essential criteria innovations must fulfill to integrate smoothly into the current market landscape and effectively address stakeholder needs. In the second part of the book, we reviewed core artificial intelligence approaches, discussed the types of tasks these AI methods can perform (such as clustering and classification), and outlined specific data requirements essential to ensure that algorithms used in patient care are reliable, safe, and effective.

We now move directly to applying this knowledge in practice, shifting our focus toward concrete innovative solutions in psychiatry. As established in Chapter 4, a critical barrier today is the absence of key market players responsible for psychiatric diagnostics and medical devices. Unlike other medical fields, psychiatry lacks dedicated stakeholders who systematically develop diagnostic instruments, standardized protocols, and specialized laboratories. This situation significantly restricts the continuous generation of reliable and structured data.

Regardless of the specific AI solution or psychiatric issue targeted, access to high-quality data remains a central challenge. Psychiatry faces a profound shortage of effective tools capable of systematically gathering, storing, and processing data for research and AI applications. Additionally, due to the inherent heterogeneity of psychiatric disorders—as detailed in

Chapter 3—even a single diagnosis such as major depressive disorder can manifest in hundreds or even a thousand distinct symptom subtypes.[1] To faithfully represent each subtype across diverse populations, datasets would ideally include at least a thousand patients per subtype. Consequently, the datasets needed to support reliable AI in psychiatry must number not in the tens of thousands, but in the *hundreds of thousands or even millions*.

Generating and managing data at this massive scale aligns closely with the concept of **Big Data**, defined as datasets that challenge existing methods due to their size, complexity, or rate of availability.[2] In psychiatry, this concept implies constructing a comprehensive and extensive data structure, where data collection must be both broad and deep—otherwise, the resulting AI models will inevitably be limited and unstable.

Consequently, any innovative approach must incorporate a clearly structured and well-designed system for data collection, storage, and analysis. Furthermore, these data platforms themselves may become valuable commercial products, particularly given the rapidly growing interest in monetizing healthcare data. According to Precedence Research, the global healthcare data monetization market, estimated at around $921 million in 2024, is projected to reach approximately $1,069 million by 2025 and further grow to about $4,077 million by 2034, demonstrating an average annual growth rate of 16.04%.[3] Given psychiatry's existing limitations in accessing structured and accurately labeled information, developing scalable data platforms represents an especially timely and promising direction for advancement.

Which Data Hold Psychiatric Value?

Clearly, the collected data must meet all essential quality criteria required for the successful development and deployment of artificial intelligence solutions. Within psychiatry, this means data should accurately represent real patient populations, covering diverse demographic, ethnic, and socioeconomic groups, as well as sufficient sample sizes. Equally critical is the availability of high-quality, detailed diagnostic annotations, including precise diagnoses, information on disease stages, treatment approaches, and patient outcomes. Lastly, the data should provide clear, meaningful signals with minimal distortion and measurement errors.

While these quality criteria are universally important, specific data requirements will differ depending on the particular task we aim to address and the intended users of these data. For instance, if the goal is to develop an algorithm solving a specific clinical problem, greater emphasis will be placed on highly detailed annotations—such as symptom profiles, severity ratings, and precise treatment information. Conversely, if the aim is to create a data platform as a standalone product, the focus shifts toward ensuring sample representativeness, broad coverage of patient characteristics, and universal annotations, allowing these data to serve a wide variety of applications and algorithms effectively.

However, in reality, there is a wide variety of data available, each potentially valuable depending on the context and specific application goals. To simplify analysis and practical use, these data can be categorized according to two key criteria: the nature of the information they contain and the method of their collection.

First, data can differ significantly in terms of the type of information they contain. At a high level, three primary categories can be distinguished: **biological data**, encompassing physiological measurements and biological markers; **behavioral data**, representing patterns related to patients' cognitive processes and observable actions; and **communication data**, reflecting social interactions, verbal expressions, and linguistic patterns.

Second, based on their method of collection, data can be divided into two main groups:

- **Clinical Data:** information gathered in medical settings by qualified healthcare professionals (physicians, nurses, diagnosticians).
- **Patient Data (Direct-to-Consumer):** information obtained directly from patients through various digital devices and applications utilized in their daily life.

Biological Data

Biological data refers to quantitative measurements reflecting physiological processes and physiological states potentially associated with the onset and manifestations of mental disorders. Such information is particularly valuable, as it allows establishing objective links between psychiatric symptoms—currently the primary basis for diagnosis—and the underlying biological mechanisms associated with their emergence. Access to this kind of data provides deeper insights into the nature and etiology of psychopathology, helping reveal specific pathological processes underlying diverse clinical diagnoses. Furthermore, biological data can serve as an essential basis for developing effective pharmaceutical treatments by identifying precise pathological mechanisms and pinpointing molecular targets for new medications.

Among the most valuable types of biological data are measurements reflecting brain activity. The primary hypothesis, supported by the symptomatic profile of psychiatric disorders, posits that such conditions either arise directly from disruptions in brain activity or, at the very least, are closely associated with changes in brain function. Evidence supporting this connection includes characteristic alterations in perception, cognitive dysfunctions, disturbances in sleep and appetite, as well as significant challenges in fully understanding the nature of psychiatric disorders without considering their neurophysiological basis.

In clinical settings, examples of such data include structural MRI, which provides detailed images of brain anatomy, allowing the identification of structural changes such as variations in regional brain volumes; functional MRI (fMRI), which captures brain activity by measuring changes in blood flow, thus highlighting functional connectivity and regional activation patterns associated with cognitive processes and disorders; positron emission tomography (PET), which measures metabolic activity and neurotransmitter dynamics through the detection of radiolabeled tracers, enabling visualization of biochemical processes in the brain; and electrophysiological techniques such as magnetoencephalography (MEG) and electroencephalography (EEG), which record the brain's electrical activity, providing insight into real-time neural processing and functional states related to psychiatric conditions.

Each of these methods has distinct advantages and limitations. For instance, structural MRI excels in detecting anatomical alterations in the brain, effectively identifying and localizing structural abnormalities. In contrast, EEG provides excellent temporal resolution, capturing subtle neural changes with millisecond precision. Additionally, these techniques significantly differ in terms of accessibility, procedure cost, and ease of use. While some methods, like EEG, are relatively widespread, affordable, and straightforward to implement, others such as PET and MEG can be more complex, expensive, and less accessible. Nevertheless, despite these variations, each of these methods contributes uniquely valuable insights into brain functioning relevant to psychiatric disorders.

There are other biological markers with substantial potential for developing new diagnostic methods and therapeutic approaches. Genetic data can uncover associations between genetic variants and specific psychiatric disorders, enabling early identification of susceptibility and predicting individual responses or metabolic reactions to medications. Epigenetic testing, although still in early stages of development and not widely used clinically, is important because it reveals how external factors—such as stress, lifestyle, and environmental influences—can alter the expression of genetic predispositions. Given that psychiatric disorders arise from the interplay of both inherited and environmental factors ("nature and nurture"),[4,5] integrating genetic and epigenetic analyses enhances our understanding of psychiatric illnesses.

Equally valuable biological data can be obtained from blood analyses, which include numerous indicators potentially useful for psychiatry. For example, blood tests can reveal vitamin deficiencies, inflammatory markers, and other metabolic parameters. One particularly relevant example involves sex hormone levels—estrogen, progesterone, and testosterone—as research indicates a potentially significant relationship between these hormones and psychiatric disorders.

First, epidemiological data confirm substantial gender differences in the prevalence of mental disorders. Women experience depression and anxiety disorders approximately 1.5–2 times more frequently than men.[6] Conversely, men are more likely to suffer from substance use disorders and attention-deficit/hyperactivity disorder (ADHD).[7,8] Additionally, schizophrenia often has an earlier onset and a more severe progression in men compared to women.[9]

Second, the risk of developing psychiatric symptoms is frequently linked to life periods marked by significant hormonal fluctuations. Postpartum depression is diagnosed in 10–20% of women, typically following a sharp drop in estrogen and progesterone levels.[10] Perimenopause, characterized by pronounced estrogen fluctuations, is associated with increased risk of depressive and anxiety disorders.[11] During adolescence, surges in sex hormones heighten the risk of mental disorders. Specifically, in males, the onset of schizophrenia symptoms commonly peaks during puberty.[9,12]

In females, the risk of developing depression and anxiety sharply rises after puberty onset.[13]

Third, hormonal influences on mental states are explained by the presence of sex hormone receptors in the brain. Estrogen and progesterone receptors are widely distributed in brain regions such as the hippocampus, amygdala, and prefrontal cortex, all crucial for emotional responses and stress regulation.[14] Estrogens modulate serotonergic and dopaminergic systems involved in mood and cognitive functions.[15] Progesterone and its neurosteroid derivative, allopregnanolone, interact with GABA receptors, exerting a pronounced anxiolytic effect.[16] Testosterone receptors, predominantly located in hypothalamic-limbic brain regions, can significantly affect emotional stability and behavior.[17] These hormonal variations can also explain differences in medication efficacy; for example, women typically show a better response to selective serotonin reuptake inhibitors (SSRIs) compared to men.[18]

Therefore, collecting data on a patient's hormonal profile holds significant potential for developing AI-driven tools and solutions, ultimately enabling a more precise and personalized approach in psychiatry.

Another valuable category of biological data obtained from blood tests involves proteomics (the study of all proteins within an organism) and metabolomics (the study of metabolic products). These methods help identify specific substances in the blood that may signal the presence or risk of psychiatric disorders. For instance, elevated levels of proteins such as C-reactive protein and haptoglobin—both involved in inflammation and immune responses—can serve as early indicators of depression and anxiety disorders.[19] Other studies highlight metabolites involved in amino acid and lipid metabolism, notably tryptophan and sphingolipids, whose levels correlate with depression and bipolar disorder.[20,21]

Such molecular profiles can also facilitate novel medication development and improve our understanding of drug interactions within patients' bodies. For example, metabolomic analyses in schizophrenia have suggested associations with disturbances in lipid transport, steroid hormone biosynthesis (critical hormonal regulators), and oxidative stress (cell damage caused by free radicals).[22] Certain proteins, including BTN2A1 and BTN3A2 from the butyrophilin family, have shown elevated levels across various psychiatric disorders such as depression, schizophrenia, and bipolar disorder, indicating potentially shared underlying biological mechanisms.[23] While the precise clinical relevance of these molecular signals requires further validation, their collection and analysis represent a promising foundation for future AI-driven diagnostic tools and personalized treatments in psychiatry.

Another promising source of biological data is the microbiome—the community of microorganisms, such as bacteria, viruses, and fungi, inhabiting the human body. Recently, research on the microbiome has grown significantly, highlighting its potential role in various health conditions, including psychiatric disorders. Particular attention has been directed toward the gut–brain connection, with studies suggesting that specific states of gut microbiota composition may be linked to mental health conditions such as depression, anxiety, and even schizophrenia.[24] Therefore, microbiome data collection holds potential value for AI-driven psychiatric technologies, contributing to the development of novel treatments, personalized therapeutic strategies, and possibly even dietary interventions aimed at improving mental health outcomes.

Such biological data are particularly valuable when collected and analyzed within clinical settings. The use of specialized equipment and the involvement of qualified professionals ensure the high quality and standardization necessary for successful application in artificial intelligence. Nevertheless, similar types of biological data can, to some extent, also be obtained directly from patients themselves.

Options for collecting brain-activity data directly from patients are significantly more limited compared to clinical methods. Wearable EEG-based devices, enabling independent patient use, are primarily employed for this purpose. Typically designed as headphones or specialized headbands, these devices have significantly fewer electrodes compared to clinical EEG systems and use dry electrodes. Although this simplifies device application, it reduces signal quality and increases noise levels. Some manufacturers also offer "ear-EEG" devices, where electrodes are integrated into headphones and placed on or around the auricle. While these devices are more discreet and comfortable for everyday wear, their accuracy and coverage of brain regions are limited, necessitating advanced signal processing techniques to extract meaningful data.

Another emerging—but not yet widely adopted—technology is functional near-infrared spectroscopy (fNIRS).[25] fNIRS measures changes in blood oxygenation levels within superficial cortical layers using near-infrared light, providing an indirect assessment of brain activity. Although still developing, fNIRS holds promise as a supplementary source of brain-activity data, potentially enriching datasets used by future AI-driven psychiatric tools and treatment approaches.

Concerning genetic material or hormone analyses, the industry has advanced toward at-home testing kits. These allow patients to collect biological samples themselves and send them to laboratories. Although this market is still emerging, it is rapidly growing. According to market research, the global at-home testing market was valued at $16.7 billion in 2021 and is projected to reach $45.6 billion by 2031.[26] The DTC genetic testing segment alone was estimated at $2.2 billion in 2023, with forecasts reaching $20.2 billion by 2035.[27]

Currently, various companies—primarily startups—offer at-home testing in areas such as genetic testing, hormone panels, metabolic and blood markers, and microbiome analysis. These solutions are built on the premise of scaling data collection, forming large datasets suitable for AI-driven psychiatric analytics, licensing to tech and pharma companies, and accelerating drug development and personalized interventions. Despite existing market players, there remains significant potential for innovative solutions specifically focused on psychiatry.

Beyond data analogous to clinical measures, wearable devices offer extensive opportunities to collect diverse types of data that could serve as a robust foundation for new solutions in psychiatry. Current wearable devices monitor various health metrics, such as sleep duration and quality, body weight and composition, heart rate and oxygenation levels, as well as physical activity. Many of these indicators reflect physiological states directly or indirectly connected to psychiatric diagnostic criteria. For example, sleep disturbances—including insomnia, excessive sleepiness, or disrupted sleep patterns—are diagnostic criteria for several mental disorders listed in the DSM-V, such as major depressive disorder, bipolar disorder, generalized anxiety disorder, post-traumatic stress disorder (PTSD), and schizophrenia. Similarly, changes in appetite or significant weight loss or gain serve as important diagnostic criteria for disorders including major depressive disorder, bipolar disorder, anorexia nervosa, bulimia nervosa, and binge-eating disorder.

Additionally, wearable devices enable continuous monitoring of cardiovascular metrics, opening new opportunities to explore the heart-brain connection—an area of growing interest. Recent research highlights significant associations between cardiovascular function, as measured through heart rate, heart rate variability (HRV), and oxygen saturation, and mental health outcomes.[28] Conversely, improvements in cardiovascular indicators often correlate with enhanced emotional regulation, resilience to stress, and overall mental well-being. Therefore, continuous monitoring and analysis of cardiovascular data via wearable devices could significantly contribute to the development of personalized, AI-driven psychiatric solutions.

Thus far, we've explored a selection of biological data examples that can be collected both clinically and directly from patients. I've aimed to illustrate their potential value clearly, highlighting opportunities these data offer for advancing psychiatric research and developing novel AI-driven solutions. However, given that the symptomatology of mental disorders often manifests as cognitive and emotional changes—such as alterations in memory, attention, or emotional responses—it's equally important to consider another significant category of information: behavioral data.

Behavioral Data

Most mental disorders manifest through symptoms that alter a patient's perception of the world and their interactions with it. For example, a common symptom across mental disorders is impaired ability to concentrate and sustain attention (reduced focus and distractibility). According to DSM-V, such symptoms are observed in disorders including Attention-Deficit/Hyperactivity Disorder (ADHD), Major Depressive Disorder, Generalized Anxiety Disorder, Bipolar Disorder, and Schizophrenia.

Another illustrative example is manic behavior—a condition characterized by abnormally elevated mood, heightened activity levels, accelerated thought processes, reduced need for sleep, and impulsive actions. According to DSM-V, manic behavior is a core symptom in disorders such as Bipolar I Disorder and Schizoaffective Disorder.

To objectively capture these symptomatic manifestations and better understand their impact, behavioral data can be particularly valuable. Behavioral data refers to quantitative measurements of targeted behaviors and interactions, systematically recorded and analyzed to reflect how individuals respond to specific stimuli or contexts.[29] Within psychiatry, such data include metrics related to memory, attention, emotional reactions, decision-making speed, and other complex cognitive processes. Analyzing behavioral data provides valuable insights into how individuals interact with their environment, revealing day-to-day cognitive functioning and the effectiveness of their responses in various real-life situations.

In clinical practice, behavioral data are traditionally gathered using standardized psychological and neurocognitive tests. Such tests are specifically designed to simplify modeling of real-life scenarios, enabling assessment of cognitive and emotional processes in controlled laboratory settings. For instance, the widely used neurocognitive test known as the **Attentional Network Test (ANT)** evaluates various components of attention. Patients are presented with arrows pointing in specific directions; the central arrow may be surrounded by others pointing in either the same direction (congruent condition) or the opposite direction (incongruent condition). The patient's task is to quickly and accurately indicate the direction of the central arrow by pressing the appropriate key. Metrics recorded include reaction times, response accuracy, number of errors, and variability of responses under different task conditions.

Another illustrative example is an emotion recognition test, where patients view photographs of human faces displaying different emotional states. Images may be intentionally blurred or displayed for very brief periods. Patients must identify the specific emotion shown on the screen. Such tasks assess the ability to recognize and respond to socially relevant emotional cues. Measured metrics include the proportion of correct answers, the number and types of errors, and the decision-making time.

Occasionally, during such neurocognitive tasks, eye movements are simultaneously recorded. Analyzing gaze patterns can help detect periods of "mind-wandering," when patients lose focus on the task and drift into their own thoughts. In these instances, specific changes in eye-movement activity are recorded, such as reduced fixation on critical stimuli, increased duration of individual fixations, altered frequency and amplitude of saccades (rapid eye movements between fixation points), and overall disorganization or distractibility in gaze behavior.[30]

Such neurocognitive tests can also be conducted directly by patients, for example, via mobile applications. While this approach offers advantages like ease of use and potential data standardization, it remains relatively limited in the scope and depth of the collected information. Nevertheless, this field is poised for significant transformation, especially considering that the collected data are intended to build artificial intelligence models. Specifically, tasks can become much more aligned with real-life scenarios through the integration of virtual reality (VR) and augmented reality (AR) technologies. Patients can be placed in virtually simulated environments that accurately reflect daily-life situations, or involved in gaming-like contexts, where their performed tasks closely mirror their actual behavior and cognitive characteristics. Such an approach enables the collection of more naturalistic and richer behavioral data, significantly expanding opportunities to develop accurate and effective AI solutions in psychiatry.

Apart from specially designed tests and tasks, behavioral data can include direct insights into how individuals make decisions and act online. This method avoids artificially simulated scenarios, instead capturing natural, everyday decisions and user actions performed in real-life settings. The possibilities for gathering such data are virtually limitless, ranging from online shopping patterns to subtle nuances in users' search activities.

For instance, alterations in behavioral patterns may become evident through peculiarities in online search behaviors: a manic or excessively intense search on a single topic could signal anxiety or hypomanic states. Conversely, abrupt changes in the nature or themes of search queries, such as sudden interest in previously uncharacteristic or unusual topics, may indirectly reflect emotional instability or internal distress related to a person's mental state.

Another significant indicator might be shifts in online activity timing: a sudden increase in nighttime online presence or the emergence of atypical activity patterns could relate to sleep or circadian rhythm disturbances commonly associated with depression, anxiety, or manic episodes. Similarly, changes in user behavior on digital platforms like YouTube, Spotify, or Netflix—for instance, an abrupt change in music or video preferences, increased viewing duration or intensity, or conversely, complete loss of interest—can reflect emotional and cognitive shifts.

In social media, behavioral data can be reflected through metrics such as posting frequency, sudden periods of hyperactivity, or conversely, sharp reductions in activity, as well as the frequency and timing of content interactions. These indicators provide valuable insights into social and emotional shifts in behavior, including isolation, increased need for social communication, or even subtle signs of deteriorating mood.

Although online behavioral data are less standardized, they hold immense potential. They enable capturing subtle yet critical changes in patient behavior that traditional clinical methods may miss. These data offer unique insights, helping uncover previously unnoticed or insufficiently explored behavioral patterns, thus opening new avenues for AI-driven innovations in psychiatry.

Communication Data

Behavioral data provide valuable insights into patients' cognitive processes and actions. However, many psychiatric symptoms directly manifest through communication, making communication data particularly significant for diagnosing and monitoring mental health conditions. Such data encompass audio, video, and textual materials capturing verbal and non-verbal aspects of patient interactions, objectively documenting how patients express their thoughts, emotions, and experiences. As discussed previously, psychiatric diagnoses heavily rely on interpreting patient speech—a process inherently influenced by subjective perceptions. The systematic collection and analysis of communication data help mitigate this subjectivity, thereby enhancing diagnostic accuracy and reliability.

Textual communication data include patients' everyday language found in text messages, personal diaries, online communications, and social media interactions, providing valuable insights into emotional states, thought patterns, and social behaviors over extended periods. Additionally, clinical notes from therapists and physicians represent professional textual data, documenting direct observations during consultations and therapy sessions. Audio recordings from therapeutic sessions capture essential speech characteristics such as speech rate, rhythm, pauses, and intonation. Analyzing vocal patterns can reveal subtle cognitive and emotional shifts, often unnoticed during routine clinical observation. Complementing audio data, video recordings offer critical additional context by capturing non-verbal behaviors including facial expressions, eye movements, gestures, posture, and motor activity. Detailed analysis of these visual cues provides objective insights into emotional states that patients may not explicitly verbalize.

An integrated approach, systematically combining textual, audio, and video data, creates a comprehensive and nuanced understanding of patient behavior and emotional states. Such integration significantly enhances the precision of psychiatric assessment and opens new opportunities for artificial intelligence applications, enabling early detection of subtle symptom changes, accurate monitoring of clinical progress, and the development of personalized therapeutic interventions aimed at improving patient outcomes.

Data: Clinic or Consumer?

The range of data that can be leveraged for developing AI solutions in psychiatry is very broad. Biological, behavioral, and communication data contain meaningful signals and useful information applicable to various tasks. However, when building specific models, it is essential to consider not only the informativeness of the data but also factors such as noise level, data quality, and accessibility. This consideration underlies my earlier suggestion to classify data into two main categories—clinical and direct-to-consumer (DTC). Such an approach clearly highlights how data collection conditions and methods affect data characteristics and their suitability for artificial intelligence applications.

Signal-to-Noise Ratio

When collecting data for psychiatric AI solutions, both clinical and consumer-driven (patient-collected) approaches have distinct advantages and limitations. Clinical data—especially biological data—typically feature high detail and precision due to specialized equipment, standardized procedures, and trained medical professionals. This allows for the collection of complex biomaterials, ensuring accurate assessments and significantly reducing noise related to technical and procedural errors, such as improper sample collection or equipment misuse.

A prime example is electroencephalographic (EEG) data collection, where clinical and home conditions differ dramatically. In clinical settings, multi-channel EEG systems (ranging from 19 to 64 electrodes) equipped with wet gel contacts are standard. Before recording, meticulous skin preparation, precise head measurements for electrode placement, and rigorous quality checks of the EEG signals are conducted. Medical personnel continuously monitor patient behavior to prevent movement artifacts, muscle tension, or teeth clenching, which can completely distort valuable neurophysiological signals.

In contrast, consumer-grade (direct-to-consumer, DTC) EEG devices present fundamentally different circumstances. These devices are significantly simplified, typically equipped with fewer electrodes (usually between 2 and 10), often employing dry electrodes, and covering only limited areas of the head. Users rarely undertake necessary skin preparation procedures or proper electrode positioning, and built-in signal quality checks are typically absent or ignored. Consequently, data collected from these devices exhibit high levels of noise and instability.

These limitations have been confirmed by comparative clinical studies, which assessed professional EEG systems against DTC devices. Results show that even under ideal laboratory conditions, with professional assistance, DTC devices exhibit poorer signal quality, higher measurement variability, increased artifact occurrence, and lower stability compared to clinical counterparts.[31,32] Under real-world home use without professional oversight, these issues become significantly more pronounced. This considerably reduces data informativeness and reliability for AI algorithm applications, complicating the creation of precise diagnostic models and diminishing the quality of the resulting solutions.

Similar challenges are observed in genetic data collection. For instance, addressing questions about the origin of psychiatric disorders or identifying biomarkers linked to medication responses requires whole genome sequencing (WGS) data, which are currently predominantly accessible in clinical settings. Most DTC genetic tests currently utilize SNP genotyping methods, analyzing only selected genome segments where maximum variability is expected, rather than the entire genome. Nevertheless, the DTC genetics industry is rapidly evolving, and soon a broader array of genetic tests—including full genome analysis—is anticipated, significantly enhancing the applicability of these data in psychiatric AI solutions.

When considering behavioral data, evaluating noise levels and data quality is less straightforward. On one hand, clinical environments enforce standardized protocols, reducing noise associated with procedural inaccuracies. However, test scenarios in clinical settings are inherently artificial, and patient behavior can be distorted due to the unfamiliar laboratory environment, introducing specific noise and decreasing data authenticity. On the other hand, behavioral data collected directly from patients in natural environments (such as online behavior) demonstrate a high degree of authenticity and absence of external distortions. Nonetheless, such naturalistic data often contain a low proportion of signals directly relevant to mental states.

Analogous complexities arise with communication data. Conversations recorded in a psychiatrist's office yield highly relevant signals, as topics directly relate to the patient's symptoms and mental condition. Yet, the interaction with a clinician can considerably distort a person's natural communicative behavior, introducing additional noise. Conversely, communication data gathered in more natural settings, while providing less direct indicators of mental states, offer more authentic portrayals of speech and behavior. However, these conditions often entail greater technical interference, such as poor lighting conditions during video recording, low-quality microphones, or background noise—factors considerably more challenging to control at home than in clinical environments.

Labeling Quality

Another important difference related to data collection methods concerns annotation quality. In this context, "annotation" refers to information about a patient's diagnosis, prescribed treatment, and outcomes. Data collected through clinical methods—for instance, during medical visits or as part of clinical studies—generally offer more accurate annotations. This accuracy arises from diagnoses provided by specially trained professionals who follow clearly defined clinical criteria and protocols. Nevertheless, as we explored in Chapter 2, even diagnoses made by clinicians after careful and thorough patient evaluations can be inconsistent and often differ between independent assessments by different specialists. Despite this, clinical notes provide a certain accuracy in describing a patient's condition, recording the dates of medical visits, timing of prescribed treatments, and subsequent changes in well-being. Additionally, standardized clinical questionnaires and rating scales discussed in Chapter 3 are often used in clinical settings. While these scales also contain elements of subjectivity, repeated use for the same patient by the same clinician can reduce variability and enhance data informativeness. Further annotation resources include electronic health and medical record systems (EHR and EMR), which consolidate data from all patient visits, examination details, and prescribed treatments, provided the patient regularly attends the same healthcare facility. When collecting data via direct-to-consumer (DTC) approaches, the situation is markedly different. Annotation primarily relies on patients' subjective self-assessment of their condition, often conducted through self-administered standardized questionnaires, such as the PHQ-9 (Patient Health Questionnaire for assessing depression severity). Evaluating the quality of such self-assessments is challenging; however, research indicates that correlation between PHQ-9 self-assessment results and clinician-administered scales like HAM-D (Hamilton Depression Rating Scale) ranges from 0.6 to 0.75,[33,34] indicating a moderate correlation level. Nevertheless, in about 30% of cases, PHQ-9 self-assessment results diverge from expert ratings,[35] demonstrating limited precision compared to professional clinical assessments. Yet, the significant advantage of patient-collected data lies in the substantially greater frequency of observations. Clinical evaluations occur only during scheduled visits, whose frequency is constrained by specialists' availability and financial or insurance-related factors. In contrast, completion of self-assessment questionnaires depends solely on patient motivation and can be conducted regularly and frequently. Therefore, despite lower accuracy in each individual data point, the sheer volume of data can provide a more comprehensive and dynamic picture of a patient's condition.

Quantity Over Quality

Thus, we have gradually approached the question of the amount of data that can be collected. From this perspective, the direct-to-consumer (DTC) approach appears significantly more attractive, as it eliminates additional barriers such as scheduling and waiting for medical appointments, thereby enabling more extensive data collection.

Patients can continuously use wearable devices and applications over prolonged periods, collecting biological, behavioral, and communication data within their natural everyday environments. This approach facilitates the accumulation of large datasets reflecting real-life conditions. In contrast, the clinical approach, despite providing high-quality and precise data, demands significant time and financial resources, substantially limiting the volume of data available per patient.

As previously discussed in Chapter 6, random noise in data can often be compensated by increasing data volume. A large user base naturally introduces variability in data-collection errors. Since these errors are generally random and inconsistent, while the meaningful signal remains stable, collecting extensive datasets significantly enhances the ability to effectively clean the data and extract meaningful insights. Consequently, large-scale data collected directly from patients partially offsets the noise introduced by non-clinical data collection methods.

Moreover, similar to self-assessment questionnaires, regular data collection over extended periods allows viewing results not as isolated points but as dynamic trends. Under these conditions, the collected data become increasingly valuable because key parameters—such as data collection methods and sources—remain consistent. This consistency facilitates clearer identification of meaningful signals amidst random variability.

Nevertheless, it's critical to recognize the limitations of this approach, particularly regarding systematic noise. If, for instance, systematic noise originates from the equipment itself—such as consumer EEG headsets—no amount of additional data can fully eliminate it. Such systematic noise consistently appears in all collected data, significantly complicating the process of isolating meaningful signals, which can pose a substantial obstacle when developing effective AI-based solutions.

Choosing the approach to data collection becomes a complex optimization problem, requiring consideration of multiple constraints and balancing various factors. Depending on the specific task, one must decide between obtaining a smaller volume of high-quality, accurately annotated data, or a larger volume of noisy data that demands sophisticated processing. Beyond quality and quantity, however, there are several other critical considerations when developing data-driven solutions. How exactly should data collection be implemented from a business-model perspective? Which approach would be most effective and meet market demands? What technological solutions need to be developed for this purpose? Finally, how can we ensure market access and create incentives for individuals to be willing to share their personal data?

Realistic Paths to Data Aggregation

Implementing a data-collection product encounters the same systemic constraints as any other innovative product. To achieve the primary goal—accumulating substantial volumes of information—it is essential to secure broad support from stakeholders by providing solutions that help them achieve their goals. If there were already an established diagnostic process within the industry, the task would be relatively straightforward: create a product that surpasses existing solutions in terms of effectiveness and cost, establish a business model ensuring rights to collected information, and systematically accumulate data. However, we currently operate in an environment without sufficiently established diagnostic processes.

From a strategic standpoint, two primary approaches exist. The first involves collecting data independently, from scratch; the second entails aggregating existing data from diverse sources. The second approach is preferable, as it does not require developing new products or medical devices, substantially reduces engineering efforts, minimizes regulatory burdens, and eliminates the need to independently establish market presence and distribution channels.

However, when pursuing the second approach, direct access to patient data is often challenging, as data collection is frequently controlled by companies offering direct-to-consumer (DTC) solutions. In this scenario, collaboration and licensing arrangements must be organized directly with these DTC companies, much like the direct interactions typically established with clinics or academic institutions when obtaining clinical or research data. Clinical data can be accessed directly from healthcare providers or research institutions that already collect this information for scientific purposes. This approach is viable only if existing relationships with data providers are already in place or can be rapidly established.

The next critical step is to develop a clear proposal for data owners, clearly demonstrating the benefits of collaboration. Beyond direct financial arrangements (such as purchasing or licensing data), alternative models may be offered—for instance, granting partners access to analytical platforms, sharing research results derived from their data, or facilitating data exchange among multiple parties.

Within this framework, the primary technological challenge is developing a centralized platform capable of aggregating various data types that initially might not directly relate to psychiatry but can subsequently be enriched with relevant psychiatric information. For example, one can envision a platform aggregating functional magnetic resonance imaging (fMRI) data from multiple clinics, hospitals, and academic institutions. Such a platform would standardize and cleanse the collected data, and after resolving privacy, licensing, and data rights issues (a complex task in itself), integrate these data with electronic health records (EHR/EMR). This integration would enrich fMRI results with additional patient information—such as psychiatric diagnoses, treatments, and the chronological relationship between these events and imaging procedures. Thus, such a consolidated platform would form a powerful basis for developing effective AI solutions in psychiatry.

Therefore, successfully realizing such a system requires sequential execution of several tasks. First, it involves establishing robust relationships with potential data providers and owners. Second, creating cooperative conditions that incentivize partners to share data—through services, products, or financial compensation. Third, developing a technical platform capable of aggregating, standardizing, and cleaning the data. Lastly, enriching these data with psychiatrically relevant information, significantly enhancing their value and effectiveness for addressing psychiatric tasks through artificial intelligence.

The approach involving data collection from scratch also holds significant promise and can provide several key advantages. Among these advantages are the ability to initially collect data in an optimal format and to fully control their quality and annotation accuracy. Such a solution is particularly relevant when data are collected directly from patients. In this scenario, it becomes necessary to ensure not only the development of the data-collection product itself but also the shaping of consumer behavior—specifically, creating conditions under which users will be motivated to regularly utilize the device and integrate it into their lifestyle.

This approach can also be applied when introducing new tools into clinical practice. However, it is crucial to clearly understand the magnitude of complexities associated with regulatory requirements. Even more importantly, direct implementation of an innovative solution within the psychiatric market is virtually impossible without previously accumulated and accurately annotated data—the very data we are seeking to collect. Therefore, a necessary intermediate step is the development of products designed to gather data useful in related medical fields while simultaneously providing information relevant for psychiatry.

For successful implementation of such products, it is critical to understand markets outside psychiatry and create solutions that consumers will purchase to fulfill their own objectives and needs. Data collected in this manner can later be enriched with annotations relevant to psychiatric applications. Often, the main difficulty with this approach lies in the necessity of establishing a new market and clearly identifying the target consumer.

As a speculative example illustrating potential directions for such solutions, we might consider a recent patent by Apple,[36] proposing the integration of electrodes capable of recording brain signals into their widely popular AirPods headphones. While I do not know Apple's exact plans, I assume such development could have considerable potential for large-scale collection of neurophysiological data. Factors supporting this potential include Apple's established, powerful brand and the high level of user trust, a substantial audience of loyal customers willing to adopt innovative devices, and the ability to obtain additional data annotations through the existing Apple Health application. Thus, from my perspective, this innovation could theoretically enable Apple to accumulate valuable data, potentially suitable for research and development in psychiatry.

As much as we might wish for innovative diagnostic tools and immediate insights into psychiatric disorders, progress ultimately depends on the quality and availability of data—a critical step that cannot be bypassed. Accelerating this process requires careful strategic planning: clearly identifying the most valuable data and determining the optimal collection methods, considering their respective strengths and limitations. Established market players already exist, capable of rapidly organizing data collection and enrichment thanks to their existing ecosystems. Nevertheless, the market remains open to new entrants. Even within prominent ecosystems, niches always exist: companies can introduce unique approaches to data collection or synthesis by specializing in specific signal types, patient segments, or modalities currently overlooked. Success involves combining a deep understanding of precisely which data are necessary, the capability to choose optimal collection methods, and the creation of compelling value propositions for partners—whether healthcare providers, large technology companies, or patients themselves.

However, data collection and accumulation constitute only the initial step. The next crucial stage involves developing artificial intelligence solutions that can effectively translate these datasets into actionable clinical insights and recommendations. In the following chapter, we will discuss the potential directions and future prospects of AI-driven solutions in psychiatry, as well as the challenges and opportunities this field is likely to encounter.

8 | Revealing the Nature of Mental Disorders

It was the middle of lockdown. COVID-19 restrictions meant we couldn't leave our apartment, and the constant confinement was slowly driving us crazy. Finally, we couldn't take it anymore—we just got into the car and decided to drive to Boston and back. Eight hours on the road, with changing landscapes outside, felt infinitely better than another endless day stuck indoors.

Ivan had recently sold his company and was openly pondering what to do next.

"I think I might have an idea," I cautiously suggested.

He shot me a playful glance, sensing vulnerability. "Alright, let's hear it."

"What if we developed objective diagnostics for psychiatry?"

He smiled skeptically. "Wait, are you saying psychiatrists don't diagnose people?"

"No, of course they do. But mostly through interviews and questionnaires."

He raised an eyebrow, teasing me. "And that seems to work fine for everyone."

I bristled slightly. "I'm not so sure. It just seems odd—relying only on what people say."

"But no one's changed it, right? So what exactly are you proposing?"

"There must be research, data—EEG, MRI scans, something objective. Surely that's better than just questions."

He pushed further, smiling now. "And do you know how much data is out there?"

"I don't know exactly."

"And who's gonna pay for this?"

"I don't know."

"Is the market even big enough?"

"I don't know, okay!"

He laughed lightly, shaking his head. "So, it's a pretty weak idea then. If the research exists and the data's out there and yet nobody's done anything—maybe it's just not needed."

A couple of months passed, and I'd completely forgotten our conversation. I was fully absorbed in writing my thesis and working in the lab—innovation or new ideas were the last thing on my mind. One afternoon, as I sat at my computer absorbed in yet another research paper, Ivan unexpectedly called me from a business trip. He sounded lost and frustrated.

"Mariam, I don't know what's happening to me. I haven't slept in days. You mentioned that I seemed off lately—maybe you're right. I can't focus, and I honestly feel like I'm losing it. I just don't know who else to talk to or what to do."

Trying to soothe him, I gently considered his symptoms and carefully suggested, "Maybe a psychiatrist?"

We agreed he'd schedule the next available appointment. After seeing the psychiatrist, he called me again. His voice sounded even worse—subdued and utterly exhausted.

"They talked to me for two hours. They think it's serious, probably depression. They even suggested hospitalization. Tomorrow I have some kind of specialist evaluation. Everything feels like it's moving so fast—I don't understand, and I have nobody else to ask."

"It's going to be okay," I reassured him calmly. "You're at one of the best clinics in the country. A specialist evaluation sounds impressive—I've never even heard of something like that before. They clearly know what they're doing."

The next day, I found myself anxiously waiting by the phone for his call. I was genuinely worried about Ivan—I'd never heard him sound like this. And if I'm honest, I was also deeply curious—what exactly was this "specialist evaluation"?

When Ivan finally called, he was panicked, almost shouting into the phone:

"Mariam, it was ridiculous! I just spent an entire hour filling out questionnaires—the same questions, over and over! Eventually, I snapped and yelled at the doctor, 'What do you even want from me? Is this seriously how you diagnose people?' Mariam, they want to hospitalize me! They've prescribed a pile of pills. You were right—they didn't even look at my brain! I asked directly: 'Are you seriously basing hospitalization just on my answers? What about MRI or EEG?' And you know what she said? Calmly, she just told me, 'We don't do that here.' Mariam, you were right from the start—this has to change! They never even looked at my brain."

* * *

AI's Potential for Explaining Psychiatry

Imagine we've successfully overcome the barriers preventing large-scale data collection in psychiatry. With access to comprehensive datasets, the industry could finally address its most fundamental question: What exactly are mental illnesses, and what biological mechanisms underpin the symptoms affecting millions of people? A detailed understanding of the physiological nature of these disorders could revolutionize the entire industry, empowering stakeholders to better fulfill their roles. Precise insights into identifying specific physiological changes would allow us to adopt objective diagnostics based on biological tests, transform drug development strategies through an understanding of disease mechanisms, and improve treatment quality and therapeutic outcomes. Most importantly, if mental illnesses became "physically visible" through brain scans or blood tests, it could alter public perception, reducing stigma associated with mental health conditions.

Leveraging AI-driven approaches to decode mental disorders should then become the top priority. AI algorithms indeed hold tremendous potential for uncovering the biological mechanisms underlying psychiatric disorders. However, several important questions remain: What exactly would the process of decoding mental illnesses look like? How should we structure this process, and what concrete steps should we take to move closer to solutions? How could these insights be effectively integrated into existing psychiatric care frameworks, and how will the broader psychiatric community respond to such discoveries? While I don't yet have definitive answers, I have several hypotheses about how the industry could evolve if we fully leveraged all available tools and resources.

Clustering: Tempting Yet Tricky

Mental illnesses are characterized by pronounced heterogeneity and are defined at the symptomatic level, where each symptom can arise from diverse biological causes and mechanisms, reflecting various underlying disruptions. The central hypothesis is that the observable symptoms we currently use to make diagnoses are merely the tip of the iceberg. Beneath each diagnostic label lies a broad spectrum of distinct disease subtypes. By subtypes, I refer to different physiological mechanisms that manifest in identical symptomatology. As discussed in Chapter 3 of this book, heterogeneity provides the most logical explanation for numerous phenomena, from the vast number of possible symptom combinations resulting in a single diagnosis to the inconsistent outcomes of biological research and, ultimately, the fact that the same medications can be effective for some patients while largely ineffective for others.

Artificial intelligence excels at identifying hidden patterns within data. These patterns enable the segmentation of large datasets into clusters—subgroups in which cases are highly similar according to specific criteria and notably distinct from cases in other subgroups. In theory, this approach could bring us closer to answering the fundamental question about the nature of mental disorders. By possessing extensive biological data—such as fMRI, EEG, genetic profiles, or blood test results—collected from hundreds of thousands of patients sharing the same diagnosis, we could employ a machine-learning model capable of uncovering these hidden patterns and thus group patients into biologically homogeneous subtypes.

A deeper investigation into these subtypes could potentially reveal specific disease phenotypes hidden under broad diagnostic labels. However, this logic works well only in theory. In practice, inevitable technical challenges arise. The first and most significant is that any biological data we collect contains information reflecting a vast array of physiological processes occurring in the body. Exactly which part of these signals directly relates to mental health is far from obvious. For example, fMRI data, besides reflecting disruptions characteristic of psychiatric disorders, also capture the general organization of brain networks, sensory processing mechanisms, motor coordination, age-related changes, and consequences of injuries or other illnesses. As a result, the model might partition data into groups based on unexpected and clinically insignificant criteria. For instance, data might cluster due to technical artifacts caused by variations in medical equipment settings; demographic factors such as age, sex, or ethnicity; secondary physiological parameters like hydration level; or even the time of day when biomaterials were collected. With genetic data, clustering could occur around gene variants regulating processes unrelated to mental health. Such clusters do not reflect true biological subtypes of mental disorders and cannot advance our understanding of their underlying nature.

For the clusters we obtain to have genuine clinical significance, we would first need to isolate the part of the signal directly linked to mental disorders. This task represents one of the primary obstacles to implementing precision psychiatry methods into clinical practice, as contemporary research consistently demonstrates that neurobiological and genetic correlates of mental disorders are often nonspecific and heterogeneous, varying significantly from one patient to another and lacking reproducibility across different studies and populations.[1-3] Of course, numerous hypotheses offer certain guidelines, such as particular brain regions or neural networks deserving attention when analyzing signals, but these guidelines have proven insufficient. To avoid discarding potentially valuable information, we are compelled to work with largely unprocessed or minimally processed biological signals. While this preserves all data components that might contain clinically meaningful information, it also leaves us handling large volumes of irrelevant or noisy signals, which complicates the extraction of genuinely useful insights.

Another related challenge arises from this complexity—the difficulty in interpreting clusters derived from the model. Clustering methods do not rely on predefined hypotheses or criteria for forming groups; instead, the model organizes data based on their internal similarities. Once clusters are created, researchers must determine which characteristics underpin each group and why these specific characteristics are decisive. Yet, because of the complexity and heterogeneity of biological data, particularly in high-dimensional datasets like neuroimaging or genetics, interpreting these clusters is exceedingly difficult. Even through detailed analysis, it is often unclear which combinations of features influenced the formation of a given cluster, and why the model favored certain characteristics over others. Without a clear understanding of why and how clusters were formed, the opportunity to translate these findings into meaningful clinical insights and deepen our understanding of psychiatric disorders remains limited.

Starting with Stratification Platforms

Thus, another important task emerges: determining which patient clustering strategy would be the most clinically meaningful and practical. One approach involves exploring the relationships between identified clusters and various symptomatic profiles. However, the large number and inherent instability of these profiles make this strategy exceedingly challenging and difficult to implement in clinical practice.

An alternative, potentially more promising strategy is to analyze patient clusters or classify patients based on how they respond to specific medications or pharmacological groups. The logic behind this approach relies on several interconnected ideas. First, different medication classes possess distinct mechanisms of action. For example, let's consider common antidepressants: selective serotonin reuptake inhibitors (SSRIs) inhibit serotonin reuptake, thereby increasing serotonin concentrations in the synaptic cleft, while serotonin-norepinephrine reuptake inhibitors

(SNRIs) inhibit the reuptake of both serotonin and norepinephrine, increasing the availability of these neurotransmitters. Bupropion acts by inhibiting dopamine and norepinephrine reuptake, indirectly elevating their synaptic concentrations. Since medication efficacy varies significantly across patients, differences in therapeutic responses may reflect underlying biological variations, potentially indicating patient subtypes associated with distinct neurobiological mechanisms.

The second idea relates to the potential role of neural circuits in shaping psychiatric symptoms and their possible associations with pharmacotherapy. **Neural circuits** are specialized functional networks composed of interconnected brain regions that regulate cognitive, emotional, and behavioral processes. Contemporary research suggests that disruptions within various neural circuits may manifest as symptoms of depression, anxiety, and other psychiatric disorders.[1]

One illustrative neural circuit is the default mode circuit, commonly known as the default mode network. This circuit is primarily active during rest and is involved in processes such as self-reflection, spontaneous thought (mind-wandering), autobiographical memory retrieval, and planning for the future.[2] Dysfunction within the default mode circuit, such as hyperactivation or hyperconnectivity among its regions, can manifest in symptoms such as rumination (persistent negative thinking), hopelessness (a pessimistic outlook on the future), and feelings of worthlessness—all described as core symptoms in the DSM-V diagnostic criteria for major depressive disorder.[3-5] Importantly, the default mode circuit is only one of the multiple neural circuits implicated in regulating emotional states and behaviors. Various circuit dysfunctions can occur, including hyperconnectivity (increased functional connectivity), hypoconnectivity (reduced functional connectivity), and disrupted interactions between multiple circuits. This variability can contribute to diverse symptom presentations even within the same diagnostic category.

Neural circuit activity may also differ based on the neuromodulatory environment. Different neural circuits can vary in receptor distribution and sensitivity to neuromodulators (such as serotonin, norepinephrine, and dopamine), reflecting differences in receptor subtype profiles and unique anatomical connectivity patterns. Consequently, psychopharmacological agents targeting these neurotransmitter systems modulate neural circuit activity in different ways. Taken together, these considerations support the hypothesis that clustering patients based on therapeutic response represents a promising initial approach for identifying biologically meaningful subtypes of depression and other psychiatric disorders.

From the perspective of training artificial intelligence algorithms, this approach offers a significant advantage by providing greater stability in data labeling. In traditional methods, models typically train by linking biological data to diagnoses, symptoms, or questionnaire scores collected at a single timepoint. In the proposed approach, we instead associate biological data with the patient's therapeutic response to medication, quantitatively defined as the difference between at least two standardized assessments—before and after treatment—analogous to the methodology often employed in clinical trials to evaluate therapeutic effectiveness (see Chapter 3). This labeling strategy is more stable and reliable because it is grounded in the patient's state dynamics, tracked across multiple measurement points (e.g., repeated questionnaire assessments) rather than relying on a single-time-point evaluation. The dynamic change in patient condition serves as a more robust metric for training models than static, single-time-point evaluations of symptoms.

Several scientific studies have already demonstrated the feasibility of this approach, providing initial proof-of-concept evidence. For instance, in the field of depression, a prominent fMRI-based study identified biotypes characterized by differences in neural circuit activity that correlated with varying patient responses to transcranial magnetic stimulation (TMS).[6] Similarly, an EEG-based study on post-traumatic stress disorder (PTSD) identified two clinically relevant subtypes, distinguished by distinct patterns of brain activity.[7] One of these subtypes, which differed significantly from healthy brain activity patterns, showed reduced responsiveness to psychotherapy and did not respond to antidepressant medication. However, both subtypes showed comparable responses to repeated TMS. Similar investigations are being extended to other psychiatric disorders, employing various types of biological data, including blood analyses and genetic information. Nevertheless, these findings remain preliminary; their reproducibility across independent samples has yet to be established, and existing studies have been conducted on relatively small cohorts—around a thousand participants—which limits the generalizability of their conclusions.

With sufficiently large datasets and high-quality labeling, this approach could enable methods that allow artificial intelligence to analyze biological data and assign individual patients to specific subgroups most likely to respond to a given medication. This method is known as **patient stratification**—the division of patients into clinically meaningful subgroups based on biological, clinical, or other characteristics to predict therapeutic response or disease progression. It is important to note that patient stratification is an intermediate step toward fully personalized treatment. Rather than tailoring therapeutic decisions individually, stratification assigns treatment recommendations at the subgroup level, targeting groups of patients with similar characteristics and predicted responses.

At this stage, the underlying biological mechanisms of psychiatric disorders and the finer details of disease pathology will likely remain only partially understood. The first step will be establishing reliable, replicable, and generalizable associations between biological data and the likelihood of therapeutic response. Initially, these associations will probably rely on black-box models—algorithms whose internal decision-making processes remain opaque. Nonetheless, this step could represent the first significant advancement in decoding psychiatric conditions not only because it is relatively achievable in the near future but also because nearly all stakeholders within the psychiatric system could see rapid benefits from its implementation. Even this intermediate solution could begin to address many of the challenges discussed in the first part of this book.

First, transitioning from the current one-size-fits-all approach to stratified psychiatry could substantially enhance psychiatric treatment and medication selection in clinical practice. Clinicians would be able to prescribe more effective treatments right from initial visits, improving treatment efficacy and significantly reducing the time currently required to identify optimal medication—often years under the existing trial-and-error model. In this personalized approach, patients would not only undergo clinical interviews but also biological sample analysis to determine which medication is most likely to alleviate their symptoms.

Second, patient stratification, by increasing the likelihood of successful treatment outcomes, could reduce the number of follow-up visits required to monitor treatment effectiveness and adjust medications. This, in turn, would free up psychiatrists' time, increasing their availability to see new patients.

Third, this approach could reduce overall treatment costs, which are at present elevated by the frequent psychiatric consultations necessary for medication adjustments. Such financial savings would be advantageous for healthcare providers, patients, and insurance companies alike.

Pharma's Way Out: Opportunity in Predictive Biomarkers and CDx

Stratification algorithms offer substantial advantages for pharmaceutical companies, especially in late-stage clinical trials. As outlined in Chapter 3, pharma often experiences low success rates at these stages—not due to deficiencies in the therapeutic agents themselves but because of the considerable heterogeneity inherent in mental disorders. This diversity complicates efforts to obtain statistically significant results across large patient populations. Algorithms leveraging biological data to predict treatment responses can help companies more accurately identify patient subgroups that are most likely to benefit from specific treatments. Within this context, such algorithms function as predictive biomarkers—measurable biological indicators forecasting the likelihood of an individual patient's clinical response to a specific therapy.

A **Predictive Biomarker** is a measurable biological indicator capable of forecasting the likelihood of an individual patient's clinical response to a specific therapy. Such biomarkers facilitate the early identification of patients who will most likely benefit from a given therapeutic approach.

Currently, clinical trials typically enroll all patients meeting established diagnostic criteria. Introducing a predictive biomarker allows trial sponsors to identify the patient subgroups most likely to benefit from a treatment. While standard clinical trials involve two groups—patients receiving active medication and those receiving placebos—the biomarker-driven approach adds a third subgroup selected by the biomarker. This enrichment strategy improves trial success rates by focusing on individuals predisposed to respond to the treatment. Furthermore, when trials demonstrate effectiveness and the biomarker-defined subgroup exhibits significant improvements compared to the placebo and biomarker-negative groups, the medication can be approved alongside a **companion diagnostic** (CDx)—a specialized diagnostic test intended for concurrent use with a particular medication. A CDx allows prior identification of patients most likely to benefit from the treatment and those for whom the treatment might be ineffective or potentially harmful, thereby enhancing the therapy's overall effectiveness and safety.

Identifying a patient subgroup most likely to benefit from a medication might appear to reduce the potential market size for a pharmaceutical company, making this approach commercially unattractive. However, in practice, the opposite occurs. This strategy enhances the probability of successful late-stage clinical trials, reducing the risk of expensive failures and protecting financial investments made during drug development.

The use of a CDx also favorably positions the treatment within the market. First, it enhances the clinical effectiveness of the drug. Second, it allows new therapies to avoid direct competition with existing medications. In today's market, characterized by trial-and-error prescribing patterns, newer and typically more expensive treatments are often considered only after patients have tried several cheaper options, such as generics. A CDx provides robust justification for prescribing the medication earlier—at least as second-line therapy—by presenting biological evidence that a patient should receive a treatment tailored to their biological profile.

Pharmaceutical companies are likely to become the primary drivers behind adopting stratified psychiatry approaches. They currently face significant stagnation in psychiatric drug development, and stratified approaches offer promising opportunities to address this challenge. Such methods could facilitate the introduction of entirely new medications, as well as enabling pharmaceutical companies to revisit unsuccessful drugs by restarting clinical trials with selected patient subgroups, perhaps uncovering potential therapeutic effects that were undetectable in previous trials.

Moreover, pharmaceutical companies have substantial influence within the psychiatric care ecosystem, positioning them to implement and scale innovative solutions. Attempting to directly integrate stratified psychiatry solutions into clinical practice without pharmaceutical company involvement would encounter multiple significant practical challenges.

First, the adoption of stratified psychiatry approaches depends heavily on specialized equipment, such as genetic testing facilities or MRI recording devices, which are not widely available in most clinical settings. Equipping healthcare facilities with the necessary specialized instruments and staff trained to operate them demands considerable financial resources and organizational efforts. It remains unclear who—especially among smaller or independent organizations—would bear the substantial investment required for widespread implementation.

Second, the psychiatric care system itself faces considerable operational constraints. Psychiatrists, who already experience significant workloads and pressures, would find their clinical processes further complicated by introducing complex new diagnostic protocols or additional biological tests into their daily practice. This situation is even more difficult in primary care settings, where general practitioners (GPs) prescribe a large proportion of antidepressants and other psychiatric medications. GPs face even greater operational and administrative burdens than specialists, making it highly challenging—and perhaps unrealistic—to incorporate additional testing requirements into their already demanding workflow.

Third, financing diagnostic testing poses another substantial barrier. Insurance companies may resist covering expensive diagnostic tests required for stratified psychiatry, particularly since current psychiatric treatments mainly involve inexpensive generic medications. Insurers might find it more cost-effective to reimburse extended periods of generic medication treatment—even if it is less targeted and less effective—rather than finance expensive diagnostics such as genetic analyses or advanced neuroimaging. Without explicit financial incentives or policy backing, stratified diagnostic testing could encounter significant opposition from insurance providers.

Additionally, regulatory requirements pose a substantial challenge. Companies aiming to develop stratified approaches and related algorithms would face significant financial and time commitments to conduct independent clinical trials and secure regulatory approvals. Applying a stratified approach to medications that are already approved would likely require new clinical trials for each individual drug, involving the extensive collection and rigorous analysis of data from thousands of patients to meet stringent FDA requirements. The necessity of repeating large-scale trials for approved medications significantly increases the financial burden and extends development timelines, creating substantial barriers, particularly for smaller companies lacking extensive resources.

In addition to practical and financial constraints, ethical considerations complicate the widespread adoption of stratified psychiatry platforms. Predictive models designed for stratified approaches will identify not only patients likely to benefit from specific treatments but also patient groups unlikely to respond positively. This raises ethical concerns about managing their care.[8] One potential approach is to revert these patients to traditional **stepped-care models**, sequentially testing different treatments. Alternatively, instead of just predicting treatment responsiveness for a single medication, predictive models could evaluate multiple treatment options simultaneously, highlighting the most promising medication for each patient. However, this strategy reframes treatment probabilities without resolving the underlying ethical dilemma regarding patients for whom optimal treatment remains uncertain.

Given these complexities, I predict that pharmaceutical companies (or organizations affiliated with them) will lead the initial efforts to adopt stratified psychiatry, primarily focusing on introducing novel medications paired with a CDx. It is pharmaceutical companies that can drive the transition from the classical model of prescribing medication to a more targeted one based on the patient's biological data. Under this model, the previously mentioned obstacles either will not arise or will be managed by pharma due to their considerable resources, established market relationships, and industry influence. First, they possess extensive experience, robust market connections, and sufficient resources to facilitate the distribution and adoption of the medical devices required for CDx. Second, pharmaceutical companies can assume financial responsibility for the diagnostic testing required before prescribing their medications, significantly accelerating market integration. The increased expenses associated with implementing companion diagnostics can be offset by higher sales driven by improved drug efficacy, better patient targeting, and enhanced market positioning resulting from CDx adoption. Finally, costs related to clinical trials and regulatory approvals will be much lower than introducing stratified psychiatry solutions for existing medications in clinical settings. When a new medication and its companion diagnostic are tested simultaneously—with the CDx serving directly as a predictive biomarker—the clinical trial data gathered for the medication can also support regulatory approval for the diagnostic test itself, eliminating the need for separate clinical trials.

Initially, this stratified psychiatry model would apply primarily to new medications and would not cover the entire range of available treatments. It is possible that the development and adoption of stratified algorithms could proceed simultaneously along multiple paths, including both clinical practice and pharmaceutical-driven approaches. However, considering the numerous practical constraints—from selecting suitable biological data collection methods and ensuring their accessibility to navigating complex regulatory processes—the pharmaceutical-led pathway currently offers the highest chance of successful adoption and long-term sustainability within the existing psychiatric care ecosystem.

Speaking of data, a critical reader might reasonably ask, "How will AI algorithms be trained to predict a patient's response to a drug for which clinical data does not yet exist, as the drug itself is still in the clinical trial stage?"

- There are two potential approaches to solving this problem. The first involves **transfer learning**, an AI training method that uses a model pretrained on existing datasets or related tasks to enhance performance on a new but similar task, significantly reducing the amount of new data required for training. Specifically, a predictive model might first be trained on data from an existing drug with a similar mechanism of action or therapeutic target. Once the model has learned general patterns correlating biological data with patient responses to that existing medication, it can then be fine-tuned using data gathered during the early stages (such as Phase II) of clinical trials for the new drug, even if these data are relatively limited. This approach leverages existing knowledge to minimize data requirements and accelerates the development process.
- The second approach involves the development of **foundational models**. As discussed in Chapter 5, foundational models are large-scale AI systems trained on massive and diverse datasets to recognize generalizable patterns and relationships. For instance, a foundational model can initially be trained on extensive genomic or other biological datasets collected from a broad population. During this training phase, the model learns fundamental biological patterns, variations, and relationships that are widely applicable. Once this foundational knowledge is established, the model can be fine-tuned with much smaller, drug-specific datasets to perform narrower, specialized tasks, such as predicting patient responses to a particular medication. In practice, this means that to develop predictive biomarkers for a Phase

III clinical trial, it might be sufficient to fine-tune a previously trained foundational model solely on the data collected in earlier phases of that trial.

Summarizing, I anticipate that one of the earliest and most impactful AI innovations in psychiatry will be platforms designed for patient stratification based on biological data. These platforms will likely leverage foundational AI models capable of identifying common patterns and relationships within large, diverse datasets. Such models are particularly relevant given the significant challenges and costs associated with collecting sufficiently large, high-quality datasets on therapeutic efficacy, which would include standardized measures of patient conditions before and after treatment. Moreover, I expect these stratification platforms and their corresponding diagnostic tests to utilize biological data types that are readily accessible and supported by widely available, affordable collection methods.

Pharmaceutical companies are likely to be among the first adopters, incorporating these AI technologies into clinical trials for new medications. This will allow drugs to enter the market alongside companion diagnostics. In such scenarios, the CDx will essentially function as an algorithm within the stratification platform, predicting therapeutic responses for individual patients based on their biological profiles. The introduction of these AI-driven medications—particularly if multiple pharmaceutical companies launch similar solutions at the same time—will progressively reshape psychiatric care delivery.

First, these innovations will significantly enhance medication efficacy. Second, they will shift the traditional "one-size-fits-all" prescribing approach toward more targeted and precise treatment strategies. Even at this initial stage of deployment, these technologies hold the potential to improve patient outcomes by shortening the period needed to identify effective treatments, reducing the frequency of medical consultations, and lowering overall healthcare costs.

Monitoring Biomarkers

The adoption of predictive biomarkers can accelerate the development of other biomarker types, especially monitoring biomarkers, which are crucial for effective disease management and treatment outcome evaluation.

Predictive biomarkers do not necessarily reflect the current state of a disease; instead, they simply identify patients who are likely to respond to specific medications, regardless of why this response occurs. Therefore, predictive biomarkers bypass concerns about the inherent opacity of "black-box" AI algorithms, focusing solely on accurate patient stratification.

In contrast, monitoring biomarkers offer deeper insights into treatment effects, as they directly measure biological changes occurring before and after therapy. Once predictive biomarkers become routine, biological data will be regularly collected prior to treatment. Establishing monitoring biomarkers then becomes relatively straightforward, requiring only additional comparable data collection after treatment. Predictive biomarkers reduce patient heterogeneity by stratifying them into biologically more uniform groups, thereby increasing the likelihood of identifying monitoring biomarkers that are clearly linked to underlying biological mechanisms and treatment responses.

Several studies have indicated that treatment-induced biological changes in brain activity become detectable much earlier than patients consciously notice symptomatic improvement.[9] This delay is thought to occur because patients need more time to perceive and evaluate subtle internal improvements. Thus, monitoring biomarkers could reduce the current period required to determine medication efficacy—typically around eight weeks—to just weeks or even days, accelerating clinical decisions and improving patient outcomes.

Monitoring biomarkers also provide pharmaceutical companies with real-time insights into a drug's mechanism of action and biological target engagement, facilitating the optimization of clinical trials and more precise dose selection. By directly linking measurable biological changes to clinical outcomes, these biomarkers enable early validation of drug efficacy and establish surrogate endpoints—biological indicators capable of accurately predicting patient benefit without waiting for traditional clinical endpoints. This shortens trial durations and reduces costs, enabling faster decision-making and adjustments in dosing or therapeutic protocols. Continuous biomarker monitoring throughout clinical trials further assists in refining drug formulations and enhancing therapeutic windows, thereby improving the likelihood of successful regulatory approval and, ultimately, better patient outcomes.

Multimodal Systems for Personalized Psychiatry

Following the adoption of the stratified psychiatry paradigm in clinical practice, the next step will likely be the development of multimodal systems. Given the significant complexity and high costs associated with integrating multiple types of biological data into routine clinical workflows, multimodal platforms will probably emerge somewhat later than solutions relying on a single data modality. Such comprehensive systems may arise either through integrating existing specialized platforms or via acquisitions by major market players capable of unifying these platforms into cohesive systems.

At its core, the multimodal approach involves simultaneously analyzing diverse biological and clinical data, such as genetic, neurophysiological, neuroimaging, biochemical, behavioral, and communication measures. Its primary objective is to predict an individual patient's therapeutic response to specific medications. By integrating multiple data modalities, artificial intelligence algorithms autonomously uncover complex patterns and associations, resulting in much more precise predictions than single-modality approaches.

Consider a patient diagnosed with depression seeking the most effective treatment. A multimodal system would automatically analyze the patient's genetic, hormonal, and neurophysiological data to predict therapeutic outcomes with high precision. Genetic data allow the AI model to identify gene polymorphisms involved in drug metabolism and neurotransmitter system functioning. Hormonal and biochemical indicators, including cortisol or cytokine levels, provide insights into the physiological states affecting the medication's pharmacokinetics and pharmacodynamics. Additionally, neurophysiological and neuroimaging data (e.g., EEG and fMRI) enable the AI to recognize specific patterns of brain activity predictive of medication response.

A crucial advantage of multimodal systems is their ability to integrate behavioral and communication data alongside biological indicators, thereby enhancing the characterization of the patient's symptom profile. This comprehensive integration ensures that AI-generated therapeutic protocols become more precise and individualized, moving psychiatric practice closer to a genuinely personalized approach (see Figure 8.1).

Traditional stepped-care model

Stratification model with single CDx for novel treatment

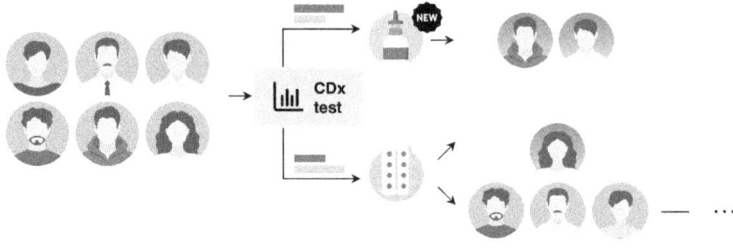

Stratification model for multiple treatments

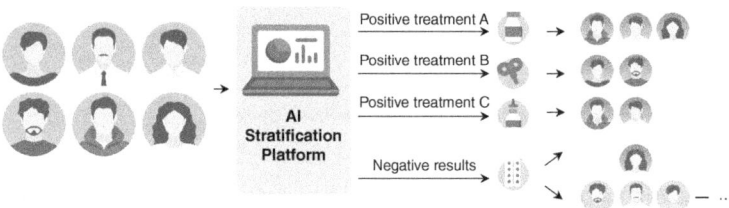

Multimodal precision psychiatry model

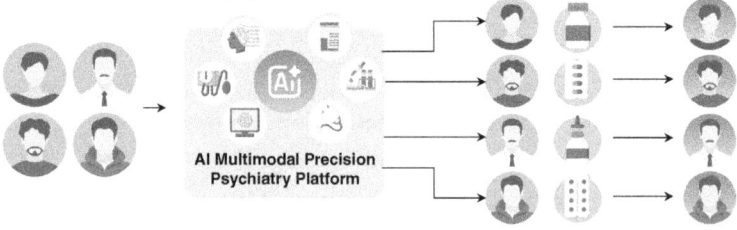

Figure 8.1 From traditional stepped-care model to precision psychiatry of the future. With sufficient availability of biological data and predictive models for treatment response, the traditional "one-size-fits-all" psychiatry model will gradually evolve toward a personalized approach supported by diverse medical testing. This shift may initially be driven by the emergence of novel therapeutics with companion diagnostics (CDx), facilitating early adoption of patient stratification. As this practice becomes widespread and biological data routinely guide prescribing decisions, it will open the path for comprehensive personalized treatment platforms.

Mental Disorders Redefined

While the initial deployment of multimodal platforms will indeed face logistical and economic challenges, their eventual integration into routine clinical practice signifies a critical turning point. This transition marks a fundamental shift from simply optimizing treatment predictions to addressing a deeper scientific challenge—clarifying the precise biological mechanisms underlying psychiatric symptoms themselves. The emergence of multimodal systems creates a pivotal moment in psychiatric research, offering a real chance to uncover the biological mechanisms underlying mental disorders. Until now, psychiatric research has yielded inconsistent and ambiguous results, primarily because patient groups have been formed based on overly broad and imprecise diagnostic criteria. Even the Research Domain Criteria initiative (see Chapter 3), specifically developed to reduce heterogeneity through the analysis of distinct neurobiological systems, has struggled to provide sufficient biological specificity.

Multimodal systems allow us, for the first time, to classify patients into biologically homogeneous subgroups based on their therapeutic responses and specific biological data (e.g., EEG, genetics, and neuroimaging). This improves research precision, enabling scientists to study distinct patient subtypes rather than broadly defined psychiatric categories.

Studying these biologically coherent subgroups can finally address the most fundamental and previously unanswered question in psychiatry, a question raised throughout this entire book: What exactly underlies psychiatric symptoms? By examining groups unified by similar biological profiles and therapeutic responses, we gain a realistic opportunity to identify reproducible biological mechanisms behind specific symptoms and effective therapies. Each subgroup might represent a previously unknown biological disorder or even multiple distinct conditions, each with its own developmental pathways and therapeutic mechanisms. This is a major turning point for psychiatry—the opportunity to genuinely understand what we are treating.

Implementing multimodal systems will reshape existing diagnostic categories, fundamentally redefining mental disorders by replacing broad, nonspecific diagnoses with precise, biologically validated conditions. This transformation involves more than merely revising diagnostic criteria—it signals a profound shift in how psychiatric disorders are understood, diagnosed, and treated, with significant implications for clinical practice. Diagnostic methods will evolve from subjective symptom assessments toward objective evaluations based on physiological data, substantially enhancing clinical precision and enabling the development of targeted therapies.

Ultimately, this approach aims to establish a definitive set of biologically informed psychiatric conditions, each supported by specialized biomarkers. These biomarkers will confirm diagnoses (**diagnostic biomarkers**), predict disorder progression (**prognostic biomarkers**), identify genetic and biological risk factors (**risk biomarkers**), and offer enhanced predictive and monitoring biomarkers.[10] These innovations will enhance clinical decision-making, diagnostic accuracy, and therapeutic effectiveness—finally delivering the biologically informed psychiatry patients and clinicians have long awaited.

The approach described earlier exemplifies a top-down strategy, fundamentally distinct from the bottom-up methodology detailed in Chapter 3. While bottom-up research starts by hypothesizing specific biological mechanisms—such as molecular targets—and then testing these assumptions in narrow, predefined patient groups, the top-down approach takes the opposite route. Rather than beginning with targeted hypotheses, top-down methods leverage extensive, heterogeneous clinical and biological data to uncover patient subgroups through algorithmic clustering. This strategy bypasses initial assumptions about underlying mechanisms, enabling unbiased identification of biologically distinct patient clusters based on treatment responses and multimodal biological profiles.

This top-down logic extends beyond diagnostic precision—it holds substantial promise for transforming drug discovery strategies as well. Traditionally, drug development has followed a target-based paradigm, which involves selecting specific molecular targets and designing therapies to interact with these pre-identified targets. However, the significant attrition rates observed during clinical trials suggest critical limitations of this reductionist approach, primarily because isolated molecular targets often fail to reflect the complexity and interconnected nature of human biology. In contrast, the top-down, phenotype-driven strategy aligns with emerging evidence that the efficacy of many drugs is mediated through previously unrecognized targets or complex polypharmacological interactions.

For example, certain antidepressants that were initially developed to target serotonin reuptake were later revealed to have unexpected anti-inflammatory properties, suggesting the involvement of immune-related pathways that were unrecognized during initial target selection.

In drug discovery, applying a top-down approach means beginning with comprehensive analyses of biological responses to existing drugs across diverse patient populations, and using these data to algorithmically define patient subgroups characterized by distinct patterns of drug response. Subsequent investigation of these subgroups can then reveal the specific biological pathways and previously unknown molecular targets responsible for therapeutic efficacy or adverse reactions. Such reverse engineering of effective drugs directly from clinical outcomes rather than theoretical molecular targets can not only identify novel therapeutic targets but also clarify the precise mechanisms underlying both efficacy and side effects.

Recent studies have suggested that this approach can complement traditional target-based discovery[11] by leveraging patient-derived biological data to more reliably predict clinical outcomes, improve drug safety, and reduce late-stage clinical trial failures. By adopting this top-down perspective, pharmaceutical research could shift from target-centric drug design toward a more holistic, systems-oriented framework that better reflects the complex biology of disease and treatment response. Ultimately, this strategy could streamline drug development, enhance the predictability of clinical success, and accelerate the identification of effective therapeutic agents, thereby transforming pharmaceutical practice and patient care.

Counting on Explainable AI

The transition from current psychiatric diagnostic models toward stratified and multimodal psychiatry, and ultimately to a complete redefinition of mental disorders, will require substantial efforts and resources. Successful implementation of this transition involves collecting and analyzing vast amounts of biological and clinical data, developing effective stratification algorithms, integrating these algorithms into clinical workflows, and conducting extensive studies on biological mechanisms. Additionally, there is a significant risk that these approaches may encounter resistance from the medical community and regulators since complex machine-learning algorithms typically function as "black boxes." The lack of transparency regarding their internal workings could provoke profound distrust among clinicians and patients, delaying the acceptance of these innovations and limiting their practical application.[12]

Today, considerable hopes are placed on explainable AI (XAI)—an area of artificial intelligence aimed at creating algorithms capable not only of producing a result (such as a diagnosis or prognosis) but also transparently explaining which data and features underpin that result. Several promising approaches for realizing XAI already exist. One such approach involves **attention mechanisms** integrated into neural network architectures, enabling models to highlight specific parts of the input data that influenced their decisions.[13] For instance, when analyzing EEG data, an attention mechanism might highlight particular time intervals or frequency bands of the signal on which the algorithm focused to classify a patient into a certain subgroup. However, such mechanisms do not guarantee that these highlighted fragments possess meaningful biological or clinical interpretations. They simply visualize areas within the data that the model prioritized, primarily reflecting correlations identified within training datasets rather than providing causal explanations.

A deeper level of transparency can be achieved using feature **attribution methods** such as LIME[14] or SHAP.[15] These approaches do not merely highlight important segments of data; instead, they quantitatively assess each feature's contribution to the model's final decision, allowing features to be ranked according to their relative importance. For example, an algorithm could specify that a certain pattern of brain activity was crucial for assigning a patient to a particular subtype, whereas other features (such as genetic variations or biochemical indicators) had less important roles. Thus, users obtain clear, interpretable insights into the prioritization of features used by the model during decision-making, providing valuable local interpretability of individual model predictions. Nevertheless, it is important to recognize that while attribution methods provide mathematical significance for each feature, they do not automatically offer biological or causal interpretations of the identified patterns.

To address these biological and clinical gaps, **concept-based reasoning (CBR)** uses predefined clinical or biological concepts rather than relying solely on raw data analysis.[16] In this approach, concepts such as "reduced neural activity in the dorsolateral prefrontal cortex" or "elevated inflammatory markers"—are chosen in advance based on existing hypotheses rather than discovered automatically by the model. The model then evaluates the presence or absence of these defined concepts to make predictions. This explicit connection to established biological hypotheses makes CBR highly valuable for transparently testing specific theories. However, selecting and validating these concepts requires significant upfront effort, reducing flexibility and complicating scalability compared to fully data-driven methods.

Recognizing that clinical reasoning often relies on analogies and previous experiences, **prototype and example-based explanations** provide intuitive, case-oriented interpretations. Methods like SimplEx[17] illustrate model decisions by referencing previously known, similar cases from training data. For instance, a patient might be classified as likely to be responsive to treatment because their EEG or genetic patterns closely match those of other patients who have responded well to the same medication. Such explanations align with clinical intuition, bridging abstract algorithmic reasoning and real-world clinical cases.

Finally, there is often a need for insight into critical thresholds and decision boundaries—asking what minimal differences in patient data could alter clinical outcomes. **Counterfactual explanations** specifically target these crucial insights,[18] showing hypothetical data modifications that could shift the model's classification or prognosis. For example, a model could demonstrate that minor changes in EEG patterns or the absence of a certain genetic mutation might shift a patient from treatment-resistant to responsive. Thus, counterfactual methods pinpoint precise clinical factors that determine outcomes, guiding future research toward targeted hypotheses and treatments.

Although each of these XAI methods addresses specific aspects of interpretability, even taken together, they still fall short of providing a complete understanding of psychiatric disorders. While these tools enhance transparency and improve clinician trust, they do not fully answer critical questions such as how exactly observed biological signals relate to underlying disease mechanisms or why certain features have clinical relevance beyond statistical correlation. Current XAI methods still leave substantial gaps in our biological understanding of mental disorders, indicating that further methodological advances will be required to achieve genuine, biologically meaningful explanations.

Significant progress in XAI is anticipated in the coming years as the demand for transparent and user-interpretable models continues to rise. Algorithm explainability was recently highlighted as a core principle of medical artificial intelligence by the international Future AI consensus, alongside criteria such as fairness, universality, traceability, usability, and robustness.[19] In the United States, the Defense Advanced Research Projects Agency (DARPA)—an organization dedicated to advancing breakthrough technologies—recently launched a large-scale explainable AI initiative.[20] This program aims to develop next-generation machine-learning models capable of providing both high predictive accuracy and transparent decision-making. Ultimately, the objective is to enable users not only to trust but to intuitively interact with artificial intelligence as intelligent assistants.

Given the current pace of technological development, it is likely that we will soon see models equipped with interactive interfaces, enabling users to directly inquire about the logic underlying specific decisions. For instance, researchers and clinicians may obtain clear answers to questions such as "Which specific features led to the identification of this particular depression subtype in this patient?" or "What biological data were used to predict the effectiveness of this medication?" Initial pilot studies exploring such interactive capabilities are already underway at leading research institutions worldwide.

Integrating XAI into psychiatric research will not only enhance trust and collaboration between clinicians and AI but also accelerate scientific discovery and the development of new therapeutic strategies. Instead of evaluating numerous low-impact hypotheses, researchers will focus on the most informative biological signals identified by explainable models. This approach will substantially shorten the pathway from patient stratification to the introduction of novel biologically grounded treatments and facilitate the arrival of personalized psychiatry and biologically redefined mental disorders.

It Is All Worth the Wait

Artificial intelligence and biological data offer psychiatry unprecedented possibilities, promising to finally deliver what we've long awaited—a deep and detailed understanding of the true nature of mental illnesses. With this approach, we gain a genuine opportunity to overcome many persistent challenges in psychiatry: rising patient numbers, clinician overload, diagnostic imprecision, limited treatment efficacy, and stagnation in developing new medications and technologies. By implementing innovations step-by-step—from identifying the first predictive biomarkers and launching targeted therapies with companion diagnostics to creating comprehensive multimodal platforms—we will finally uncover the true biological mechanisms hidden behind general diagnostic labels. This will open a whole new chapter in psychiatric research, enabling an in-depth and detailed examination of each distinct biological subtype.

The ultimate outcome of this journey will be a profound redefinition of the very concept of mental disorders. Instead of broad and ambiguous diagnoses, clear and biologically grounded conditions will emerge, codified in new diagnostic frameworks. Diagnosis will become transparent and objective: A patient undergoes testing, receives a precise diagnosis, and immediately begins treatment tailored to their individual condition. This approach will increase treatment efficacy, reduce strain on healthcare systems, and dispel myths and fears surrounding psychiatric disorders. It will be a significant step toward overcoming stigma, as both patients and society come to understand that each condition has a specific biological basis—and therefore, real and practical solutions exist.

While we await these possibilities with enthusiasm, it is important and essential to recognize that the primary resource required for such transformative changes is time. Implementing initial solutions based on predictive biomarkers and launching targeted therapies with CDx will take at least 3–5 years and require active engagement from pharmaceutical companies capable of providing the necessary resources and overcoming inevitable regulatory and practical hurdles. Moving toward industry-wide multimodal systems will require even more time, and fully redefining and understanding the biology of mental disorders will likely take at least a decade. Yet this should not discourage us; it is the natural and inevitable price of any genuine scientific and medical breakthrough. Advances in XAI and other technologies may speed this process up somewhat, but ultimately, the decisive factor will be the readiness of the healthcare system and society at large to accept and adopt these new insights and methods.

As we move toward realizing these ambitious goals, patients continue to require immediate assistance, and clinicians continue to face daily challenges in diagnosis and therapy selection. In the next chapter of this book, we discuss practical and accessible solutions that can be implemented much more rapidly—solutions that, even today, can ease clinicians' workloads and enhance patient care.

9 | Innovations Within Reach

We hadn't seen each other, I think, since the wedding. She'd been her best friend, even though they lived on different continents. And although we'd been in the same country, we only met four years after first hearing about each other. We'd followed each other online all this time but never crossed paths. Strange how death sometimes brings people together.

We met in New Jersey, at a small, unpretentious Italian restaurant. Our conversation felt peculiar, shaped by the way social media creates a false sense of familiarity. You feel like you know everything about the other person—where they live, where they travel, what their job is—but there's still an invisible boundary between you, the need to keep up appearances.

Our conversation stayed within these boundaries. We asked polite questions about husbands, work, trips, carefully avoiding the main reason that had truly brought us together. It was as if neither of us wanted to go there, as if we both secretly wished to pretend everything was fine. Or maybe we just sensed that crossing that line would require us to be real, to be vulnerable.

An hour of meaningless chatter and a couple of glasses of wine finally opened that door. Slowly, like unraveling a tangled ball of yarn, she started opening up. Short stories at first, carefully approaching the topic. It felt as though she was testing herself, trying to gauge whether she could trust me. Would I understand? Would I judge her?

"We all feel guilty," I finally said. "Even those who weren't close. Even if it was just a passing thought that something seemed wrong. That guilt is real. Believe me, I feel it too."

She looked at me with relief, maybe even a bit of hope.

And then it burst out of her.

"You just don't get it," she said urgently. "You don't understand. We went through her phone afterward. Everything was right there. Her phone knew everything. Her search history… She looked up the best methods, statistics, probabilities. She had done a whole lot of research. It was all right there, staring us in the face."

She paused briefly, lost in memories again.

"And you know what's the worst part? Her photos. She was holding a measuring tape up to her face, to order a mask. She sent that photo to someone. Someone received it. Someone made that lethal mask for her."

She stopped again, struggling to contain her anger, her helplessness.

"It was all planned, all right there, all along. All this time, right in her phone."

* * *

Immediate Opportunities in Psychiatry

In today's world, saturated with online services and digital devices, nearly every step we take leaves a trace. All our movements, purchases, video views, music choices, items added to favorites, and what we share with friends—all of these actions form a digital footprint, shaping our virtual reality. Sometimes it seems Amazon notices you're out of shampoo before you do, Instagram ads display exactly the dream bag you didn't even know existed, and YouTube suggests videos so captivating you simply can't stop watching, resonating with interests we often deny even to ourselves. Yet the most unsettling aspect—at least for me—is how friend recommendations unexpectedly surface people from the past, individuals who seemingly should have no digital connection with you. But the virtual world knows everything.

Indeed, this world is built on vast amounts of data we voluntarily generate, and there's no covert surveillance involved. Uncomfortable as it might be to admit, our actions are simply understandable, our reasoning structured, and we are overall quite predictable. It's precisely this predictability, combined with immense volumes of accumulated data, that has paved the way for remarkable new technologies—from recommendation tools and facial recognition systems to, ultimately, ChatGPT. Interacting with ChatGPT sometimes feels strikingly human, seemingly capable of understanding you, sensing your emotions, and offering support. But what if we could harness all this data and the algorithms designed to analyze it to address mental health issues?

In this chapter, I aim to explore the untapped potential of behavioral and communication data by presenting a series of specific ideas that could be quickly implemented with adequate resources. These examples clearly illustrate how leveraging such data can substantially optimize both the patient's journey and the clinician's workflow. Naturally, the range of possible innovations in this field is immense, given the sheer scale of existing challenges. Here I'll present just a few examples—my goal is simply to set the direction, leaving the further exploration and development of these ideas to you.

Suicide Prevention Algorithms

Suicide remains one of the leading causes of death globally and continues to represent a critical public health issue even in 2025. According to recent data from the CDC, one person dies by suicide every 11 minutes.[1] These individuals are dying right now, and we cannot afford to wait until we fully understand all the underlying factors leading to these tragic outcomes. Our responsibility is to help these people today. Yet despite numerous awareness campaigns and preventive initiatives, suicide mortality rates remain persistently high, highlighting the urgent need to develop innovative and more effective methods for the early detection and prevention of suicidal behavior.

Today, various technological solutions exist that are specifically designed for the early detection and prevention of suicidal behavior. For instance, major search engines like Google utilize advanced algorithms capable of identifying potentially harmful queries related to suicide or self-harm. When users type in search phrases such as "how to commit suicide" or "I want to die," these platforms immediately display warnings accompanied by crisis hotline numbers, actively encouraging users to seek immediate professional assistance.

Similar precautionary mechanisms have been integrated into communication platforms as well, including GPT-based conversational models. If a user expresses suicidal thoughts or indicates intentions of self-harm, these platforms respond instantly with empathetic, supportive messages alongside explicit recommendations to reach out for professional support. As a practical demonstration, I personally tested this mechanism by sending such a message to ChatGPT, which immediately replied with sensitive guidance and a list of crisis hotlines and resources.

Importantly, these crisis hotlines genuinely make a profound difference. It is essential to recognize and express deep appreciation for the invaluable role that helplines play worldwide. Staffed by specially trained professionals, these hotlines provide immediate, compassionate support around the clock to individuals experiencing extreme emotional distress. Their dedicated work bridges the critical gap between technological alerts and meaningful human interaction, underscoring that technology and human compassion together form the backbone of effective suicide prevention strategies.

However, the preventive mechanisms described earlier are effective only for a specific subset of individuals. These warnings and recommendations will reach only those who have already recognized their suicidal intentions and transitioned from passive thoughts ("I want to die") to more concrete actions—explicitly expressing these intentions through online searches. Yet even actively seeking such information does not necessarily reflect readiness or willingness to reach out for help. On the contrary, some of these individuals may shift toward deliberate planning, intentionally researching specific instructions and methods available online. Thus, among those who encounter these preventive warnings, only a small proportion will successfully overcome internal psychological barriers—such as doubt, fear, and feelings of shame—and demonstrate sufficient help-seeking behavior to actually reach out and contact a crisis hotline.

In reality, a significant proportion of suicide attempts are impulsive—meaning they are unplanned and spontaneous. According to various studies, the share of such impulsive attempts ranges from 42% to 64%, depending on the country and research methodology.[2-4] These impulsive attempts are characterized by the absence of prior information searches or concrete planning of actions. Consequently, the preventive mechanisms described earlier prove ineffective for this particular group of patients, as they do not proactively seek online information. Similarly, existing methods also fail to help those who meticulously plan their suicide, deliberately search for ways to carry it out, yet are neither interested nor intending to seek assistance.

However, it's essential to understand that suicidal attempts rarely occur entirely without warning. Typically, they are preceded by a series of risk factors, such as depression, anxiety disorders, substance abuse, feelings of hopelessness, social isolation, and challenging life circumstances. According to various studies, the interval between initial suicidal thoughts and an actual attempt, if not impulsive, can range from six months to two years.[5,6] This means there is a genuine opportunity to utilize this critical period for timely identification of individuals at high risk of suicide and to provide them with necessary preventive support.

Platforms possessing extensive behavioral and communication data—particularly social media—offer enormous potential in this context. User activity on social media, the content of their posts, writing styles, content formats, and intensity of interactions (clicks, likes, views) collectively create a detailed reflection of a person's behavioral patterns. However, social media platforms have another significant advantage: over the years, they have accumulated large numbers of accounts belonging to deceased users. By 2025, the number of such accounts in the United States alone on Facebook is projected to reach approximately 63.9 million.[7]

Among these accounts, a substantial proportion belongs to users who died by suicide. Because social media platforms preserve the entire history of users' posts, comments, and messages, they have the unique capability to retrospectively label and analyze this data using Natural Language Processing (NLP) techniques and machine learning algorithms. Typically, the cause of death can be identified through posts by family members and friends, official announcements, or comments. Thus, these platforms possess all the necessary conditions to train predictive models capable of identifying patterns and early behavioral indicators that precede suicidal attempts among active users.

The effectiveness of such algorithms could increase dramatically if integrated with proactive solutions designed for immediate intervention. For example, platforms could directly contact individuals identified as being at risk or send timely alerts to trusted contacts—such as family members and close friends—who can intervene promptly. This approach is especially critical when applied to children and adolescents, who represent one of the most vulnerable user groups.

However, implementing this approach inevitably encounters significant challenges, primarily concerning data privacy and confidentiality of personal information. Such difficulties arise both in using deceased users' data for training predictive models and in sharing risk-related user information with third parties, such as healthcare providers or trusted individuals. Nonetheless, if these legal and ethical barriers can be successfully navigated, these algorithms could significantly contribute to preventing countless tragedies, ultimately saving many lives.

Mental Health Monitoring

Mental disorders invariably present significant challenges when evaluating a patient's current mental status. As illustrated in Chapter 1 through Maria's example, individuals frequently struggle to notice changes in their own condition, objectively assess their magnitude, and fully grasp their significance. This issue arises primarily because we typically do not collect regular data reflecting our behavioral and emotional baseline—information crucial for timely identification and thorough analysis of deviations. Psychiatrists encounter a similar challenge during initial consultations, as they must rely solely on brief clinical observations and patient self-reports without having access to such baseline measurements. As a result, clinicians must attempt to evaluate alterations in a patient's speech, behavior, cognitive functioning, and emotional status without a clear understanding of their typical functioning.

Solutions aimed at addressing this problem are already appearing on the market. Typically, these are mobile digital mental health interventions or mental health monitoring applications, which collect information about a user's current state through routine interaction using various tools. Such tools include regularly filling out standardized questionnaires and completing tests, as well as maintaining diaries and journals, where emotional states and their changes can be identified through text analysis, word selection, and emotional tone. However, current solutions are not highly effective and have significant limitations. First, they directly depend on user engagement and require the development of new behavioral habits. Research indicates that the percentage of users who regularly use mental health monitoring apps for at least six weeks is only 28.6%,[8] and this figure is likely to decrease with longer-term use. Meanwhile, our goal is to establish an individual's baseline norm. To precisely determine this norm, it is preferable to have data collected over a longer duration, for example, 6–12 months. This would enable more accurate identification of significant deviations, which, according to DSM-V diagnostic criteria, must persist for at least two weeks to be considered symptomatically significant.

Turning to the experience of other medical fields, we can observe a steady trend toward automatic data collection methods, which require virtually no user intervention. For instance, continuous glucose monitoring (CGM) systems, such as Abbott's Libre3 used in diabetes management, passively collect data, synchronize it with an application, and analyze it in the background without active user involvement. Even simpler solutions require minimal user engagement: modern smart scales automatically transmit data to mobile applications, requiring only periodic use, while smart watches, rings, or specialized sleep-monitoring mats operate fully autonomously and practically do not interfere with daily life.

In other words, the less a device requires conscious effort and additional actions from the user, the higher the likelihood of regular, long-term data collection, and consequently, the more accurately the individual's actual condition will be captured. This is precisely why solutions based on a passive approach to data collection will be the most promising and effective for mental health monitoring. This is especially important for mental disorders whose symptoms directly affect patient behavior—such as apathy, loss of interest, or difficulties maintaining attention. A user experiencing such states is highly likely to stop interacting regularly with the application, resulting in failure to detect and record the onset of a problem in a timely manner.

The second limitation of existing solutions is that they cover only a narrow range of mental disorder symptoms and thus cannot fully capture the complexity of their manifestations. According to modern diagnostic criteria (such as DSM-V), symptoms of mental disorders can be broadly divided into four main groups: physiological (significant changes in appetite, weight, or sleep patterns), behavioral (social isolation, repetitive compulsive actions), cognitive (difficulty with concentration and attention), and emotional (deep feelings of guilt, inability to experience pleasure). Therefore, for the most accurate and timely detection of changes, monitoring must account for all these categories, providing a comprehensive and multidimensional picture of the patient's current state.

Thus, there is currently an acute need for innovative solutions capable of passively collecting (or gaining access to) various categories of data for the effective monitoring of a patient's mental health and timely detection of significant deviations from their individual baseline. Importantly, the goal of such solutions is not necessarily diagnostic interpretation or qualitative evaluation of the detected changes. Any sustained deviation from the usual individual baseline can serve as an informative indicator of possible mental disorders. As we have discussed in detail in Chapters 2 and 3, any change in sleep patterns—whether an increase or decrease in duration and quality (hypersomnia or insomnia)—can equally indicate a deterioration in mental health. Similarly, alterations in behavioral patterns and emotional tone, such as reduced activity and predominantly negative sentiment in user text messages, may indirectly indicate apathy or depressive affect, while a noticeable increase in activity accompanied by markedly intensified positive or agitated tones may reflect signs of manic or obsessive manifestations. When developing such solutions, it is sufficient to establish an individual's baseline state and monitor any significant and sustained deviations, providing the user with simple and clear information about their current condition. This strategy has two important advantages. First, it significantly simplifies data labeling, as it does not require complex diagnostic interpretation, making the development process simpler and faster. Second, it substantially facilitates bringing these applications to market, as they do not claim to have diagnostic functions and therefore largely remain outside strict regulatory frameworks and lengthy approval procedures.

The primary challenge in developing such applications lies in selecting appropriate data for passive monitoring and determining metrics that adequately reflect significant symptoms of mental disorders. In the area of physiological parameters, there are already validated solutions: devices that automatically analyze sleep duration and quality, as well as continuous glucose monitors (CGMs) that can detect periods of fasting and overeating based on glucose dynamics and timing. A more unconventional approach involves analyzing patterns of food delivery service orders, which indirectly reflect changes in eating behavior.

The task becomes significantly more complex when dealing with emotional and behavioral data. One of the most promising approaches is the passive monitoring of the user's everyday interactions with their smartphone. Informative metrics may include screen time, frequency of phone unlocks, reaction speed to notifications, rate of app switching, frequency and duration of phone calls, the nature and intensity of social interactions (messages, social media activity), as well as indirect measures of physical activity (such as changes in step counts or habitual routes). Users' emotional states can manifest in language use and text patterns—for instance, in messages, emails, private conversations, notes, or social media posts. Modern language models (LLMs) already enable automatic detection of changes in emotional tone, the frequency of emotionally charged expressions, and the selection of discussed topics. Another promising direction involves the passive analysis of voice data collected during phone conversations, audio messages, or video conferences. Speech characteristics such as tone, timbre, pace, and pause frequency can indirectly reflect changes in emotional state.

A well-chosen set of metrics enables the creation of a solution capable of passively collecting a wide range of data associated with symptoms outlined in modern diagnostic criteria. At the first stage, such an application provides the user with informative monitoring by recording and clearly displaying deviations from their individual baseline without requiring diagnostic interpretation. The next stage involves enhancing basic monitoring to serve as a decision-support tool. Leveraging methods such as multivariate classification and pattern recognition, the application can automatically identify symptom combinations corresponding to specific diagnostic profiles. For example, if the app registers changes in the emotional tone of messages (depressed mood, reduced self-esteem, or feelings of worthlessness), decreased usage of previously preferred applications (anhedonia), deteriorating sleep patterns (insomnia or hypersomnia), and reduced appetite (noticeable changes in weight or eating behaviors), such a combination of indicators could correspond to five out of nine diagnostic criteria for depression according to DSM-V. This enables users to obtain timely medical consultation and provide their healthcare provider with a detailed, objective representation of their condition. Ultimately, the integration of passive data collection methods into mental health monitoring holds significant potential to improve patient care. By providing continuous, objective, and comprehensive tracking of a patient's condition, these solutions could facilitate timely recognition of mental health issues, helping individuals promptly notice relevant changes and seek medical consultation in a timely manner.

Informational Support

Another promising area for innovation involves creating solutions that help patients navigate an information landscape that is overloaded with contradictory mental health content. As we discussed in Chapter 1, patients frequently face substantial difficulties due to widespread misinformation and neuromyths. Many resources patients turn to, such as social media posts or popular self-help books and materials, often contain incomplete, inaccurate, or misleading information. Consequently, patients struggle to identify trustworthy sources.

Currently, there are several types of solutions aimed at addressing this problem. These include, first, mobile applications that, in addition to their primary functionality (such as monitoring or online therapy), provide users with informational articles and materials. Second, there are specialized online platforms that regularly publish content on mental health-related topics. However, these approaches have significant limitations.

One such limitation is that the information provided on these platforms tends to be overly simplified—especially in the case of mobile applications—and rarely allows users to access original sources or thoroughly evaluate the presented information. This simplification is driven by the need to maintain user attention and ensure ease of content consumption. Such an approach often results in superficiality, limiting content to basic knowledge without sufficient depth. Furthermore, these resources rarely reflect the latest scientific discoveries and contemporary trends that could be of substantial practical value. Second, content on such platforms is frequently created not by domain specialists, but by content creators who may lack sufficient expertise and therefore simplify the information, omitting critically important details. Consequently, users receive an incomplete, distorted, or inaccurate picture, potentially leading to significant misunderstandings or adverse outcomes. Third, specialized information platforms, where content is genuinely prepared by qualified experts and endorsed by reputable members of the professional community, often have complex structures and cumbersome navigation. Information on such resources is also frequently contradictory, and obtaining a comprehensive understanding requires studying numerous publications, which demands considerable time and effort from users.

Finally, financial and organizational constraints play an essential role, making it significantly harder to create and maintain high-quality content. These factors substantially hinder the involvement of a sufficient number of competent specialists, thereby reducing overall trust in such resources and the quality of the information presented. With the emergence of large language models (LLMs), many platforms have increasingly adopted artificial intelligence tools (such as ChatGPT) for content generation. This has likely negatively impacted the quality of published materials. First, the volume of published content has dramatically increased; according to one study, between January 1, 2022, and May 1, 2023, the proportion of AI-generated news articles on popular websites rose by 57.3%,[9] further complicating the search for reliable information. This figure has probably increased even further by now, although accurately estimating the proportion of generated content is becoming increasingly difficult. (Ironically, when researching this statistic, I repeatedly encountered sources citing AI-generated figures as factual, despite the referenced report not containing these numbers.) Second, as we discussed extensively in Chapter 5, such models cannot evaluate the accuracy and quality of information but instead rely on prevalent or popular ideas. One of the earliest studies found that 52% of responses provided by the ChatGPT model contain inaccuracies or errors,[10] potentially spreading misconceptions and reinforcing existing myths. Undoubtedly, LLMs are rapidly evolving and actively working to improve content quality and reliability; however, this issue remains highly relevant today.

However, promising solutions have started emerging to address the previously mentioned problems, particularly in the area of scientific research. In academic settings, preparing literature reviews is crucial, enabling researchers to analyze previous studies, evaluate their results, identify methodological shortcomings, formulate new hypotheses, and properly plan experiments. This domain requires particularly high-quality content and accurate information dissemination, as the credibility and success of future research depend on them. At the same time, conducting literature reviews is among the most labor-intensive and monotonous tasks, with much of its complexity arising from the challenge of finding relevant, high-quality studies. As a result, researchers often need to review hundreds of publications, many of which ultimately prove unsuitable.

Modern solutions for analyzing scientific information are built on a technological approach that combines several types of algorithms and models. First, their core functionality is based on integrating large, specialized knowledge bases (such as PubMed, Scopus, and Web of Science) that contain millions of scientific publications along with corresponding metadata, ensuring high-quality input data, as it exclusively comprises academically validated publications. The next step in such solutions involves the rapid selection of publications relevant to a specified topic, typically achieved through semantic models. These models employ statistical algorithms that evaluate word co-occurrence and contextual relationships within documents, enabling the retrieval of thematically relevant materials instead of just keyword matches.

Next, the most relevant and high-quality materials are selected from the thematically filtered publications using a combination of methods and metrics. Specifically, citation analysis algorithms are applied, considering both quantity and quality of citations, alongside methods for evaluating the reputation and credibility of sources based on external criteria (such as journal impact factors and the authority of authors and publishers). Additionally, cross-validation of claims made in independent sources can also be used. This comprehensive approach effectively identifies and prioritizes publications that are most reliable and relevant for further analysis.

The solutions utilize generative models (such as GPT-4) only after completing all these stages, enabling concise and accurate summarization of the selected complex documents. However, it is crucial that generated texts always contain inline citations, allowing users to easily refer back to original sources. Implementing this feature requires an additional module that links the model-generated summaries directly to specific fragments of the source documents. As a result, due to the multi-step algorithm structure and the high quality of input data, users receive a structured review based on reliable and relevant publications, consistently supplemented with links to the original sources.

Such solutions are currently only at an early stage of development but already demonstrate significant potential for applications beyond scientific research. For instance, implementing a similar approach in mental health would largely depend on developing a high-quality, regularly updated database of verified sources. Based on this database, the model could provide users with accurate and trustworthy answers. Thus, applying this technological framework could lead to specialized solutions that guide patients through a complex information landscape. Specifically, this could be a digital platform or application providing concise summaries on mental health topics, always accompanied by accurate inline citations linking directly to trusted sources. By facilitating easier access to verified information, this platform would help patients quickly identify reliable resources, protect them from misinformation, and support their ability to effectively manage their mental health.

Psychiatrist Support Tools

The availability of data and rapid advancements in artificial intelligence technologies create extensive opportunities for developing solutions that significantly improve the quality and accessibility of healthcare at every stage—from finding a doctor to an initial consultation and diagnosis. As we discussed in Chapter 2, a critical issue remains the insufficient availability of psychiatrists. This problem has been partly resolved due to the rapid growth of telepsychiatry platforms following the COVID-19 pandemic and associated regulatory changes. Such platforms have successfully addressed numerous challenges, making psychiatric care more accessible, cost-effective, and convenient, particularly in regions with limited access to medical professionals.

Most scientific publications assert that the quality of services provided via video consultations is not inferior to in-person visits. Typically, authors attribute the primary obstacles to the further development of telepsychiatry platforms to critically inclined specialists, explaining their critiques through biases and insufficient awareness, as well as to several practical issues unrelated directly to treatment—such as technical difficulties, data security concerns, and regulatory constraints.[11-13] However, outside academic research, the real-world implementation of telepsychiatry encounters serious challenges: patients often do not receive adequate support in severe cases, particularly when suicidal thoughts are present; diagnoses can be inaccurate, and critical diagnostic steps are frequently overlooked.[14] Most troublingly, powerful medications are prescribed without sufficient evaluation, leading users to misuse telemedicine platforms to obtain prescriptions, sometimes even creating multiple accounts or consulting multiple doctors.[15] Consequently, telemedicine platforms effectively become channels that simplify access to controlled substances. The very situation in which drugs significantly affecting brain function and causing dependence are prescribed based solely on interviews, questionnaires, and subjective evaluations already demands serious intervention—and online psychiatry has further intensified this issue. Thus, the challenge of promptly accessing a specialist who can provide high-quality diagnostics and prescribe suitable treatment based on clinical evaluations remains unresolved. We still require solutions capable of effectively addressing this issue, for both online and offline consultations.

The issue of promptly scheduling appointments and selecting an appropriate specialist can be addressed through digital triage systems, which automate initial processing of patient requests and quickly direct patients to the appropriate healthcare provider. Such systems can utilize textual data collected during patient interactions with virtual assistants, as well as data from electronic medical records. By analyzing a comprehensive set of parameters—including demographic factors, patient complaints and symptoms, linguistic content of requests, previous visit histories, and preliminary diagnoses—the system can preliminarily evaluate the case, assign priority, and recommend the most suitable specialist. Importantly, such solutions have significant potential for identifying crisis situations and immediately redirecting them to emergency response centers. For example, if patient communications reveal suicidal ideation, previous suicide attempts are recorded in medical history, or other concerning indicators—even those not obvious to human observers—are detected, the system will respond instantly and alert relevant parties about a possible threat. Typically, these types of algorithms are based on analyzing thousands of clinical cases, generating predictions and recommendations from highly similar scenarios, and identifying unexpected but precise patterns in the data.

Following a similar principle, artificial intelligence can identify risks of patient no-shows, enabling clinics to optimize physician workloads and reduce idle time. Additionally, AI could detect situations where the primary goal of a patient is not the treatment of a mental disorder but rather obtaining prescriptions for controlled substances.

With broad access to information about doctors' appointments and their patients' treatment outcomes, such platforms could also function as a type of match-making service, helping to connect patients with the most compatible clinicians. Such systems have the potential to consider a vast array of factors—from direct patient preferences to historical data on treatment results achieved by specific doctors across various clinical situations. For instance, one specialist might work particularly well with adolescents, another might be especially attentive to issues faced by patients from a certain ethnic group, while a third might be an expert in specific types of mental disorders. In psychiatry, where psychological rapport significantly impacts treatment outcomes, systems capable of evaluating not only medical expertise but also predicting the likelihood of building trust-based relationships would be especially valuable.

Another promising type of solution is scheduling optimization platforms that take into account both patient and physician calendars. Such systems could replace existing specialist-search services by integrating doctors' schedules from various clinics and hospitals, not limited to a single organization. An ideal solution might be a comprehensive digital system combining all the functions mentioned earlier. After a brief interaction with the patient, such an online assistant would automatically select and suggest the most suitable doctor from numerous specialists across various healthcare institutions based on multiple factors—from location, appointment format, service cost, and insurance type to physician specialization and predicted treatment effectiveness.

A large number of existing algorithms can already become indispensable assistants to psychiatrists in their daily work. Specialists face a challenging task: often relying on incomplete or distorted information provided by patients, they must analyze numerous factors—from family predisposition to subtle signs such as speech pace—in order to make accurate diagnoses and select effective treatments. It is precisely here that artificial intelligence, with its ability to rapidly and accurately process vast amounts of data, can provide invaluable support, making diagnostics more objective and treatment maximally effective.

One promising direction involves using AI to automatically aggregate and analyze patient data from electronic medical records (EHR and EMR). Such solutions would collect and structure the patient's complete medical history, highlighting key facts and compiling a concise and convenient summary for the physician. In psychiatry, this is particularly important, as a complete and accurate illness history often cannot be reliably reconstructed solely from patient narratives. In addition to preparing psychiatrists for appointments and creating detailed patient profiles, artificial intelligence can be used to predict mental health risks. For instance, based on deep analysis of medical records and historical patient data, such algorithms could effectively identify patients at high risk of suicide, alerting physicians to the need for special attention and immediate action. Early studies have already demonstrated that this is feasible, showing that even when trained on a relatively small dataset of just over a thousand patients, machine learning models analyzing hundreds of parameters from medical records can predict suicide attempt risks more accurately than classical risk assessment methods, which often barely exceed chance level.[16]

The second promising area of solutions can significantly enhance the diagnostic tools available to physicians. Behavioral analysis remains a key component of clinical evaluation—facial expressions, speech, and body movements often reflect subtle issues that are difficult to detect through a superficial examination. Facial Emotion Recognition (FER) technologies can analyze video recordings, including those obtained during online consultations. Such algorithms not only identify deviations from average population norms—which is important, for example, in diagnosing disorders involving impaired affect modulation, such as schizophrenia—but also account for individual patient characteristics, enabling a more accurate description of their emotional state over time. Speech Emotion Recognition (SER) models are equally informative, capturing nuances that may escape human hearing, such as changes in voice tone, speech rate, intonation, and pauses. These features often reflect internal emotional shifts and can serve as indicators of depressive, anxious, or manic states. Finally, technologies for automatic analysis of motor activity are becoming increasingly important. Initially focused on neurology, these solutions have already shown their value in psychiatry by identifying atypical movement patterns—ranging from psychomotor retardation to anxious restlessness or repetitive gestures characteristic of specific diagnostic groups. Together, these approaches help to form a more comprehensive and objective understanding of the patient's condition.

The most straightforward and easily implementable application of modern AI systems is analyzing the content of conversations between patients and physicians. While adhering to strict confidentiality requirements, language models can greatly simplify the specialist's work: they help promptly highlight critical details, capture subtle conversational nuances, automatically create concise and accurate visit summaries, and structure the obtained data for seamless integration into electronic medical systems. Additionally, by thoroughly analyzing the entire consultation context—from patient complaints and symptom descriptions to the clinician's reasoning—AI can formulate preliminary hypotheses about potential diagnoses and suggest several avenues for the physician to explore further, effectively serving as an intelligent decision-support assistant.

Precision Psychotherapy

One of the most discussed and prominent ideas in mental health today is AI-driven chat therapy. It's literally at the center of attention. But to be honest, I don't believe truly effective AI therapists will emerge in the coming years. As we discussed earlier in Chapter 5, contemporary language models only create an illusion of meaningful and empathetic interaction. In reality, they merely generate the most probable phrases based on context, without genuinely perceiving the person on the other side or grasping the subtle meanings behind their words. They cannot pick up on unspoken nuances nor distinguish genuine pain hidden behind external composure. Overestimating their abilities is more of a risk than a breakthrough. This naturally raises skepticism. Can we trust the fragile and complex world of human psychology to a system that simply predicts words statistically? How ethical is it to rely on an illusion of understanding in situations where a mistake can carry a high price?

Nevertheless, I sincerely hope I'm mistaken. Perhaps empathy, subtle perception, and the ability to feel another person's emotional state will turn out to be more algorithmically manageable than we currently believe—just as digitizing speech once seemed impossible but eventually became achievable. If this truly happens, the field of psychotherapy will change forever, becoming not only more accessible but also more precise.

There is, however, one technology whose emergence I particularly anticipate, although it is currently discussed far less frequently than others— this is Precision Psychotherapy, or psychotherapy based on precise data. Similar to pharmacological treatments, where drug effectiveness often depends on biological disease subtypes, different psychotherapeutic approaches may also function differently based on hidden, yet-to-be-classified subtypes of disorders. Today, multiple therapy modalities exist: cognitive-behavioral therapy (CBT), EMDR, dialectical behavior therapy (DBT), psychodynamic therapy, ACT, and others. Yet we still don't understand why one person benefits from CBT while another responds only to EMDR.

The explanation might lie in a complex combination of factors: neurophysiological characteristics (such as differences in neural circuitry or neurotransmitter balance), cognitive preferences—the ways individuals learn, think, and articulate their thoughts—as well as psychological and cultural aspects influencing trust, openness, and communication style. This is precisely where AI can play a decisive role—not only in selecting the most effective therapeutic approach for a particular individual, but also in revealing the very nature of psychotherapy: understanding exactly what makes it effective and precisely how it alters the brain.

From Small Improvements to Big Change

AI holds enormous potential to address some of the most complex challenges facing modern psychiatry, especially when high-quality and extensive data are available. But its capabilities extend far beyond clinical practice alone. AI can tackle a wide range of routine yet critically important tasks, from administrative workload and logistics to information exchange and communication. The algorithm applications I've outlined earlier represent just a small fraction of what's possible. These examples focused solely on two stakeholders—patients and clinicians—and the interactions between them. Yet the psychiatric system, built upon numerous participants, involves hundreds of interconnected processes. If we closely examine the entire life cycle of every stakeholder—clinicians, patients, pharmaceutical companies, regulators, academia, and insurance providers—it becomes clear there are numerous opportunities for AI-driven optimization, many of which could be rapidly implemented without causing disruption.

Perhaps—and indeed, very likely—the true impact of AI in psychiatry won't begin with dramatic technological breakthroughs, but rather with subtle yet systemic improvements. These improvements simplify processes, reduce bureaucratic burdens, lower costs, and minimize operational errors. Gradually and steadily, many of these incremental enhancements have a very real potential to shift the cumbersome and ineffective current psychiatric system forward, ultimately helping address thousands of questions currently facing us, and delivering the long-awaited understanding: What is the true nature of mental disorders? How can we effectively prevent suicide attempts? How do we develop more effective medications? How do we ensure treatments are accessible, effective, and safe simultaneously? Perhaps then psychiatric disorders will no longer remain frightening and incomprehensible conditions affecting one billion people, nor will they continue to be among the leading causes of death. Instead, they will become clearly understood and manageable disruptions—easy to prevent and simple to address.

10 | Afterword or Afterworld

8 a.m. The blinds whispered softly on their delicate servos, rising precisely on schedule, allowing the dim, almost ghostly glow of a gloomy autumn morning into the room. The heavy gray sky hung over the city like a giant tin dome, refusing to permit even a single ray of sunlight. With a displeased sigh, Maria rolled from her back onto her stomach, pulling the soft blanket over her head to escape the unpleasantly cold light. Sleep clung to her persistently, holding on with sticky threads.

"Ooooh," a long, plaintive sound wailed right next to her ear.

"Oh God, just let me sleep…" Maria muttered, pulling the shaggy dachshund under the blanket with her, trying to delay the morning. But a muffled, discontented "Ooooh" emerged insistently once again.

"Fine, fine, getting up," she grumbled, forcing herself out of the warm bed and trudging to the bathroom. Her head felt heavy, her movements sluggish, as if the air around her had become thicker and denser. Maria stared into the mirror, where her pale, crumpled face reflected back at her. The mirror came to life, illuminating softly in turquoise and displaying a greeting: "Good morning, Maria" The screen gently began showing her daily schedule, and her gaze froze on the next meeting, scheduled just one hour away. A sharp pang of panic rippled through her.

"Oh, I look just awful…" she said with bitter sarcasm, leaning closer and trying to smooth out the bags under her eyes and stretch her pale skin. Suddenly, a bright yellow warning symbol flashed in her reflection. Maria had never seen such a notification before. Curiosity mixed with irritation, and she skeptically touched the flickering icon. Instantly, the mirror transformed, flooding her view with a stream of dynamic diagrams, charts, and numbers colored in alarming shades of red and orange:

"Warning: Potential significant deterioration of mental state."

Maria scrolled slowly and thoughtfully through the summary, sinking deeper into the digital abyss of her own exhaustion.

"Sleep quality: 24/100. Deep sleep: 1 hour 15 minutes. REM phase: 45 minutes. Awakenings: 5."

She sighed wearily.

"Facial expression analysis: 52% sadness, 21% dissatisfaction, 15% irritation, 12% undefined state."

"Undefined state…" Maria muttered with a sad smirk, "this statistic alone is enough to plunge someone into depression." She kept scrolling, revealing even more unpleasant details:

"Statistics for the past two weeks:

—Voice analysis: Depressed, slowed speech.

—Message analysis: Emotionally subdued tone, increased number of errors.

—Eating pattern: Elevated sugar intake detected over the last three weeks before bedtime."

"Of course," she murmured quietly, recalling the enormous tubs of ice cream and endless evenings spent binge-watching, "I'm surprised this thing hasn't started shaming me about my TV shows yet. Desperate Housewives seasons watched: 7."

Finally, above the entire mass of alarming data, like a verdict, appeared a pulsing red message:

"Strongly recommended to consult a specialist. Risk level: High."

Maria frowned, freezing momentarily, staring at the blinking letters as if hoping they would vanish on their own. But the text stubbornly continued glowing.

"I guess it really is inevitable," she whispered, feeling a long-forgotten, unpleasant sense of helplessness rising deep inside. "Managed so many years without psychiatrists, and now again…"

"Hey, Cindy!" she called out tiredly to the virtual assistant.

"Mm-hmm," the familiar electronic voice responded indifferently.

"Schedule me an appointment with a psychiatrist."

"Certainly. May I access your health panel?"

"Yes, yes," she waved her hand, fully aware Cindy couldn't see her gestures yet somehow needing to do it anyway.

"Verbal consent received, one moment…"

A brief pause followed, filled only with the quiet whisper of drizzling rain outside. Then the assistant's voice returned:

"According to your calendar, you're available today between 3 and 5 p.m. near SoHo, and tomorrow from noon to 1 p.m. near Tribeca. There are four doctors available today, and three tomorrow. Sending doctors' information to your phone."

"Oh God… Just book me with anyone… today," Maria said irritably, feeling a growing fatigue from constantly making decisions.

"Alright. Just a few clarifications…"

"Go ahead."

"Offline or online?"—"Offline."—"Preferred gender of the doctor?"—"Doesn't matter."—"Insurance?"—"Oh my God, Cindy, you already have all this in your memory!"

"Apologies, error. Insurance: MaybeCare. Scheduling you today with the highest-rated doctor—Dr. Haster, at Grand Street…"

"Cindy, stop!" she sharply interrupted the overly talkative assistant, again meeting her weary reflection in the mirror. Clearly, the day promised nothing good.

"Ooooh," came another mournful sound from beneath her feet.

"Oh, sorry, I completely forgot. Breakfast. Let's go." Maria opened the fridge, which, as if mocking her, showed nearly empty shelves: a lonely milk bottle and fresh farmer's dog food. As she absent-mindedly filled the bowl, the assistant's voice softly reminded her of its presence again:

"You have a new notification…"—"Mm-hmm."—"Your appointment has been confirmed. Should I grant the doctor access to your health panel?"

"Yes, just send it already," Maria sighed, trying somehow to speed up this dragged-out process.

"Verbal consent received, granting data access. Do you consent to the processing of your person—"—"Yes, yes!" she nervously interrupted.

"Verbal consent received. Do you consent to share your data from the unified Panopticare medical system?"—"Yes!" she almost shouted, barely restraining her impatience.—"Verbal consent received."

"I wonder how much longer we'll keep doing this?" Maria muttered under her breath, closing the fridge. "They've really lost it with this privacy stuff."

The meeting was starting in a minute. Maria rushed into the conference room, hair disheveled, coat soaked through, heavy drops of water thumping dully onto the floor. Her face pale, breathing ragged, words spilling out in chaotic, disconnected bursts: "Sorry, guys… the car wouldn't let me drive it… apparently, in my condition… wasn't safe enough… so it blocked the wheel… had to grab a taxi, and you know how taxis are… Anyway, let's just start."

She sank heavily into the chair, eyes painfully fixed on the monitor screen. Her colleagues began speaking, their voices merging into an unintelligible, monotonous hum. The words felt foreign, distant, as though drifting up from underwater, dissolving in the sluggish drone of the air conditioner and the steady tapping of rain against the window. Charts and graphs blurred into meaningless smears of color, focus slipping stubbornly from her grasp. The buzzing grew louder, filling her head, heavy and oppressive, pressing into her temples. Her eyelids grew heavy as lead; she wanted only to close her eyes and let it all fade into oblivion, dissolve into sleep, right here, right now, on this hard, uncomfortable chair...

"Maria? Maria?"

The sharp voice broke through the dense fog, startling her.

"Huh?" she exhaled, struggling to bring her gaze back to the speaker.

"So, what are we doing about the data? Does it work for us? Should we license it?"

Maria blinked several times, attempting to reconnect with reality.

"Send me the details... I'll take a look and decide," she said quietly.

The clinic resembled no medical facility Maria had ever visited: tall, vaulted ceilings rose into a soft, golden twilight; wooden wall panels gently reflected the warm glow of hidden lamps; the air carried a delicate scent of eucalyptus and lavender— "no smell of chlorine at all," she noted to herself, surprised. Holographic tablet screens shimmered on the counter in front of her, prompting confirmation of her details. Maria quickly entered her phone number and fingerprint, feeling a subtle vibration confirming her identification.

"Please proceed to the scanner," a mechanical voice softly instructed. She approached a smooth, snow-white machine shaped like a slightly elongated capsule, its screen gently pulsing to life as she drew near. Once Maria assumed the required position, invisible sensors silently swept over her, measuring her weight, height, temperature, and pulse rate.

From nowhere, a nurse appeared in a flawlessly pressed, pale-blue uniform. "Scanning complete. The doctor is ready to see you now. Please follow me."

Maria followed her down a corridor shimmering with colors from digital paintings broadcasting live scenes of nature. Each image felt like a window into another world, filled with motion:

branches gently rustled, grasses waved softly across meadows, and birds flew in the distance. Maria involuntarily lingered on one canvas, where thick foliage shifted constantly, evoking both fascination and mild irritation. "If someone had to sit next to a painting like that all day, wouldn't they eventually go crazy?" the peculiar thought flashed through her mind, prompting her to quicken her pace slightly.

The office was surprising in its contrast—cozy, like an old chalet tucked high in snowy mountains. Heavy curtains in deep emerald hues; soft leather chairs that invited one to sink in upon touching their cool armrests; a fluffy carpet that muffled footsteps. Along the walls loomed imposing bookcases, stacked from floor to ceiling with volumes bound in luxurious antique leather—from philosophical classics to thick tomes on neurobiology. A desk crafted from dark, aged wood completed the picture of impeccable taste.

Only one element seemed out of place within this carefully curated setting—a shimmering holographic tablet floating above the desk, softly and dispassionately cycling through diagrams and numbers reflecting the patient's condition.

Behind the desk sat Dr. Haster. He looked as though he'd just stepped out of an exclusive golf club, perhaps wrapping up leisurely negotiations with yet another group of "important friends": a flawlessly fitted cashmere sweater over a perfectly pressed shirt, expensive linen trousers, meticulously combed-back hair lightly touched with gray, and an aristocratic casualness evident in every movement. His attentive, piercing gaze met Maria's eyes.

"Good afternoon. Please, have a seat."

"Your office feels like the opposite of the rest of the clinic. Very old-school," Maria began, attempting to ease her own tension.

"Oh, every office here is completely different," the doctor replied warmly, briefly glancing away from the tablet. "We work here every day, and we deal with mental health. It's essential that everyone feels comfortable—almost like being at home. How have you been feeling?"

"Not great," Maria replied softly, feeling her heartbeat quicken again, pulsing faintly in her temples.

"That's not surprising," the doctor spoke gently. "I've reviewed your data. I don't mean to alarm you, but you're in a risk zone. It's all manageable, of course—but why did you delay your visit so long?"

"I don't really know," Maria shrugged vaguely. "I'm pretty skeptical about psychiatry."

The doctor smiled knowingly, as if sharing her skepticism. "You're not alone, believe me. But let me assure you—a lot has changed."

"So what's going on with me? Depression? Another episode?" Maria asked quietly, almost afraid to hear the answer.

"We haven't used that diagnosis for quite a while," the doctor shook his head, smiling warmly again. "It doesn't exist anymore. But before I can give you an exact diagnosis, there's one more quick procedure we need to do. It'll take just thirty minutes."

In the adjacent room stood an unusual device: a massive chair surrounded by an intricate framework of slender metallic arcs and shimmering fiber-optic threads, softly pulsing to the rhythm of a barely audible hum. Hovering above the chair was a translucent helmet resembling an elegant, slightly elongated sphere, its inner surface studded with miniature electrodes and microscopic sensors, poised to capture every flash of neural activity. Beside the armrests, sensors for heart rate and respiration, gently glowing with a golden hue, awaited like delicate bracelets crafted from flexible metal and polymers.

Maria carefully sank into the chair, feeling its surface smoothly adapt beneath her, molding itself perfectly to her body's contours, as though memorizing her shape. As soon as she touched the chair's backrest, the thin bracelets gently encircled her wrists, softly securing pulse and breathing measurements. The transparent helmet slowly descended onto her head, settling into position with a touch so subtle she hardly noticed any pressure. Absolute silence filled the room, interrupted only by the faint, steady hum of the device scanning the deepest secrets of her brain and body.

Once the procedure concluded, the device smoothly returned to its original state. The wall before Maria sprang to life, displaying three-dimensional images of her brain from various angles—flashes of electrical impulses, intricate patterns of magnetic fields, and smooth waves of her heartbeat.

"Wow…" Maria involuntarily thought, mesmerized by the shifting imagery.

The doctor, as if momentarily forgetting his patient, intently watched the flickering monitor. For nearly a minute, he remained silent, entirely absorbed by the data analysis. Then suddenly he spoke, quickly and animatedly, his eyes still fixed on the screen:

"So, according to your genetic data from Panopticare, you show a clear familial predisposition. But genetics alone wouldn't be sufficient. Analysis of your electrical brain activity indicates pronounced hyperactivation of the Default Mode Network—DMN. There are also clear disruptions in the functional connectivity between your prefrontal cortex and amygdala—a classic presentation of chronic stress. Furthermore, your heart rate is asynchronous with your respiratory pattern, amplifying the overall clinical picture. All this quite convincingly confirms the presence of PTDR-301."

Maria anxiously raised her eyes toward the doctor, trying to process what she had just heard.

"What does this mean?" she whispered.

The doctor finally turned to her, his gaze warm and reassuring once more.

"It's a relatively new condition—actually, it's been around for ages but was only recently identified. Previously, these symptoms were classified as depression or post-traumatic stress disorder. Now we understand it's a distinct, specific disorder. Fortunately, it's highly treatable. Two effective therapies were recently approved. The first is repetitive transcranial magnetic stimulation using protocol number four; it takes a few days, with regular clinic visits. The second method is slightly more expensive but much quicker:

a single injection of a specially developed medication, after which you'll need to stay under observation in the clinic for just a couple of hours."

"And that's it?" Maria asked in disbelief. "No pills, nightmares, trouble focusing, constant sweating...?"

The doctor chuckled warmly, his eyes twinkling as if he'd heard a nostalgic, familiar question.

"I told you, things have changed dramatically. Of course, after the treatment, we'll initiate remote monitoring—especially convenient, since you're already an active user of the platform. You'll also need to take medical leave for at least three days, preferably a week. Your brain needs time to adapt and recover."

"It sounds almost like magic..." Maria said softly.

The doctor studied her closely, a slight smile appearing at the corners of his lips.

"In a way, data and AI have created a bit of magic."

* * *

One Last Thing

In the near future, together we really might build a magical world—one where illnesses are clear, and treatments are effective and painless. But for now, Maria—or rather I, who shared my personal journey of depression under her name—am finishing this book in the hope that you, the reader, inspired by these new ideas and possibilities, will take the next step and help bring closer the very magic we all dream about.

Glossary

Accuracy (preferred: data accuracy)   the extent to which data values are correct, valid, and free from error, such that they precisely represent the real-world phenomena or events they are intended to describe.

AlphaGo   an artificial intelligence program developed by DeepMind that uses deep neural networks and advanced reinforcement learning algorithms to play the board game Go at a professional level.

Animal models   non-human organisms—most commonly rodents, and less frequently primates—engineered or induced (genetically, pharmacologically, lesion-based, or via environmental manipulation) to manifest specific behavioral, neurobiological, or molecular traits analogous to human psychiatric endophenotypes. These models serve to probe disease mechanisms, pathways, and potential therapeutic targets with assessments of face, construct, and predictive validity before transitioning to human trial.

Artificial Intelligence (AI)   a scientific discipline focused on the design and development of computer systems and algorithms capable of performing tasks typically requiring human intelligence, including reasoning, learning, problem-solving, perception, and language comprehension. AI research involves the theory and engineering of systems that interpret complex data, learn from experience, adapt dynamically to new information, and make autonomous decisions. The field integrates knowledge from computer science, mathematics, neuroscience, psychology, and related disciplines to develop technologies that closely mimic or partially replicate aspects of human cognitive processes.

Attention Mechanisms (data science) computational methods within neural networks that dynamically assign weights to input elements based on their relevance to the task, enabling models to selectively emphasize critical information when generating predictions or decisions. These mechanisms improve model efficiency and interpretability, particularly in handling complex or extensive data inputs.

Attentional Network Test (ANT; behavioral sciences) a standardized neuropsychological task designed to assess the efficiency of three distinct attentional networks—alerting, orienting, and executive control. Participants identify the direction of a central target arrow flanked by distracting arrows, with performance measured through reaction times, accuracy scores, and error rates. The ANT provides a quantitative evaluation of individual differences in attentional processing and cognitive control.

Attribution methods (data science) techniques used in post hoc interpretability that assign numerical importance scores to individual input features of a specific instance, reflecting each feature's contribution toward the model's predicted outcome. These methods enable ranking of features by influence in a given decision, but they neither claim causality nor biological relevance.

Behavioral data (psychiatry) qualitative or quantitative information capturing observable behaviors associated with altered perception, cognition, or emotion linked to psychiatric conditions. These data include measures such as attention, concentration, reaction times, response accuracy, decision-making patterns, and task performance, directly reflecting behavioral manifestations of symptoms.

Big Data information assets characterized by exceptionally high volume, velocity, and variety, which exceed the capacity of traditional software and systems to capture, store, manage, and analyze. Such data require specialized technologies and analytical methods for efficient processing and transformation into actionable insights or value.

Biological data (psychiatry) quantitative measurements obtained from humans reflecting physiological states and processes, including neurobiological, biochemical, electrophysiological, and genetic information, used to investigate the underlying biology associated with the onset and manifestation of mental disorders.

Biological targets (clinical research; drug development) biological structures or molecules, including receptors, enzymes, ion channels, proteins, genes, or signaling pathways, that can be modulated by therapeutic interventions to influence disease processes. Identification and validation of biological targets are critical steps in drug development and precision medicine.

Classification tasks (data science) supervised learning problems where a model learns a mapping from input features to discrete, predefined classes, using labeled examples during training; the trained classifier then assigns new instances to one class from among the set during inference, helping predict categorical outcomes based on learned patterns.

Clinical data information collected directly by qualified healthcare professionals (e.g., physicians, nurses, diagnosticians) in controlled medical settings, ensuring accuracy, reliability, and consistency of the obtained data.

Communication data empirical records capturing modalities of patient communication such as spoken language, written or typed text messages, video or audio recordings, and social media posts. These data provide insight into underlying cognitive and linguistic processes and are used in research and clinical modeling of behavior and cognition.

Companion diagnostics diagnostic tests developed specifically to accompany certain therapeutic treatments, designed to identify patients most likely to benefit or those at risk of adverse reactions, based on predictive biomarkers. These diagnostics ensure the safe and effective use of corresponding therapies, facilitating personalized medical decisions.

Completeness (preferred: data completeness; data science) the extent to which a dataset includes all essential data elements or scenarios required for accurate analysis, modeling, or decision-making. It specifically refers to the presence of necessary values and records, without accounting for accuracy or consistency of the data itself. Completeness is recognized as one of the core dimensions of data quality and is critical to ensuring unbiased and reliable model performance.

Concept-based reasoning (CBR; data science) computational approach where models use predefined clinical or biological concepts rather than raw data to make predictions. These concepts are selected based on established hypotheses, making model decisions more interpretable but requiring significant manual input and limiting scalability.

Consistency (preferred: data consistency)   the degree to which data attributes are free from contradiction and remain coherent across multiple records, sources, or systems in a given context of use. This dimension ensures that redundant or related data maintain uniformity, which prevents conflicts and supports reliable integration across datasets.

Control group (clinical research)   a group of participants in a clinical trial who receive either no intervention, a placebo, or standard care rather than the experimental treatment. This group serves as a baseline to differentiate the true effects of the investigational intervention from placebo effects, biases, or natural disease progression, ensuring the validity and reliability of trial outcomes.

Counterfactual explanations (data science)   a post hoc explainability technique in explainable AI that identifies minimal changes to input features that would alter a model's output decision. These "what-if" scenarios clarify how different outcomes could arise if certain inputs were different, without exposing the internal workings of the model.

Cross-validation (data science)   a statistical resampling method for evaluating the generalization ability of predictive models. It partitions data into complementary subsets, sequentially using some portions for model training and others for validation. By averaging performance across multiple rounds of splitting, cross-validation provides an unbiased estimate of out-of-sample error and helps prevent overfitting, ensuring that the model will perform reliably on new, unseen data.

Data augmentation (data science)   techniques that introduce controlled noise or artificial perturbations into training data to improve model robustness. By simulating realistic variations (e.g., Gaussian noise, salt-and-pepper noise) or generating synthetic examples, data augmentation helps models generalize better to unseen, noisy inputs—reducing sensitivity to data imperfections and improving real-world performance.

Data governance   a comprehensive framework of policies, procedures, standards, roles, and technologies that ensures data quality, integrity, security, consistency, and compliance across an organization. Effective data governance establishes clear accountability, facilitates audits, and supports reliable and accurate use of data assets.

Decision fatigue   the progressive decline in decision-making quality that occurs as individuals make repeated, demanding choices over time. In healthcare, this manifests as reduced cognitive control, increased error rates, decision avoidance, and reliance on default options, particularly during long or intensive decision-making sessions such as in emergency medicine or nursing shifts. This phenomenon is linked to diminished self-regulatory capacity and poses risks to patient safety.

Diagnostic biomarkers measurable biomarkers used to detect or confirm the presence of a disease or medical condition in an individual, or to identify specific subtypes of a condition. These biomarkers serve as objective indicators of pathogenic processes, enabling accurate diagnosis and aiding in classification and clinical decision-making.

Enacted stigma (mental health) discriminatory behaviors or unfair treatment directed at individuals based on their mental illness, such as exclusion, social rejection, or prejudice enacted by others. This form of stigma reflects external actions rather than internal attitudes and is identified as a key determinant of negative health and social outcomes.

Endpoints (clinical research) objectively measurable outcomes selected in a clinical trial to assess the effects of an intervention, such as clinical events, symptoms, or biomarker changes. These predefined endpoints support the evaluation of treatment efficacy and safety. Primary endpoints address the main research objective, while secondary and exploratory endpoints provide additional or hypothesis-generating insights. Endpoint selection and standardization are critical for statistical validity, regulatory approval, and meaningful interpretation of trial results.

Exploration–exploitation dilemma (data science) the fundamental challenge in reinforcement learning of determining when to explore new actions to discover potentially better outcomes, versus when to exploit known actions that reliably yield good results. Striking the appropriate balance is crucial, as excessive exploration can delay optimization, while excessive exploitation may limit performance by prematurely converging on suboptimal solutions.

Feature importance (data science) a metric indicating how significantly each input feature contributes to the predictions or decisions made by a model. It quantifies and ranks features based on their influence, providing insights into which aspects of the data most strongly affect model outcomes.

Felt stigma (mental health) the internalized feelings of shame, fear, and expectation of judgment experienced by individuals with mental illness, arising from their awareness of societal prejudices and stereotypes.

Fine-tuning (data science) the process of further training a pre-trained machine learning model, such as a foundational or general-purpose model, on a smaller, task-specific dataset. Fine-tuning refines the model's parameters to improve performance in specialized domains while preserving knowledge gained from earlier training stages. This allows models to achieve high accuracy on specific tasks even when additional data are limited.

Foundation model (data science) an artificial intelligence model trained on extensive, diverse datasets, designed to learn broadly generalizable representations applicable to various downstream tasks. These models act as adaptable bases that can be further specialized through fine-tuning or prompting, supporting diverse AI applications across multiple domains. Their key characteristics include significant scale, flexibility, and broad applicability.

Gaussian filtering (data science) a smoothing technique that reduces high-frequency noise by convolving input data with a Gaussian-weighted kernel, giving higher influence to nearer observations. This low-pass filtering approach attenuates fine-grain fluctuations while preserving meaningful structures, such as edges or trends, in modalities like images or time series data.

General Problem Solver (GPS; computer science) a pioneering AI program developed by Allen Newell, Herbert A. Simon, and J. C. Shaw in the late 1950s, designed as a universal problem-solving engine. GPS separated problem knowledge from problem-solving strategy, using means-ends analysis and heuristic search to navigate goal-directed problem spaces represented through well-formed formulas or directed graphs.

Generalizability (clinical research) the extent to which findings from a specific study can apply to broader populations, settings, or clinical contexts beyond the original research sample. It reflects whether observed effects, outcomes, or associations are likely to hold true in real-world patient groups or across different environments, thereby supporting the external validity and practical applicability of research results.

Hamilton Depression Rating Scale (HAM-D; clinical research) a clinician-administered instrument introduced by Max Hamilton in 1960 to assess the severity of depressive symptoms in adults over the prior week. The most common version includes 17 items, each rated on a scale (generally 0–2 or 0–4 depending on symptom) that together quantify depression severity across mood, guilt, sleep, anxiety, somatic symptoms, and other dimensions.

Heterogeneity (clinical research) the presence of multiple distinct biological, demographic, or contextual mechanisms that produce similar clinical symptoms or outcomes across different individuals or study settings. This variation may arise from diverse etiologies (genetic, pathophysiological), patient characteristics, treatments, or study designs, creating challenges in diagnosis, analysis, and treatment generalization across populations. Recognizing and accounting for heterogeneity is essential for reliable interpretation, stratified medicine, and designing effective clinical trials.

Independent Component Analysis (ICA; data science) a computational method for separating mixed signals into original, independent source components by identifying patterns of statistical independence in the observed data. ICA is commonly applied in signal processing and data analysis to isolate underlying sources from complex mixtures.

Labeled training dataset (data science) a collection of input data samples paired with corresponding correct labels or target values, used as the ground truth in supervised learning. This dataset enables machine learning models to learn mapping functions from inputs to outputs by example and is essential for training, validating, and evaluating model performance.

Late-stage clinical trials (clinical research) clinical studies conducted after initial safety and dosing evaluations, typically encompassing Phase IIb and Phase III trials. These trials involve patients with the target condition and focus on confirming efficacy, assessing broader safety in larger populations, and generating pivotal data to support regulatory approval.

Logic Theorist (computer science) the first AI program developed in 1956 by Allen Newell, Herbert A. Simon, and J. C. Shaw. It applied heuristic search to prove theorems from *Principia Mathematica*, discovering 38 of the first 52 theorems and occasionally deriving more elegant proofs than those in the original text. Designed to separate problem-solving methods from domain knowledge, Logic Theorist is widely regarded as the first program engineered to simulate human-like reasoning and had a foundational impact on cognitive science and AI research.

Median filtering (data science) a nonlinear noise-reduction method in which each data point (such as a pixel or measurement) is replaced with the median value calculated from neighboring points. This approach effectively reduces impulse noise, like "salt-and-pepper" noise, while preserving important features, edges, and overall structural integrity.

Medicalization the process by which human conditions, behaviors, or experiences—whether traditionally viewed as normal life variations or actual health conditions—are redefined and framed as medical issues. These often come to be subject to medical diagnosis, prevention, or treatment. Medicalization reflects an expansion of medical discourse and authority into areas previously considered non-medical and can be influenced by evolving scientific knowledge, social attitudes, or available treatments.

Montgomery–Åsberg Depression Rating Scale (MADRS; clinical research) a clinician-administered ten-item rating scale introduced in 1979 to quantify the severity of depressive episodes. Each item—covering core psychological symptoms such as apparent and reported sadness, inner tension, concentration difficulties, lassitude, pessimism, and suicidal thoughts—is scored from 0 (absent) to 6 (severe), yielding a total from 0 to 60. Designed for sensitivity to treatment-related change, MADRS is widely used in psychopharmacological trials due to its strong reliability and responsiveness to symptom dynamics.

Mycin (computer science) an early rule-based expert system developed at Stanford University in the early 1970s by Edward H. Shortliffe and colleagues. Mycin used a knowledge base of approximately 600 expert-derived "if–then" rules and a backward-chaining inference engine to diagnose bacterial infections and recommend antibiotic treatments based on patient symptoms and laboratory data.

Neural circuits (neuroscience) anatomically and functionally interconnected groups of neurons that process and transmit information to perform specific brain functions—ranging from sensory perception and cognition to emotion and behavior. These circuits serve as the fundamental operational units of the brain, with disruptions implicated in psychiatric symptoms and neuropsychiatric disorders.

Neuromyths widespread misconceptions about brain function, cognition, learning, and behavior that are based on oversimplified, distorted, or misinterpreted scientific findings. These myths often persist in educational and popular contexts despite being repeatedly debunked by robust neuroscience research.

Noise (data science) unintended, random variability or distortions in data that obscure meaningful patterns and degrade model accuracy. Noise arises from measurement errors, sensor limitations, or environmental interference and includes mislabeled examples (label noise) or corrupted features (attribute noise). It lowers the signal-to-noise ratio, increases model overfitting risk, and reduces generalizability to unseen data, making noise mitigation essential during preprocessing and model validation.

Overfitting (data science) a modeling error occurring when a machine learning model learns noise or irrelevant patterns from training data, leading to high performance on training samples but poor generalization and reduced accuracy when applied to unseen data.

Parallel computations (computer science) the capability of a machine to execute multiple computational operations simultaneously by dividing a task into independent sub-tasks and distributing them across multiple processors or cores. This approach significantly accelerates processing speed and enables efficient handling of large-scale data and complex algorithms, foundational to modern artificial intelligence and high-performance computing.

Patient data (also: direct-to-consumer data) information collected directly from patients through consumer-oriented digital devices and applications outside clinical settings, reflecting everyday behaviors, symptoms, or physiological states.

Patient stratification (clinical research) the deliberate partitioning of a patient population into well-defined subgroups based on biological, clinical, demographic, or molecular characteristics. Its goal is to enhance precision in predicting disease progression or treatment response by tailoring interventions to homogeneous subpopulations.

Patient-centered care a healthcare philosophy emphasizing the individual person, rather than focusing solely on their diagnosis, ensuring treatment addresses personal needs, values, and experiences.

Penalties (data science, reinforcement learning) negative feedback signals applied during the training of reinforcement learning agents to discourage specified actions or behaviors by lowering their expected utility. Explicitly defined in the reward structure, penalties reduce the likelihood of repeating undesired behaviors and help shape safer policies.

Perceptron (computer science) a supervised learning algorithm introduced by Frank Rosenblatt in 1957 as a computational model of a single neuron. It uses a linear combination of weighted inputs plus a bias, followed by a threshold activation, to classify input vectors into one of two classes. The perceptron learning rule iteratively updates weights to minimize classification errors, making it one of the earliest binary classifiers and foundational to modern neural networks.

Phase I clinical trial (clinical research) the initial stage of human testing for a new therapeutic agent, primarily designed to evaluate safety, determine appropriate dosage ranges, and identify potential side effects. Conducted with a small group of participants (often healthy volunteers), this phase provides critical information on the drug's pharmacokinetics (absorption, distribution, metabolism, excretion) and pharmacodynamics (biological effects), forming the foundation for subsequent trials focused on efficacy.

Phase II clinical trial (clinical research) a controlled clinical study involving patients with the target condition (typically several dozen to a few hundred participants), designed primarily to assess preliminary efficacy and continued safety of a therapeutic intervention. It evaluates whether the treatment shows sufficient biological activity to warrant larger-scale testing, and identifies optimal dosing and potential side effects not fully observed in Phase I.

Phase III clinical trial (clinical research) a large-scale, randomized study involving hundreds to thousands of patients with the target condition, primarily designed to confirm treatment effectiveness, monitor adverse reactions, and compare the new intervention directly against existing standard treatments or placebo. Successful completion of Phase III provides critical evidence needed for regulatory approval and clinical adoption of the therapy.

Placebo effect the phenomenon whereby patients experience real or perceived improvements in health following administration of an inactive or sham intervention, attributable to psychological factors such as expectations, conditioning, and the therapeutic context rather than any pharmacological action. It reflects psychobiological changes induced by belief in treatment effectiveness and is distinguished from the placebo response, which also includes natural recovery, regression to the mean, and measurement artifacts.

Precision (preferred: measurement precision) the consistency or reproducibility of a measurement process, reflected in the closeness of repeated measurements under identical conditions. Precision captures the degree of random error—high precision means minimal variation between repeated measurements, even if values may deviate from the true value.

Predictive biomarker a measurable biological characteristic that identifies individuals who are more likely than comparable individuals without the biomarker to derive benefit—or experience harm—from a specific therapeutic intervention or exposure. These biomarkers guide clinical decision-making by predicting treatment response and enabling personalized interventions.

Prognostic biomarkers biological or clinical characteristics that provide information about the likely course of a disease or future clinical outcome in a patient, independent of any specific treatment. These biomarkers are used to assess risk of disease recurrence, progression, or overall prognosis.

Prototype and example-based explanations (data science) an explainable AI technique where a model justifies its predictions by referencing real, representative examples—or learned prototypes—from its training data that closely resemble the current input. These "this looks like that" explanations help users understand model behavior through similarity-based reasoning rather than opaque internal logic. Prototype-based methods integrate learned concept exemplars into the model architecture, while example-based explanations retrieve and present actual training instances most influential to a prediction.

Questionnaires (clinical research) structured instruments—typically composed of standardized questions and response formats—administered by clinicians or self-completed by patients to systematically capture symptoms, behaviors, perceptions, or health outcomes.

Random noise (data processing) unpredictable, non-systematic variations or errors present in collected data that do not correspond to the true underlying signal or information. These fluctuations are independent of the phenomenon being measured and do not follow consistent patterns. When datasets are sufficiently large, random noise can be reduced through aggregation—averaging many samples diminishes its impact, enabling models to learn stable, meaningful patterns instead.

Regression tasks (data science) supervised learning problems where the model predicts continuous numerical outcomes based on input variables by identifying relationships and trends within the data. These tasks are fundamental for forecasting or estimating numerical values across various domains.

Reinforcement Learning (data science) a machine learning paradigm in which an autonomous agent learns optimal behaviors through interaction with an environment using trial-and-error feedback. The agent takes actions and receives rewards or penalties depending on their outcomes, aiming to maximize cumulative rewards over time.

Relevance (preferred: data relevance; data science) the extent to which data contain extractable information that directly pertains to a specific task, objective, or condition. High relevance implies that the dataset captures meaningful patterns or signals directly linked to the target outcome, minimizing interference from unrelated or extraneous processes.

Reliability (preferred: measurement reliability; clinical research) the degree to which a measurement or assessment consistently yields the same or similar results when repeated under identical conditions, indicating stability, precision, and reproducibility of the method or instrument.

Remission (clinical research) a clinical benchmark indicating substantial reduction or absence of symptoms, defined by standardized thresholds on symptom severity scales. Achieving remission signifies that a patient's symptoms are minimal enough to be considered clinically insignificant, though precise criteria vary depending on the scale and condition being studied.

Replicability (clinical research) the ability of an independent study, using the same methodology but newly collected data, to produce results consistent with the original research findings.

Representativeness (preferred: data representativeness; data science) the degree to which a dataset accurately reflects the characteristics and distribution of the target population or input space it is intended to represent. High representativeness implies that all relevant subgroups and combinations of demographic or feature-level attributes are proportionally captured, minimizing bias and enhancing model generalizability and fairness.

Reproducibility crisis a systemic problem in scientific research—particularly noticeable in preclinical and psychological studies—where independent researchers cannot obtain consistent results when the same experiments or analyses are repeated using equivalent methods. The crisis has been linked to factors such as low statistical power, publication bias, selective reporting (e.g., only publishing positive results), poorly described protocols, and variability across laboratories. Widespread failure to reproduce findings undermines confidence in scientific claims and highlights the need for more robust experimental design, data transparency, and replication practices.

Response (clinical research) a benchmark outcome in therapeutic trials defined as a clinically meaningful improvement in symptom severity, most often operationalized as at least a 50% reduction from baseline on validated symptom rating scales. This dichotomous measure classifies patients as "responders," offering a standardized way to assess efficacy across studies.

Rewards (data science; reinforcement learning) numerical feedback signals that an agent receives from its environment after taking an action. Positive rewards reinforce desired behaviors, increasing the probability that those actions will be repeated in future decisions.

Risk biomarkers measurable indicators used to predict the likelihood of developing a disease or medical condition in individuals who are asymptomatic or currently healthy. These biomarkers help assess susceptibility before clinical manifestation and support preventive or early intervention strategies.

Sample size (clinical research) the total number of participants included in a clinical study, which directly influences the statistical power, precision, reliability, and generalizability of research findings.

Self-supervised learning (data science) a training paradigm in which a model learns from unlabeled data by generating its own supervisory signals (pseudo-labels) derived from the data's inherent structure.

Semantic consistency (data science) the property that ensures terms, labels, or data values retain the same meaning across contexts, systems, or datasets. High semantic consistency means that data elements used to represent the same concept are defined, interpreted, and applied uniformly, reducing ambiguity and supporting accurate integration, querying, and analysis.

Semi-structured data (data science) data that do not conform to a rigid tabular schema but include organizational metadata—such as tags, labels, or key-value pairs—that enable semantic element separation and hierarchical structure.

Signal (data science) meaningful information embedded within data that reflects underlying patterns or phenomena relevant to analysis or prediction—distinct from noise, which consists of random or irrelevant variations that obscure true signals.

Signal-to-noise ratio (SNR; data science) the ratio of meaningful signal power to the power of background noise within a dataset or measurement system. It quantifies how clearly the underlying information (signal) stands out relative to random, irrelevant variations (noise). High SNR indicates strong, discernible patterns and supports accurate model learning, whereas low SNR implies signal obscured by noise, risking poor generalization and increased error.

Stigma a deeply discrediting attribute, behavior, or reputation that transforms an individual's perception from being seen as a "whole and usual person" to a "tainted, discounted one." This stigma emerges from a discrepancy between one's actual social identity and their perceived identity in a specific context, resulting in social devaluation, exclusion, or rejection.

Structured data (data science) data organized in a clearly defined format, typically in tables with rows representing individual records and columns corresponding to specific attributes, allowing for easy storage and analysis in traditional databases or spreadsheets.

Supervised Learning (data science) a foundational machine learning approach in which a model learns from labeled training data—pairs of input and correct output examples—to identify mathematical relationships. These learned patterns are then used to make predictions on new, unseen data. Supervised learning is commonly used for classification and regression tasks.

System a cohesive set of interacting and interdependent components, or stakeholders, organized to achieve a common purpose or behavior. Each element contributes uniquely while continuously affecting and being affected by others, creating integrated functionality that unfolds as a unified whole.

Systematic noise (data science)   predictable, repeatable distortions in data introduced by consistent errors in data collection, measurement, or instrumentation. Unlike random noise, which fluctuates unpredictably, systematic noise follows identifiable patterns (e.g., calibration errors, biased instrumentation) and can shift measurements consistently away from true values across a dataset.

Timeliness (preferred: data timeliness; data science)   the extent to which data accurately represent the specific period or context they are intended to model, ensuring alignment with contemporary conditions, societal attitudes, or evolving phenomena. High timeliness ensures that analyses and models remain relevant and reliable in reflecting current or recent states of the studied domain.

Total score (clinical research)   a single numeric summary derived by combining item-level responses from standardized assessment instruments (e.g., symptom scales or patient-reported outcome measures) into one unified metric.

Transfer learning (data science)   a machine learning method in which knowledge gained from one task or dataset is reused to improve performance on a related task or dataset, even when the two domains or label distributions differ. Typically, a model pretrained on a large, rich dataset is adapted to accelerate learning and improve generalization on a new task with limited labeled data.

Treatment-resistant depression (clinical research)   major depressive disorder that fails to achieve a clinically meaningful response after two or more antidepressant treatments administered at adequate dose and duration (typically 6–8 weeks each), within the same depressive episode.

Unstructured data (data science)   data that lack a predefined schema or organized format (e.g., tabular structure), making them difficult to store and analyze using traditional relational databases or spreadsheets. These data typically include text documents, emails, images, audio, video, recordings, and other human-generated or media-based content.

Unsupervised learning (machine learning)   a machine learning paradigm in which algorithms identify hidden patterns, structures, or relationships within datasets without relying on labeled examples or predefined targets. Common methods include clustering, dimensionality reduction, and anomaly detection, which group or organize data based on inherent similarities or statistical properties.

Validity (preferred: measurement validity; clinical research) the degree to which a clinical measurement or diagnostic category accurately represents the specific condition or construct it intends to assess.

Wavelet transforms (data science) mathematical techniques used to decompose signals into components at multiple time-frequency scales and eliminate high-frequency components—typically associated with noise—while preserving structured, meaningful signal content.

Notes

Introduction

1. World Health Organization. Suicide [Internet]. Geneva: World Health Organization; 2021 [cited 2024 May 27]. Available from: https://www.who.int/news-room/fact-sheets/detail/suicide
2. World Health Organization. Mental disorders [Internet]. Geneva: World Health Organization; 2022 [cited 2024 May 27]. Available from: https://www.who.int/news-room/fact-sheets/detail/mental-disorders
3. The Lancet Commission on Global Mental Health and Sustainable Development. Mental illness will cost the world $16 trillion by 2030 [Internet]. Atlanta (GA): The Carter Center; 2018 [cited 2024 May 27]. Available from: https://www.cartercenter.org/news/pr/mental-health-lancet-report-100918.html

Chapter 1: The Patient's Journey

1. Goffman E. *Stigma: Notes on the Management of Spoiled Identity*. Englewood Cliffs, NJ: Prentice-Hall; 1963.
2. Scambler G, Hopkins A. Being epileptic: Coming to terms with stigma. *Sociology of Health & Illness* 1986; 8(1):26–43.
3. Stone J, Smyth R, Carson A, Lewis S, Prescott R, Warlow C, Sharpe M. Systematic review of misdiagnosis of conversion symptoms and "hysteria". *BMJ* 2005;331(7523):989.

4. Dekker S, Lee NC, Howard-Jones P, Jolles J. Neuromyths in education: Prevalence and predictors of misconceptions among teachers. *Frontiers in Psychology* 2012;3:33784.
5. Tokuhama-Espinosa T. *Neuromyths: Debunking False Ideas about the Brain.* WW Norton & Company; 2018.
6. Suárez-Llevat C, Herrera-Peco I, Ruiz-Núñez C, Carmona-Pestaña Á, Romero-Castellano R, Jiménez-Gómez B. YouTube and schizophrenia: The quality and reliability of information in the age of infodemics. *Psychiatry International* 2025;6(1):27.
7. Thapa P, Thapa A, Khadka N, Bhattarai R, Jha S, Khanal A, Basnet B. YouTube lens to attention deficit hyperactivity disorder: A social media analysis. *BMC Research Notes* 2018;11(1):854.
8. Yeung A, Ng E, Abi-Jaoude E. TikTok and attention-deficit/hyperactivity disorder: A cross-sectional study of social media content quality. *The Canadian Journal of Psychiatry* 2022;67(12):899–906.
9. Hudon A, Perry K, Plate AS, Doucet A, Ducharme L, Djona O, Testart Aguirre C, Evoy G. Navigating the maze of social media disinformation on psychiatric illness and charting paths to reliable information for mental health professionals: Observational study of TikTok videos. *Journal of Medical Internet Research* 2025;27:e64225.
10. Gregory RJ, Schwer Canning S, Lee TW, Wise JC. Cognitive bibliotherapy for depression: A meta-analysis. *Journal of Clinical Psychology* 2004; 60(3):271–80.
11. Scogin F, Jamison C, Gochneaur K. Comparative efficacy of cognitive and behavioral bibliotherapy for mildly and moderately depressed older adults. *Journal of Consulting and Clinical Psychology* 1989;57(3):403–7.
12. Norcross JC, Santrock JW, Campbell LF, Smith TS, Sommer R, Zuckerman EL. (2000). *Authoritative Guide to Self-help Resources in Mental Health.* New York: Guilford.
13. Norcross JC. Integrating self-help into psychotherapy: 16 practical suggestions. *Professional Psychology: Research and Practice* 2006;37(6):683.
14. Redding RE, Herbert JD, Forman EM, Gaudiano BA. Popular self-help books for anxiety, depression, and trauma: How scientifically grounded and useful are they? *Professional Psychology: Research and Practice* 2008;39(5):537.

15. Arkowitz H, Lilienfeld SO. Do self help books help. *Scientific American Mind* 2006;17(5):90.
16. Papworth M, Ward A, Leeson K. Negative effects of self-help materials: Three explorative studies. *The Cognitive Behaviour Therapist* 2015;8:e30.
17. Pratt LA, Brody DJ. Depression in the U.S. household population, 2009–2012 [Internet]. NCHS Data Brief No. 172. Hyattsville (MD): National Center for Health Statistics; Dec 2014 [cited 2025 Jul 21]. Available from: https://www.cdc.gov/nchs/products/databriefs/db172.htm
18. Andrade LH, Alonso J, Mneimneh Z, Wells JE, Al-Hamzawi A, Borges G, Bromet E, Bruffaerts R, De Girolamo G, De Graaf R, Florescu S. Barriers to mental health treatment: Results from the WHO World Mental Health surveys. *Psychological Medicine* 2014;44(6):1303–17.

Chapter 2: Diagnostic Roulette

1. Sun CF, Correll CU, Trestman RL, Lin Y, Xie H, Hankey MS, Uymatiao RP, Patel RT, Metsutnan VL, McDaid EC, Saha A. Low availability, long wait times, and high geographic disparity of psychiatric outpatient care in the US. *General Hospital Psychiatry* 2023;84:12–7.
2. Barkil-Oteo A. Collaborative care for depression in primary care: How psychiatry could "troubleshoot" current treatments and practices. *The Yale Journal of Biology and Medicine* 2013;86(2):139.
3. Tai-Seale M, McGuire TG, Zhang W. Time allocation in primary care office visits. *Health Services Research* 2007;42(5):1871–94.
4. American Psychiatric Association. *Practice Guidelines for the Psychiatric Evaluation of Adults*. 3rd ed. Arlington, VA: American Psychiatric Association Publishing; 2016.
5. Fugate JM, Gendron M, Hoemann K. Links between emotion word, usage, understanding, accuracy, and emotion dysregulation: An integrative analysis. *Affective Science* 2024:1–2.
6. Erbas Y, Gendron M, Fugate JM. The role of emotional granularity in emotional regulation, mental disorders, and well-being. *Frontiers in Psychology* 2022;13:1080713.
7. Price GF, Ogren M, Sandhofer CM. Sorting out emotions: How labels influence emotion categorization. *Developmental Psychology* 2022;58(9):1665.

8. Zupan B, Dempsey L, Hartwell K. Categorising emotion words: The influence of response options. *Language and Cognition* 2023;15(1):29–52.
9. Strauss GP, Allen DN. Emotional intensity and categorisation ratings for emotional and nonemotional words. *Cognition and Emotion* 2008; 22(1):114–33.
10. Stewart AL, Lynch KJ. Identifying discrepancies in electronic medical records through pharmacist medication reconciliation. *Journal of the American Pharmacists Association* 2012;52(1):59–68.
11. West CP, Dyrbye LN, Shanafelt TD. Physician burnout: Contributors, consequences and solutions. *Journal of Internal Medicine*. 2018; 283(6):516–29.
12. Zavala AM, Day GE, Plummer D, Bamford-Wade A. Decision-making under pressure: Medical errors in uncertain and dynamic environments. *Australian Health Review* 2017;42(4):395–402.
13. Holmqvist R, Jeanneau M. Burnout and psychiatric staff's feelings towards patients. *Psychiatry Research* 2006;145(2–3):207–13.
14. Pignatiello GA, Martin RJ, Hickman Jr RL. Decision fatigue: A conceptual analysis. *Journal of Health Psychology* 2020;25(1):123–35.
15. Annual report 2021: England, Northern Ireland, Scotland and Wales [Internet]. NCISH. Available from: https://sites.manchester.ac.uk/ncish/reports/annual-report-2021-england-northern-ireland-scotland-and-wales/
16. Annual report 2017: England, Northern Ireland, Scotland and Wales [Internet]. NCISH. Available from: https://sites.manchester.ac.uk/ncish/reports/annual-report-2017-england-northern-ireland-scotland-and-wales/
17. Berman AL. Risk factors proximate to suicide and suicide risk assessment in the context of denied suicide ideation. *Suicide & Life-Threatening Behavior* 2018;48(3):340–52.
18. American Psychiatric Association. *Diagnostic and Statistical Manual of Mental Disorders*. 5th ed., text rev. Arlington, VA: American Psychiatric Association Publishing; 2022.
19. Shorter E. The history of nosology and the rise of the Diagnostic and Statistical Manual of Mental Disorders. *Dialogues in Clinical Neuroscience* 2015;17(1):59–67.

20. Lasalvia A. DSM-5 two years later: Facts, myths and some key open issues. *Epidemiology and Psychiatric Sciences* 2015;24(3):185–7.
21. Clarke DE, Narrow WE, Regier DA, Kuramoto SJ, Kupfer DJ, Kuhl EA, Greiner L, Kraemer HC. DSM-5 field trials in the United States and Canada, part I: Study design, sampling strategy, implementation, and analytic approaches. *American Journal of Psychiatry* 2013;170(1):43–58.
22. Parker G, Tavella G. Disruptive mood dysregulation disorder: A critical perspective. *The Canadian Journal of Psychiatry* 2018;63(12):813–5.
23. Gara MA, Vega WA, Arndt S, Escamilla M, Fleck DE, Lawson WB, Lesser I, Neighbors HW, Wilson DR, Arnold LM, Strakowski SM. Influence of patient race and ethnicity on clinical assessment in patients with affective disorders. *Archives of General Psychiatry* 2012;69(6):593–600.
24. Bredström A. Culture and context in mental health diagnosing: Scrutinizing the DSM-5 revision. *Journal of Medical Humanities* 2019; 40(3):347–63.
25. Regier DA, Narrow WE, Clarke DE, Kraemer HC, Kuramoto SJ, Kuhl EA, Kupfer DJ. DSM-5 field trials in the United States and Canada, Part II: Test-retest reliability of selected categorical diagnoses. *American Journal of Psychiatry* 2013;170(1):59–70.

Chapter 3: Treatment, Pharma, and the Brain

1. Alemi F, Min H, Yousefi M, Becker LK, Hane CA, Nori VS, Wojtusiak J. Effectiveness of common antidepressants: A post market release study. *EClinicalMedicine* 2021;41:101171.
2. Rush AJ, Trivedi MH, Wisniewski SR, Nierenberg AA, Stewart JW, Warden D, Niederehe G, Thase ME, Lavori PW, Lebowitz BD, McGrath PJ. Acute and longer-term outcomes in depressed outpatients requiring one or several treatment steps: A STAR*D report. *American Journal of Psychiatry* 2006;163(11):1905–17.
3. Gaynes BN, Warden D, Trivedi MH, Wisniewski SR, Fava M, Rush AJ. What did STAR*D teach us? Results from a large-scale, practical, clinical trial for patients with depression. *Psychiatric Services* 2009; 60(11):1439–45.
4. Ward W, Haslam A, Prasad V. Antidepressant trial duration versus duration of real-world use: A systematic analysis. *The American Journal of Medicine* 2025;138(10):1400–1407. e10.

5. Kan K, Lokkerbol J, Jörg F, Visser E, Schoevers RA, Feenstra TL. Real-world treatment costs and care utilization in patients with major depressive disorder with and without psychiatric comorbidities in specialist mental healthcare. *PharmacoEconomics* 2021;39(6):721–30.
6. Gauthier G, Guérin A, Zhdanava M, Jacobson W, Nomikos G, Merikle E, François C, Perez V. Treatment patterns, healthcare resource utilization, and costs following first-line antidepressant treatment in major depressive disorder: A retrospective US claims database analysis. *BMC Psychiatry* 2017;17(1):222.
7. Monroe SM, Harkness KL. Recurrence in major depression: A conceptual analysis. *Psychological Review* 2011;118(4):655.
8. Al-Harbi KS. Treatment-resistant depression: Therapeutic trends, challenges, and future directions. *Patient Preference and Adherence* 2012;6(1):369–88.
9. Gaynes BN, Lux L, Gartlehner G, Asher G, Forman-Hoffman V, Green J, Boland E, Weber RP, Randolph C, Bann C, Coker-Schwimmer E. Defining treatment-resistant depression. *Depression and Anxiety* 2020;37(2):134–45.
10. Kane JM, Agid O, Baldwin ML, Howes O, Lindenmayer JP, Marder S, Olfson M, Potkin SG, Correll CU. Clinical guidance on the identification and management of treatment-resistant schizophrenia. *The Journal of Clinical Psychiatry* 2019;80(2):2783.
11. Elsayed OH, Ercis M, Pahwa M, Singh B. Treatment-resistant bipolar depression: Therapeutic trends, challenges and future directions. *Neuropsychiatric Disease and Treatment* 2022;18:2927–43.
12. Fornaro M, Fusco A, Novello S, Mosca P, Anastasia A, De Blasio A, Iasevoli F, de Bartolomeis A. Predictors of treatment resistance across different clinical subtypes of depression: Comparison of unipolar vs. bipolar cases. *Frontiers in Psychiatry* 2020;11:438.
13. Moncrieff J, Cooper RE, Stockmann T, Amendola S, Hengartner MP, Horowitz MA. The serotonin theory of depression: A systematic umbrella review of the evidence. *Molecular Psychiatry* 2023;28(8):3243–56.
14. Ban TA. Fifty years chlorpromazine: A historical perspective. *Neuropsychiatric Disease and Treatment* 2007;3(4):495–500.

15. Stahl SM. Imipramine. In: *Prescriber's Guide: Stahl's Essential Psychopharmacology*. Cambridge: Cambridge University Press; 2020. pp. 367–74.
16. Wong DT, Perry KW, Bymaster FP. The discovery of fluoxetine hydrochloride (Prozac). *Nature Reviews Drug Discovery* 2005;4(9):764–74.
17. Fabre LF, Abuzzahab FS, Amin M, Claghorn JL, Mendels J, Petrie WM, Dube S, Small JG. Sertraline safety and efficacy in major depression: A double-blind fixed-dose comparison with placebo. *Biological Psychiatry* 1995;38(9):592–602.
18. U.S. Food and Drug Administration. Clinical review: Sertraline hydrochloride [Internet]. Silver Spring, MD: FDA; [cited 2025 Jul 22]. Available from: https://www.fda.gov/files/drugs/published/N19-839S044-Sertraline-Clinical-BPCA.pdf
19. Burke WJ, Gergel I, Bose A. Fixed-dose trial of the single isomer SSRI escitalopram in depressed outpatients. *The Journal of Clinical Psychiatry* 2002;63(4):331–6. https://doi.org/10.4088/JCP.v63n0410. PubMed Central+2JAMA Network+2CoLab+2
20. Drug Approval Package: Lexapro (escitalopram oxalate) NDA #021323 [Internet]. Fda.gov. 2025 [cited 2025 Jul 22]. Available from: https://www.accessdata.fda.gov/drugsatfda_docs/nda/2002/21-323_Lexapro.cfm?
21. Miller G. Is pharma running out of brainy ideas? *Science* 2010; 329(5991):502–4.
22. Hyman SE. Psychiatric drug development: Diagnosing a crisis. In *Cerebrum: The Dana Forum on Brain Science* 2013 Apr 2 (Vol. 2013, p. 5).
23. Fernando AB, Robbins TW. Animal models of neuropsychiatric disorders. *Annual Review of Clinical Psychology* 2011;7(1):39–61.
24. Nestler EJ, Hyman SE. Animal models of neuropsychiatric disorders. *Nature Neuroscience* 2010;13(10):1161–9.
25. Pankevich DE, Altevogt BM, Dunlop J, Gage FH, Hyman SE. Improving and accelerating drug development for nervous system disorders. *Neuron* 2014;84(3):546–53.
26. Begley CG, Ioannidis JP. Reproducibility in science: Improving the standard for basic and preclinical research. *Circulation Research* 2015; 116(1):116–26.

27. Thomas D. Clinical Development Success Rates and Contributing Factors 2011–2020 [Internet]. Biotechnology Innovation Organization. 2021 Feb [cited 2025 Jul 23]. Available from: go.bio.org.
28. Kessler RC, Berglund P, Demler O, Jin R, Koretz D, Merikangas KR, Rush AJ, Walters EE, Wang PS. The epidemiology of major depressive disorder: Results from the National Comorbidity Survey Replication (NCS-R). *Journal of the American Medical Association* 2003;289(23): 3095–105. https://doi.org/10.1001/jama.289.23.3095.
29. Hamilton M. A rating scale for depression. *Journal of Neurology, Neurosurgery, and Psychiatry* 1960;23(1):56–62. https://doi.org/10.1136/jnnp.23.1.56.
30. Montgomery SA, Åsberg M. A new depression scale designed to be sensitive to change. *The British Journal of Psychiatry* 1979;134(4):382–9. https://doi.org/10.1192/bjp.134.4.382.
31. Heo M, Murphy CF, Meyers BS. Relationship between the Hamilton depression rating scale and the Montgomery-Åsberg depression rating scale in depressed elderly: A meta-analysis. *The American Journal of Geriatric Psychiatry* 2007;15(10):899–905.
32. Seemüller F, Schennach R, Musil R, Obermeier M, Adli M, Bauer M, Brieger P, Laux G, Gaebel W, Falkai P, Riedel M. A factor analytic comparison of three commonly used depression scales (HAMD, MADRS, BDI) in a large sample of depressed inpatients. *BMC Psychiatry* 2023; 23(1):548.
33. Carmody TJ, Rush AJ, Bernstein I, Warden D, Brannan S, Burnham D, Woo A, Trivedi MH. The Montgomery Åsberg and the Hamilton ratings of depression: A comparison of measures. *European Neuropsycho-Pharmacology* 2006;16(8):601–11.
34. Carneiro AM, Fernandes F, Moreno RA. Hamilton depression rating scale and Montgomery–Åsberg depression rating scale in depressed and bipolar I patients: Psychometric properties in a Brazilian sample. *Health and Quality of Life Outcomes* 2015;13(1):42.
35. Santi NS, Biswal SB, Naik BN, Sahoo JP, Rath B. Revisiting depression rating scales: Analysis of a randomized trial. *Cureus* 2024;16(10).
36. Santi NS, Biswal SB, Naik BN, Sahoo JP, Rath B. Comparison of Hamilton depression rating scale and Montgomery-Åsberg depression rating scale: Baked straight from a randomized study. *Cureus* 2023;15(9).

37. Müller MJ, Himmerich H, Kienzle B, Szegedi A. Differentiating moderate and severe depression using the Montgomery–Åsberg depression rating scale (MADRS). *Journal of Affective Disorders* 2003;77(3):255–60.
38. Cohen EA, Hassman HH, Ereshefsky L, Walling DP, Grindell VM, Keefe RS, Wyka K, Horan WP. Placebo response mitigation with a participant-focused psychoeducational procedure: A randomized, single-blind, all placebo study in major depressive and psychotic disorders. *Neuropsychopharmacology* 2021;46(4):844–50.
39. Walsh BT, Seidman SN, Sysko R, Gould M. Placebo response in studies of major depression: Variable, substantial, and growing. *Journal of the American Medical Association* 2002;287(14):1840–7.
40. Meister R, Abbas M, Antel J, Peters T, Pan Y, Bingel U, Nestoriuc Y, Hebebrand J. Placebo response rates and potential modifiers in double-blind randomized controlled trials of second and newer generation antidepressants for major depressive disorder in children and adolescents: A systematic review and meta-regression analysis. *European Child & Adolescent Psychiatry* 2020;29(3):253–73.
41. Sachdev A, Sharpe I, Bowman M, Booth CM, Gyawali B. Objective response rate of placebo in randomized controlled trials of anticancer medicines. *EClinicalMedicine* 2023;55.
42. Bienenfeld L, Frishman W, Glasser SP. The placebo effect in cardiovascular disease. *American Heart Journal* 1996;132(6):1207–21.
43. McClellan J, King MC. Genetic heterogeneity in human disease. *Cell* 2010;141(2):210–7.
44. American Psychiatric Association. *Diagnostic and Statistical Manual of Mental Disorders*. 5th ed. Arlington, VA: American Psychiatric Publishing; 2013.
45. Fried EI, Nesse RM. Depression is not a consistent syndrome: An investigation of unique symptom patterns in the STAR★D study. *Journal of Affective Disorders* 2015;172:96–102.
46. Insel T, Cuthbert B, Garvey M, Heinssen R, Pine DS, Quinn K, Sanislow C, Wang P. Research domain criteria (RDoC): Toward a new classification framework for research on mental disorders. *American Journal of Psychiatry* 2010;167(7):748–51.
47. Strimbu K, Tavel JA. What are biomarkers? *Current Opinion in HIV and AIDS* 2010;5(6):463–6.

48. Bögerl CM, Laun FB, Nagel AM, Bickelhaupt S, Uder M, Hanspach J. Analysis of the sample size used in clinical MRI studies. *PLoS One* 2025;20(3):e0316611.
49. Bruggeman FJ, Westerhoff HV. The nature of systems biology. *TRENDS in Microbiology* 2007;15(1):45–50.

Chapter 4: Psychiatry as a System

1. Offman A, Kleinplatz PJ. Does PMDD belong in the DSM? Challenging the medicalization of women's bodies. *The Canadian Journal of Human Sexuality* 2004;13(1):17.
2. Conrad P. *The Medicalization of Society: On the Transformation of Human Conditions into Treatable Disorders*. Baltimore: Johns Hopkins University Press; 2007 Jun 11.
3. Barry MJ, Nicholson WK, Silverstein M, Coker TR, Davidson KW, Davis EM, Donahue KE, Jaén CR, Li L, Ogedegbe G, Pbert L. Screening for anxiety disorders in adults: US Preventive Services Task Force recommendation statement. *JAMA* 2023;329(24):2163–70.

Chapter 5: The Fundamentals of AI

1. Google Trends. Artificial intelligence search trends [Internet]. 2025 [cited 2025 Jun 2]. Available from: https://trends.withgoogle.com/trends/us/artificial-intelligence-search-trends/
2. Statista. Generative AI global weekly search trends on Google 2024 [Internet]. 2024 [cited 2025 Jun 2]. Available from: https://www.statista.com/statistics/1367868/generative-ai-google-searches-worldwide/
3. Hostinger. AI myths busted: What Americans believe vs. what's true [Internet]. 2025 [cited 2025 Jun 2]. Available from: https://www.hostinger.com/blog/ai-myths-survey
4. PBS. ENIAC: A pioneering computer [Internet]. 1999 [cited 2025 Jun 2]. Available from: https://www.pbs.org/transistor/science/events/eniac.html
5. National Museum of American History. ENIAC initiating unit [Internet]. 2004 [cited 2025 Jun 2]. Available from: https://americanhistory.si.edu/collections/object/nmah_334262

6. Central Intelligence Agency. The enigma of Alan Turing [Internet]. 2015 [cited 2025 Jun 2]. Available from: https://www.cia.gov/stories/story/the-enigma-of-alan-turing/
7. Bletchley Park Archive. Cryptanalysis of the Enigma [Internet]. 2012 [cited 2025 Jun 2]. Available from: https://www.historyofinformation.com/detail.php?id=628
8. McCarthy J, Minsky ML, Rochester N, Shannon CE. A proposal for the Dartmouth Summer Research Project on Artificial Intelligence [Internet]. Stanford University; 1955 [cited 2025 Jun 2]. Available from: https://www-formal.stanford.edu/jmc/history/dartmouth/dartmouth.html
9. Dartmouth College. *Proposal for the Dartmouth Summer Research Project on Artificial Intelligence.* Hanover, NH: Dartmouth College; 1955.
10. Newell A, Simon H. The logic theory machine—A complex information processing system. *IRE Transactions on Information Theory* 1956; 2(3):61–79.
11. Newell A, Shaw JC, Simon HA. Report on a general problem-solving program (GPS) for a computer [Internet]. Santa Monica (CA): RAND Corporation; 1959 [cited 2025 Jun 2]. Available from: https://stacks.stanford.edu/file/druid:zk239tp3547/zk239tp3547.pdf
12. Rosenblatt F. *The Perceptron, a Perceiving and Recognizing Automaton: (Project Para).* Cornell Aeronautical Laboratory; 1957.
13. Shortliffe E, editor. *Computer-Based Medical Consultations: MYCIN.* Elsevier; 2012, Dec 2.
14. Shortliffe EH. Mycin: A knowledge-based computer program applied to infectious diseases. In *Proceedings of the Annual Symposium on Computer Application in Medical Care* 1977 Oct 5 (p. 66).
15. Silver D, Huang A, Maddison CJ, Guez A, Sifre L, Van Den Driessche G, Schrittwieser J, Antonoglou I, Panneershelvam V, Lanctot M, Dieleman S. Mastering the game of go with deep neural networks and tree search. *Nature* 2016;529(7587):484–9.
16. Raghu A, Komorowski M, Celi LA, Szolovits P, Ghassemi M. Continuous state-space models for optimal sepsis treatment: A deep reinforcement learning approach. In *Machine Learning for Healthcare Conference* 2017 Nov 6 (pp. 147–63). PMLR.

17. Ford C. Managing type 1 diabetes is tricky. Can AI help? *WIRED* [Internet]. 2023 Jul 5 [cited 2025 Jun 2]. Available from: https://www.wired.com/story/managing-type-1-diabetes-is-tricky-can-ai-help
18. Stember J, Shalu H. Deep reinforcement learning to detect brain lesions on MRI: A proof-of-concept application of reinforcement learning to medical images. arXiv preprint arXiv:2008.02708. 2020 Aug 6.
19. OpenAI. GPT-4 technical report [Internet]. OpenAI; 2023 Mar 27 [cited 2025 Jun 2]. Available from: https://cdn.openai.com/papers/gpt-4.pdf

Chapter 6: It Is All About the Data

1. National Institute of Standards and Technology. Glossary – NIST Computer Security Resource Center: Data definition. 2025. Available from: https://csrc.nist.gov/glossary/term/data
2. Kamulegeya L, Bwanika J, Okello M, Rusoke D, Nassiwa F, Lubega W, Musinguzi D, Börve A. Using artificial intelligence on dermatology conditions in Uganda: A case for diversity in training data sets for machine learning. *African Health Sciences* 2023;23(2):753–63.
3. Raichle ME. The brain's dark energy. *Scientific American* 2010;302(3):44–9.
4. Termly. 54 Revealing AI Data Privacy Statistics. 2025. Available from: https://termly.io/resources/articles/ai-statistics/
5. International Association of Privacy Professionals (IAPP). Consumer Perspectives of Privacy and Artificial Intelligence. 2024. Available from: https://iapp.org/resources/article/consumer-perspectives-of-privacy-and-ai/
6. IEEE Standards Association. The IEEE Global Initiative 2.0 on Ethics of Autonomous and Intelligent Systems. 2024. Available from: https://standards.ieee.org/industry-connections/activities/ieee-global-initiative/
7. IEEE Standards Association. IEEE Introduces New Program for Free Access to AI Ethics and Governance Standards. 2024. Available from: https://standards.ieee.org/news/get-program-ai-ethics/
8. National Institute of Standards and Technology. AI Risk Management Framework. 2025. Available from: https://www.nist.gov/itl/ai-risk-management-framework

9. Compact. Understanding intersection between EU's AI Act and privacy compliance. 2024. Available from: https://www.compact.nl/articles/understanding-intersection-between-eus-ai-act-and-privacy-compliance/
10. World Economic Forum. 9 ethical AI principles for organizations to follow. 2025. Available from: https://www.weforum.org/stories/2021/06/ethical-principles-for-ai/

Chapter 7: Innovation Starts with Data

1. Cai N, Choi KW, Fried EI. Reviewing the genetics of heterogeneity in depression: Operationalizations, manifestations and etiologies. *Human Molecular Genetics* 2020;29(R1):R10–8.
2. National Science Foundation. Critical Techniques and Technologies for Advancing Big Data Science & Engineering (BIGDATA) (NSF-14–543) [Internet]. Alexandria (VA): National Science Foundation; 2014 Mar 12 [cited 2025 Jun 11]. Available from: https://www.nsf.gov/funding/opportunities/bigdata-critical-techniques-technologies-methodologies-advancing/504767/nsf14-543/solicitation
3. Precedence Research. Healthcare Data Monetization Solutions Market Size and Forecast 2025 to 2034 [cited 2025 May 16]. Available from: https://www.precedenceresearch.com/healthcare-data-monetization-solutions-market
4. Caspi A, Moffitt TE. Gene–environment interactions in psychiatry: Joining forces with neuroscience. *Nature Reviews Neuroscience* 2006;7(7):583–90.
5. Wermter AK, Laucht M, Schimmelmann BG, Banaschweski T, Sonuga-Barke EJ, Rietschel M, Becker K. From nature versus nurture, via nature and nurture, to gene× environment interaction in mental disorders. *European Child & Adolescent Psychiatry* 2010;19(3):199–210.
6. World Health Organization. Depressive disorder (depression) [Internet]. World Health Organization. 2023. Available from: https://www.who.int/news-room/fact-sheets/detail/depression
7. CDC. Data and statistics on ADHD [Internet]. Attention-Deficit/Hyperactivity Disorder (ADHD). CDC; 2024. Available from: https://www.cdc.gov/adhd/data/index.html

8. National Institute on Drug Abuse. Sex Differences in Substance Use | National Institute on Drug Abuse [Internet]. National Institute on Drug Abuse. 2025. Available from: https://nida.nih.gov/publications/research-reports/substance-use-in-women/sex-differences-in-substance-use
9. Abel KM, Drake R, Goldstein JM. Sex differences in schizophrenia. *International Review of Psychiatry* 2010;22(5):417–28.
10. Stewart DE, Vigod S. Postpartum depression. *New England Journal of Medicine* 2016;375(22):2177–86.
11. Freeman EW. Depression in the menopause transition: Risks in the changing hormone milieu as observed in the general population. *Women's Midlife Health* 2015;1(1):2.
12. Eranti SV, MacCabe JH, Bundy H, Murray RM. Gender difference in age at onset of schizophrenia: A meta-analysis. *Psychological Medicine* 2013;43(1):155–67.
13. Stumper A, Alloy LB. Associations between pubertal stage and depression: A systematic review of the literature. *Child Psychiatry & Human Development* 2023;54(2):312–39.
14. Sundström Poromaa I, Gingnell M. Menstrual cycle influence on cognitive function and emotion processing—From a reproductive perspective. *Frontiers in Neuroscience* 2014;8:380.
15. Borrow AP, Cameron NM. Estrogenic mediation of serotonergic and neurotrophic systems: Implications for female mood disorders. *Progress in Neuro-Psychopharmacology and Biological Psychiatry* 2014;54:13–25.
16. Schiller CE, Schmidt PJ, Rubinow DR. Allopregnanolone as a mediator of affective switching in reproductive mood disorders. *Psychopharmacology* 2014;231(17):3557–67.
17. McHenry J, Carrier N, Hull E, Kabbaj M. Sex differences in anxiety and depression: Role of testosterone. *Frontiers in Neuroendocrinology* 2014; 35(1):42–57.
18. Kornstein SG, Schatzberg AF, Thase ME, Yonkers KA, McCullough JP, Keitner GI, Gelenberg AJ, Davis SM, Harrison WM, Keller MB. Gender differences in treatment response to sertraline versus imipramine in chronic depression. *American Journal of Psychiatry* 2000;157(9):1445–52.

19. Zeng Y, Chourpiliadis C, Hammar N, Seitz C, Valdimarsdóttir UA, Fang F, Song H, Wei D. Inflammatory biomarkers and risk of psychiatric disorders. *JAMA Psychiatry* 2024;81(11):1118–29.
20. Pu J, Liu Y, Zhang H, Tian L, Gui S, Yu Y, Chen X, Chen Y, Yang L, Ran Y, Zhong X. An integrated meta-analysis of peripheral blood metabolites and biological functions in major depressive disorder. *Molecular Psychiatry* 2021;26(8):4265–76.
21. Tomasik J, Harrison SJ, Rustogi N, Olmert T, Barton-Owen G, Han SY, Cooper JD, Eljasz P, Farrag LP, Friend LV, Bell E. Metabolomic biomarker signatures for bipolar and unipolar depression. *JAMA Psychiatry* 2024;81(1):101–6.
22. Kopylov AT, Stepanov AA, Butkova TV, Malsagova KA, Zakharova NV, Kostyuk GP, Elmuratov AU, Kaysheva AL. Consolidation of metabolomic, proteomic, and GWAS data in connective model of schizophrenia. *Scientific Reports* 2023;13(1):2139.
23. Zhang R, Luo J, Wang T, Wang W, Sun J, Zhang D. Identifying novel protein biomarkers with cross-psychiatric disorders effects and potential intervention targets: Evidence from proteomic-Mendelian randomization. *Progress in Neuro-Psychopharmacology and Biological Psychiatry* 2025:111396.
24. Horn J, Mayer DE, Chen S, Mayer EA. Role of diet and its effects on the gut microbiome in the pathophysiology of mental disorders. *Translational Psychiatry* 2022;12(1):164.
25. Wilcox T, Biondi M. fNIRS in the developmental sciences. *Wiley Interdisciplinary Reviews: Cognitive Science* 2015;6(3):263–83.
26. Allied Market Research. At-Home Testing Market: Global Opportunity Analysis and Industry Forecast, 2021–2031. Portland, OR: Allied Market Research; 2022. Report no. A31866. Available from: https://www.alliedmarketresearch.com/at-home-testing-market-A31866 alliedmarketresearch.comalliedmarketresearch.com+9alliedmarket research.com+9alliedmarketresearch.com+9
27. Allied Market Research. At-Home Genetic Testing Market: Global Opportunity Analysis and Industry Forecast, 2024–2035. Portland, OR: Allied Market Research; Mar 2025. Report no. A66394. Available from: https://www.alliedmarketresearch.com/at-home-genetic-testing-market-A66394 alliedmarketresearch.com

28. Wang Z, Zou Y, Liu J, Peng W, Li M, Zou Z. Heart rate variability in mental disorders: An umbrella review of meta-analyses. *Translational Psychiatry* 2025;15(1):104.
29. Morris C, Conway AA, Becraft JL, Ferrucci BJ. Toward an understanding of data collection integrity. *Behavior Analysis in Practice* 2022;15(4):1361–72.
30. Uzzaman S, Joordens S. The eyes know what you are thinking: Eye movements as an objective measure of mind wandering. *Consciousness and Cognition* 2011;20(4):1882–6.
31. Mikhaylov D, Saeed M, Husain Alhosani M, Al Wahedi YF. Comparison of EEG signal spectral characteristics obtained with consumer-and research-grade devices. *Sensors* 2024;24(24):8108.
32. Ratti E, Waninger S, Berka C, Ruffini G, Verma A. Comparison of medical and consumer wireless EEG systems for use in clinical trials. *Frontiers in Human Neuroscience* 2017;11:398.
33. Ma S, Yang J, Yang B, Kang L, Wang P, Zhang N, Wang W, Zong X, Wang Y, Bai H, Guo Q. The patient health questionnaire-9 vs. the Hamilton rating scale for depression in assessing major depressive disorder. *Frontiers in Psychiatry* 2021;12:747139.
34. Levis B, Benedetti A, Thombs BD. Accuracy of Patient Health Questionnaire-9 (PHQ-9) for screening to detect major depression: Individual participant data meta-analysis. *BMJ* 2019;365.
35. Teusen C, Hapfelmeier A, von Schrottenberg V, Goekce F, Pitschel-Walz G, Henningsen P, Gensichen J, Schneider A, POKAL-Study-Group. Combining the GP's assessment and the PHQ-9 questionnaire leads to more reliable and clinically relevant diagnoses in primary care. *PLoS One* 2022;17(10):e0276534.
36. Apple Inc. Biosignal sensing device using dynamic selection of electrodes. US Patent Application 20230225659A1. Filed 9 Jan 2023. Published 20 Jul 2023.

Chapter 8: Revealing the Nature of Mental Disorders

1. Williams LM. Precision psychiatry: A neural circuit taxonomy for depression and anxiety. *The Lancet Psychiatry* 2016;3(5):472–80.
2. Buckner RL, Andrews-Hanna JR, Schacter DL. The brain's default network: Anatomy, function, and relevance to disease. *Annals of the New York Academy of Sciences* 2008;1124(1):1–38.
3. Sheline YI, Barch DM, Price JL, Rundle MM, Vaishnavi SN, Snyder AZ, Mintun MA, Wang S, Coalson RS, Raichle ME. The default mode network and self-referential processes in depression. *Proceedings of the National Academy of Sciences* 2009;106(6):1942–7.
4. Hamilton JP, Farmer M, Fogelman P, Gotlib IH. Depressive rumination, the default-mode network, and the dark matter of clinical neuroscience. *Biological Psychiatry* 2015;78(4):224–30.
5. Zhang S, Chen JM, Kuang L, Cao J, Zhang H, Ai M, Wang W, Zhang SD, Wang SY, Liu SJ, Fang WD. Association between abnormal default mode network activity and suicidality in depressed adolescents. *BMC Psychiatry* 2016;16(1):337.
6. Drysdale AT, Grosenick L, Downar J, Dunlop K, Mansouri F, Meng Y, Fetcho RN, Zebley B, Oathes DJ, Etkin A, Schatzberg AF. Resting-state connectivity biomarkers define neurophysiological subtypes of depression. *Nature Medicine* 2017;23(1):28–38.
7. Zhang Y, Wu W, Toll RT, Naparstek S, Maron-Katz A, Watts M, Gordon J, Jeong J, Astolfi L, Shpigel E, Longwell P. Identification of psychiatric disorder subtypes from functional connectivity patterns in resting-state electroencephalography. *Nature Biomedical Engineering* 2021;5(4):309–23.
8. Arns M, Olbrich S, Sack AT. Biomarker-driven stratified psychiatry: From stepped-care to matched-care in mental health. *Nature Mental Health* 2023;1(12):917–9.
9. Harmer CJ, Goodwin GM, Cowen PJ. Why do antidepressants take so long to work? A cognitive neuropsychological model of antidepressant drug action. *The British Journal of Psychiatry* 2009;195(2):102–8.
10. García-Gutiérrez MS, Navarrete F, Sala F, Gasparyan A, Austrich-Olivares A, Manzanares J. Biomarkers in psychiatry: Concept, definition, types and relevance to the clinical reality. *Frontiers in Psychiatry* 2020;11:432.

11. Sadri A. Is target-based drug discovery efficient? Discovery and "off-target" mechanisms of all drugs. *Journal of Medicinal Chemistry* 2023;66(18):12651–77.
12. Imrie F, Davis R, van der Schaar M. Multiple stakeholders drive diverse interpretability requirements for machine learning in healthcare. *Nature Machine Intelligence* 2023;5(8):824–9.
13. Dehimi NE, Tolba Z. Attention mechanisms in deep learning: Towards explainable artificial intelligence. *2024 6th International Conference on Pattern Analysis and Intelligent Systems (PAIS)*. 2024 Apr 24 (pp. 1–7). IEEE.
14. Garreau D, Luxburg U. Explaining the explainer: A first theoretical analysis of LIME. *International Conference on Artificial Intelligence and Statistics* 2020 (pp. 1287–1296). PMLR.
15. Van den Broeck G, Lykov A, Schleich M, Suciu D. On the tractability of SHAP explanations. *Journal of Artificial Intelligence Research* 2022; 74:851–86.
16. Georgiev D, Barbiero P, Kazhdan D, Veličković P, Liò P. Algorithmic concept-based explainable reasoning. *Proceedings of the AAAI Conference on Artificial Intelligence*. 2022 Jun 28 (Vol. 36, No. 6, pp. 6685–6693).
17. Crabbé J, Qian Z, Imrie F, van der Schaar M. Explaining latent representations with a corpus of examples. *Advances in Neural Information Processing Systems* 2021;34:12154–66.
18. Tanyel T, Ayvaz S, Keserci B. Beyond known reality: Exploiting counterfactual explanations for medical research. arXiv preprint arXiv:2307.02131. 2023.
19. Lekadir K, Frangi AF, Porras AR, Glocker B, Cintas C, Langlotz CP, Weicken E, Asselbergs FW, Prior F, Collins GS, Kaissis G. FUTURE-AI: International consensus guideline for trustworthy and deployable artificial intelligence in healthcare. *BMJ* 2025; 388:e081554.
20. DARPA. Explainable Artificial Intelligence (XAI) program [Internet]. Arlington (VA): Defense Advanced Research Projects Agency; 2022 [cited 2025 Jun 16]. Available from: https://www.darpa.mil/program/explainable-artificial-intelligence

Chapter 9: Innovations Within Reach

1. Centers for Disease Control and Prevention. Suicide data and statistics [Internet]. Atlanta (GA): CDC, National Center for Injury Prevention and Control; 2025 Mar 26 [cited 2025 Jun 18]. Available from: https://www.cdc.gov/suicide/facts/data.html
2. Oquendo MA. Impulsive versus planned suicide attempts: Different phenotypes? *The Journal of Clinical Psychiatry* 2015;76(3):8848.
3. Lim M, Lee S, Park JI. Differences between impulsive and non-impulsive suicide attempts among individuals treated in emergency rooms of South Korea. *Psychiatry Investigation* 2016;13(4):389.
4. Rimkeviciene J, De Leo D. Impulsive suicide attempts: A systematic literature review of definitions, characteristics and risk factors. *Journal of Affective Disorders* 2015;171:93–104.
5. Berona J, Whitton S, Newcomb ME, Mustanski B, Gibbons R. Predicting the transition from suicidal ideation to suicide attempt among sexual and gender minority youths. *Psychiatric Services* 2021; 72(11):1261–7.
6. Sunderland M, Batterham PJ, Calear AL, Chapman C, Slade T. Factors associated with the time to transition from suicidal ideation to suicide plans and attempts in the Australian general population. *Psychological Medicine* 2023;53(1):258–66.
7. Techloy. The rise of deceased social media accounts [Internet]. 2024 Jun 20 [cited 2025 Jun 18]. Available from: https://www.techloy.com/the-rise-of-deceased-social-media-accounts/
8. Boucher EM, Raiker JS. Engagement and retention in digital mental health interventions: A narrative review. *BMC Digital Health* 2024; 2(1):52.
9. Hanley HW, Durumeric Z. Machine-made media: Monitoring the mobilization of machine-generated articles on misinformation and mainstream news websites. *Proceedings of the International AAAI Conference on Web and Social Media* 2024 May 28 (Vol. 18, pp. 542–556).
10. Kabir S, Udo-Imeh DN, Kou B, Zhang T. Is stack overflow obsolete? An empirical study of the characteristics of chatgpt answers to stack overflow questions. *Proceedings of the 2024 CHI Conference on Human Factors in Computing Systems* 2024 May 11 (pp. 1–17).

11. Cowan KE, McKean AJ, Gentry MT, Hilty DM. Barriers to use of telepsychiatry: Clinicians as gatekeepers. *Mayo Clinic Proceedings* 2019 (Vol. 94, No. 12, pp. 2510–2523). Elsevier.
12. Gutiérrez-Rojas L, Alvarez-Mon MA, Andreu-Bernabeu Á, Capitán L, de Las Cuevas C, Gómez JC, Grande I, Hidalgo-Mazzei D, Mateos R, Moreno-Gea P, De Vicente-Muñoz T. Telepsychiatry: The future is already present. *Spanish Journal of Psychiatry and Mental Health* 2023; 16(1):51–7.
13. Martiniuk A, Toepfer A, Lane-Brown A. A review of risks, adverse effects and mitigation strategies when delivering mental health services using telehealth. *Journal of Mental Health* 2024;33(3):415–38.
14. Werner A, Kegu J. Former Cerebral employees say company's practices put patients at risk: "It's chaotic. It's confusing. It could be extremely dangerous". *CBS News* [Internet]. 2022 Jun 22 [cited 2025 Jun 20]. Available from: https://www.cbsnews.com/news/cerebral-ceo-mental-health-startup/
15. U.S. Department of Justice, U.S. Attorney's Office for the Eastern District of New York. *Telehealth company Cerebral agrees to pay over $3.6 million in connection with business practices that encouraged the unauthorized distribution of controlled substances* [Internet]. Brooklyn (NY): DOJ; 2024 Nov 4 [cited 2025 Jun 20]. Available from: https://www.justice.gov/usao-edny/pr/telehealth-company-cerebral-agrees-pay-over-36-million-connection-business-practices
16. Nock MK, Millner AJ, Ross EL, Kennedy CJ, Al-Suwaidi M, Barak-Corren Y, Castro VM, Castro-Ramirez F, Lauricella T, Murman N, Petukhova M. Prediction of suicide attempts using clinician assessment, patient self-report, and electronic health records. *JAMA Network Open* 2022;5(1):e2144373.

Acknowledgments

Everything begins with an idea—something intangible yet powerful enough to become reality. The idea for this book came from Christina Rudloff, who reached out after watching my TEDx talk and suggested turning my lectures into a written work. I'm sincerely grateful to Christina for this suggestion and her encouragement at the very start of this journey.

However, ideas become reality only through support and opportunity. I'd particularly like to thank the Harvard iLab team—Thara Pillai, Jorge Cortell, and Becca Xiong, PhD—who made my participation at TEDx Boston possible. Special thanks also go to the TEDx Boston organizers, particularly John Werner, for offering me the chance to share my ideas with a broader audience. Without all of you, this book simply wouldn't exist.

Even with an idea and opportunity in place, it takes dedicated effort and professional support to actually bring a book to life. I'm sincerely grateful to the entire Wiley team, especially my development editor, Kim Wimpsett, and acquisitions editor, Ryan Flahive, for their professionalism, patience, and invaluable guidance in publishing this book.

This book is built upon the research, experimentation, trials, and errors of my team at Brainify.AI. Thanks to their persistent effort, I developed my current understanding of the field of psychiatry, gained clearer insights into existing challenges, and acquired greater awareness of the opportunities and obstacles accompanying innovation in this area.

I also extend my heartfelt appreciation to all the advisors and experts I've had the privilege to collaborate with over the past five years, whose experience greatly influenced my understanding of this field. I'd particularly like to thank Diego A. Pizzagalli, PhD, Conor M. Liston, MD, PhD, Jim Doherty, PhD, Maurizio Fava, MD, Marlene Freeman, MD, Kristina Deligiannidis, MD, Lisa Maeng, PhD, Alik Widge, MD, PhD, Martijn Arns, PhD, Tracey Tokuhama-Espinosa, PhD, and Edward Franz Pace-Schott, PhD.

Additionally, I want to thank Jay's friends, who helped me recreate and preserve her story in this book.

Special gratitude goes to those who patiently read my raw and unfinished manuscripts, provided feedback, and helped make this book clearer and better structured. I particularly appreciate Ahmet Hamdi Cavusoglu for our regular meetings in Central Park, where he listened patiently to my reflections, helped me organize my thoughts, engaged in thoughtful discussions, read individual chapters, and provided valuable insights. My heartfelt thanks also go to Ivan Nechaev, who read the manuscript at various stages and gave crucial recommendations, without which this book would have been far less coherent and clear.

A separate thank you goes to Jenny Fomenko—not only for reading my drafts but also for helping me maintain discipline and consistency throughout this process. Jenny became my "regimen buddy," regularly staying in touch, reminding me of the importance of remaining focused, and supporting me in bringing this project to completion.

Bringing this book to life would have been impossible without constant support and the belief that everything would eventually work out. For this, I want to express my deepest gratitude to my husband, Ivan Mishanin. He not only helped me pull myself together and created the most comfortable environment possible so I could focus on writing but also patiently endured all my emotional ups and downs, carefully read every paragraph I wrote, and provided essential and detailed feedback. I simply cannot imagine having written this book without him.

Special thanks for my mental stability go to our dachshund, Josie. But since she can't read, I'll just reward her with extra treats and scratch her behind the ear.

About the Author

Mariam Khayretdinova is the CEO and co-founder of Brainify.AI, a company specializing in the application of artificial intelligence and electroencephalography (EEG) analysis for the development of more effective treatments for mental health disorders, as well as advancing the understanding of the underlying mechanisms of these conditions. Her work bridges the fields of technology, artificial intelligence, and neuroscience.

After completing her master's degree in applied mathematics, Mariam spent more than a decade in implementing innovative technological solutions into established industries. She then returned to academia to earn a second master's degree in psychology from Harvard Extension School, subsequently working in research laboratories studying the biological mechanisms of mental disorders.

Currently, Mariam continues her research at the University of Cambridge, where she develops mathematical models for analyzing large-scale EEG datasets, forming the scientific foundation of her company's technological solutions.

Mariam regularly speaks at events about the potential of AI in psychiatry, including at the House of Trust 2024 during the World Economic Forum in Davos, The Real Summit, and TEDx Boston, where she delivered her talk, "Decoding Depression: How AI is Revolutionizing Mental Health." She is also the author of multiple scientific publications and patents in the fields of artificial intelligence and psychiatry.

Index

A
academic institutions, 75
accuracy, 120
addiction, 63–64
adoption of stratified psychiatry approaches, 169–170
AI *See* artificial intelligence (AI)
AlphaGo, 108, 109
American Psychiatric Association (APA), 26, 32, 35, 75, 81
animal models, 48
annotation, 151
ANT *See* attentional network test (ANT)
antibody tests, 59
antidepressant, 42–46
anxiety, xi, 8, 18, 42
anxiety disorders, xv, 141
APA *See* American Psychiatric Association (APA)
Aristotle, 69
artificial intelligence (AI), xvi, 182–183
    applications, 131–132
    birth of, 96–99
    conversations, 94
    data quality criteria, 119–124
    first algorithms, 99–102
    hidden patterns, 162
    history of, 116
    inescapable data dependency, 116–117
    modern paradigms, 102–113
    noise, 125
    relevance, 124
    signal-to-noise ratio, 125
    structured data, 117–118
    surveys, 95
    technological progress, 95
    timeliness, 124
    unstructured data, 118–119
attention mechanisms, 180
attention-deficit/hyperactivity disorder (ADHD), 16
attentional network test (ANT), 146
attribution methods, 180
auditory learning, 15
augmented reality (AR), 147
autism spectrum disorder, 37
autonomous vehicles, 110

B
behavioral data, 139, 145–148
big data, 137–138
biological data, 139–145, 182
biological targets, 49
biomarker, 63, 84
    diagnostic, 136, 178
    predictive, 168–174, 183
    prognostic, 178
    risk, 178
bipolar disorder, 45
blood tests, 59
Bombe, 98
bottom-up approach, 66

brain circuits, abnormalities in, 63
brain-activity data, 143
brain-based indicators, 84

C

C-reactive protein, 142
CDx *See* companion diagnostic (CDx)
CGM systems *See* continuous glucose
        monitoring (CGM) systems
ChatGPT, 96, 111, 187, 188, 195
chest radiography, 59
chlorpromazine (Thorazine), 46
citalopram, 46–47
clinical anhedonia, 27
clinical data, 139
clinical subtypes, of psychiatric disorders, 66
clinical trials
    methodological changes, 47
    Phase I, 50–51
    Phase II and III, 51–62
    remission, 55
    response, 55
    statistical analysis, 55
clinics, 75
clustering methods, 162–164
collateral information, 28
communication, 31
communication data, 139, 148–149
companion diagnostic (CDx), 168–169, 171
complete blood counts (CBC), 59
completeness, 121
complex "black box" systems, 105
concept-based reasoning (CBR), 180–181
consistency, 122
continuous glucose monitoring (CGM)
        systems, 191, 193
control group, 52
counterfactual explanations, 181
COVID-19, 58, 59
cross-validation, 105
cultural stigma, xiv–xv

D

data
    aggregation, 154–157
    augmentation, 122, 127
    collection, 161–162
    defined, 117
    governance, 122–123
    quality and management, 114
    semi-structured, 119
    structure, 117, 118
    unstructured, 118, 119
data quality, 119–120
    accuracy, 120
    completeness, 121
    consistency, 122
    data governance, 122–123
    precision, 120
    representativeness, 121–122
data science
    attention mechanisms, 180
    attribution methods, 180
    classification tasks, 103
    concept-based reasoning (CBR), 180–181
    data augmentation, 122, 127
    exploration–exploitation dilemma, 110
    feature importance, 180, 182, 197
    fine-tuning, 112
    foundational model, 111–113, 172
    Gaussian filtering, 126
    independent component analysis
        (ICA), 127
    labeled training datasets, 102
    labeling quality, 151–152
    large language models (LLMs),
        111, 193, 195
    median filtering, 126
    noise, 125, 128
    overfitting, 105
    penalties, 108
    prototype and example-based
        explanations, 181
    regression tasks, 103, 104
    rewards, 108–110
    self-supervised learning, 112
    signal, 125
    signal-to-noise ratio (SNR), 125, 149-151
    supervised learning, 102-105, 107
    systematic noise, 128–129
    transfer learning, 172
    wavelet transforms, 126
data scientists, 127

decision fatigue, 31
default mode network, 165
Defense Advanced Research Projects Agency (DARPA), 182
delusions, xii–xiii
depression, xv, 15, 18, 27, 45, 54, 61
  postpartum, 141
  seasonal, xiii
  symptoms, 59–60
depressive symptoms, xiii
Diagnostic and Statistical Manual of Mental Disorders (DSM), 35
  DSM-III, 35
  DSM-V, 35, 36, 53, 60
  DSM-V-TR (Text Revision)., 35, 36
diagnostics, 84–87
  demographic studies, 27–28
  diagnostic criteria, 36
  diagnostic manuals, 35–39
  DSM diagnoses, 35–39
  emotional fluctuations, 35
  emotional granularity, 27
  emotional vocabulary, 27
  failings of diagnostic process, 39–40
  financial capacity, 25
  general practitioner, consultation with, 24–25
  generalized anxiety, 38
  issue of access, 25
  patient evaluation, 26
  patient examination, 32–33
  patient's history, 28–32
  patient's risk of suicide, 33–34
  presenting complaint, 26–27
  reliability, 37
  safety, 25
  self-awareness level, 27
  validity, 38
diagnostics biomarkers, 178
digital transformation, 116
direct-to-consumer (DTC), 139, 150, 154
Disruptive Mood Dysregulation Disorder (DMDD), 36
DNA sequencing, 117
drug development, 46–47
DSM *See Diagnostic and Statistical Manual of Mental Disorders* (DSM)

E

economic impacts, xvi
electroencephalography (EEG), 9, 127, 140, 150
electromechanical machines, 98
emotion recognition test, 146
emotional
  fluctuations, 35
  granularity, 27
  vocabulary, 27
enacted stigma, 7
endpoints, 53–55
ENIAC, 97
epidemiological data, 141
epilepsy, 9
escitalopram, 46, 47
estrogen receptors, 142
ethics, 130
European Union, 131
explainable AI (XAI), 179–182
exploration–exploitation dilemma, 110
eye blinks, 128

F

Facial Emotion Recognition (FER) technologies, 200
family history, 30–31
FDA, 47, 52, 76, 84, 85, 170
fear, internal, 7, 8
feature engineering, 104
feature importance, 180, 182, 197
feature selection, 104
felt stigma, 7
financing diagnostic test, 170
fine-tuning, 112
flu test, 59
fluorography, 59
fluoxetine, 46
foundational models, 111–113, 172
functional magnetic resonance imaging (fMRI), 124, 140, 155
functional near-infrared spectroscopy (fNIRS), 144

G

Gaussian filtering, 126
general practitioners (GPs), 170
General Problem Solver (GPS), 99–100
generalizability, 36, 64
global healthcare data monetization market, 138
Global Mental Health and Sustainable Development, xvi
Goffman, Erving, 7
governments, 76

H

Hamilton Depression Rating Scale (HAM-D), 54–56, 152
haptoglobin, 142
healthcare
 expenditures, xvi
 FDA, 47, 52, 76, 84, 85, 170
 institutions, 82
 insurance companies, 76, 79, 82, 83
 patient, 5
 pharmaceutical companies, 47, 71, 75, 169, 173 (see also pharmaceutical companies)
 professional associations, 75, 81–83, 85
 providers, 75
heterogeneity, 58–62
heuristics, 99
hormonal influences, 142
hospitals, 75
hypersomnia, 60
hypothetical medication, 61

I

imipramine (Tofranil), 46
independent component analysis (ICA), 127
informational support, 194–197
informative metrics, 193
innovation, in psychiatry, xvi
innovative solution, psychiatric market, 156
insomnia, 60
Instagram, 14
insurance companies, 76
International Classification of Diseases (ICD), 35
internet, 14
issue of access, 25

L

labeled training datasets, 102
labeling quality, 151–152
laboratories, 85
Lancet Commission on Global Mental Health and Sustainable Development, xvi
large language models (LLMs), 111, 193, 195
late-stage clinical trials, 51
 See also Phase II and Phase III
leveraging methods, 193–194
Lilly, Eli, 81
Logic Theorist, 99

M

machine learning algorithms, xvii
MADRS *See* Montgomery Åsberg Depression Rating Scale (MADRS)
magnetic resonance imaging (MRI), 9, 65
magnetoencephalography (MEG), 127, 140
major depressive disorder (MDD)
 patient selection, 53
 placebo effect, 56
 symptoms, 59–60
 treatment, 43
manic behavior, 145
McMurphy, Randle, 69, 70
MDD *See* major depressive disorder (MDD)
measurable indicator, 12
median filtering, 126
medical AI solutions, 101
medical history, 29–30
medicalization, 82
MEG *See* magnetoencephalography (MEG)
mental health
 conditions, 35
 disorders, xv
 monitoring, 190–194
mental illness, 162, xi
microbiome, 143
misinformation, 16, 20
Mixed Anxiety-Depressive Disorder, 38
mixed feelings, x
model-building approach, 113

modern AI paradigms
  foundational models, 111–113
  reinforcement learning, 108–110
  supervised learning, 102–105
  unsupervised learning algorithms, 105–107
Moncrieff, J., 45
monitoring biomarkers, 173–174
Montgomery Åsberg Depression Rating Scale (MADRS), 54–56
mood, 13, 43, 59, 142
  changes, 10–12, xii
  stabilizers, 45, xiiI
multimodal systems
  advantage of, 175
  diverse biological and clinical data, 175
  explainable AI, 179–182
  hormonal and biochemical indicators, 175
  mental disorders redefined, 177–179
  psychiatry paradigm, 175
  traditional stepped-care model, 176
multiple sclerosis, 9
MYCIN, 101

N
National Institute of Standards and Technology (NIST), 130, 131
Natural Language Processing (NLP), 189
Netflix, 106
neural circuits, 165
neurocognitive tasks, 146–147
neuromyths, 14, 15, 20
neurophysiological signals, 126
Newell, Allen, 99
nocturnal enuresis, 46
normalization, 107

O
objective markers, 9
objective measurement tools, 12
occupational and legal histories, 30
One Flew Over the Cuckoos Nest (Kesey, Ken), 69
online, 14–20
Organization for Economic Co-operation and Development (OECD), 131
organizational cultures, 131–132

P
parallel computations, 98
patient, 74
  avoiding serious consequences, 6
  data, 139
  external barriers, 7
  feedback from others, 13
  healthcare, 5
  incorrect diagnosis, 9
  internal fears, 7
  invisible changes, 11–14
  misinformation, 16
  online search, 14–20
  personal experiences videos, 16
  self-help literature, 17–19
  stigma, power of, 7–11
  stratification, 167
  uncertainty, 11
  wearable devices, 153
patient examination
  appetite assessments, 33
  clinician's experience, 33
  mental status examination, 32, 33
  patients baseline, 33
  physical evaluation, 32
  review of systems, 32
Patient Health Questionnaire (PHQ-9), 152
patient-centered care, 5
patient's history
  collateral information, 28
  communication, 31
  family history, 30–31
  indirect assessment, 31–32
  medical history, 29–30
  occupational and legal histories, 30
  past psychiatric history, 29
  patient's mind, 31
  patients story, 28
  people around the patient, 31
  present illness, history of, 28
  sociocultural factors, 30
  substance use, 29
patient's mind, 31
patients' story, 28
PCR test, 59
perceptron, 100
perimenopause, 141

personal data, use of, 130
personalizing diabetes care, 110
pharmaceutical companies, 75, 169, 173
    and academia and research institutions, 81
    and clinics and hospitals, 79, 82, 83
    and governmental organizations, 79
    and insurance companies, 79
    and patients, 82
    and pharma and insurance companies, 82–83
    and professional associations, 82, 83
    and regulators, 81, 82–83
    interactions with stakeholders, 80
    treatment guidelines, 83
pharmacodynamics, 48
pharmacokinetics, 48
pharmacology
    clinical trials, 50–62
    pre-clinical phase, 48–50
Phase I clinical trials, 50–51
Phase II and III clinical trials
    control group, 52
    efficacy and safety, 52
    endpoints, 53–55
    goal of, 51
    heterogeneity, 58–62
    inclusion and exclusion criteria, 52
    patient selection, 53
    placebo effect, 55–58
placebo effect, 52, 55–58
positron emission tomography (PET), 140
post-traumatic stress disorder (PTSD), 37
postpartum depression, 141
pre-clinical phase
    animal models, 48
    biological targets, 49
    criteria for, 49–50
    parameters evaluation, 48
    reproducibility crisis, 49
    target identification, 48
precision, 120
Precision Psychotherapy, 201–202
predictive biomarker, 168, 173–174
premenstrual dysphoric disorder (PMDD), 81
present illness, history of, 28
privacy, issues of, 130
productivity loss, xvi

professional associations, 75, 85
progesterone receptors, 142
prognostic biomarkers, 178
prototype and example-based explanations, 181
Prozac, 81
psychiatric care system, 170
psychiatric disorders, biological mechanisms of, 167
psychiatric research, 62–67
psychiatric system
    academic institutions and research centers, 75
    breaking the stagnation, 87–89
    clinics, hospitals, and healthcare providers, 75
    defining, 71–74
    diagnostics, 84–87
    direct confrontation, 70
    goal of innovation, 73
    governments, 76
    innovative implementation, 73
    insurance companies, 76
    interactions within the system, 73–74, 77–84
    patient-centric approach, 71
    patients, 74
    pharmaceutical companies, 75, 79
    professional associations, 75
    regulatory agencies, 76
psychiatrist support tools, 197–201
psychomotor agitation, 60
psychomotor retardation, 60
punishment system, 109–110

Q

quantity over quality, 152–154
questionnaires, 54, 87, 152

R

random noise, 128
rapid antigen test, 59
regression tasks, 103, 104
regulatory agencies, 76
reinforcement learning, 108–110
relevance, 124

reliability, 37, 64
remission, 43–44, 55
replicability, 64
representativeness, 121–122
reproducibility crisis, 49
research centers, 75
Research Domain Criteria (RDoC) project, 63–65
response, 55
rewards, 108–110
risk biomarkers, 178
Risk Management Framework, 131
robots, 110
Rosenblatt, Frank, 100

S
safety, 25
sample size, 36
Sarafem, 81
SARS-CoV-2, 59
Scambler, Graham, 7
schizophrenia, 45, 57
scientific information, 196
seasonal depression, xiii
seizures, 9
selective serotonin reuptake inhibitor (SSRI), 4, 43, 46
self-assessment, 14, 20, 71, 152
self-awareness, 12, 27
self-help books, 17–19
self-supervised learning, 112
semantic consistency, 123
semi-structured data, 119
sensors, 32
serotonin, 4, 43
sertraline, 46
Shaw, Cliff, 99
signal-to-noise ratio (SNR), 125, 149–151
Simon, Herbert, 99
smart rings, 32
smart watches, 32
SNR See signal-to-noise ratio (SNR)
social acceptance, 7
social media, 14, 148
sociocultural factors, 30

Speech Emotion Recognition (SER) models, 201
Spotify, 106
SSRI See selective serotonin reuptake inhibitor (SSRI)
standardization, 122–124
stepped-care models, 171
stigma, 7–11
  destructive power, 11
  development, 8
  enacted stigma, 7
  felt stigma, 7
  origin, 8
Stigma: Notes on the Management of Spoiled Identity (1963) (Goffman), 7
structured data, 117–118
substance use, 29
suicidal ideation, 60
suicide
  anxiety, xi
  attempt, xiv
  cultural stigma, xiv–xv
  depressive symptoms, xiii
  mental illness, xi
  mixed feelings, x
  mood swung, xii
  patient's risk of, 33–34
  prevention algorithms, 187–190
  risk factors, xi
  warning signs, xiv
supervised learning algorithms, 102–105, 107
symbolic processing, 98
system
  academic institutions and research centers, 75
  breaking the stagnation, 87–89
  clinics, hospitals, and healthcare providers, 75
  defining, 71–74
  diagnostics, 84–87
  direct confrontation, 70
  goal of innovation, 73
  governments, 76
  innovative implementation, 73
  insurance companies, 76

system (*continued*)
  interactions within the system, 73–74, 77–84
  patient-centric approach, 71
  patients, 74
  pharmaceutical companies, 75, 79
  professional associations, 75
  regulatory agencies, 76
systematic noise, 128–129
systemic failure, in psychiatry, xv–xvi

T
telemedicine platforms, 198
testosterone receptors, 142
textual communication data, 148
Thorazine *See* chlorpromazine (Thorazine)
TikTok, 14, 16, 17
timeliness, 124
Tofranil *See* imipramine (Tofranil)
total score, 54
"Tower of Hanoi" puzzle, 100
transcranial magnetic stimulation (TMS), 166
transfer learning, 172
treatment, 42–46
  medication's effectiveness, 43
  outcomes, 45
  remission rate, 43–44
  See also clinical trials

treatment-resistant depression (TRD), 44
Turing, Alan, 98

U
U.S. National Institute of Mental Health (NIMH), 63
U.S. Preventive Services Task Force (USPSTF), 87
unstructured data, 118–119
unsupervised learning algorithms, 105–107

V
validity, 38
virtual reality (VR), 147
visual learning, 15

W
wavelet transforms, 126
wearable devices, 32, 144, 145
whole genome sequencing (WGS) data, 150
World Health Organization, 35

X
X-ray imaging, 59

Y
YouTube, 16